Italian

Phrase Book & Dictionary

Other languages in the *Collins Phrase Book & Dictionary* series:

FRENCH
GERMAN
GREEK
JAPANESE
PORTUGUESE
SPANISH

These titles are also published in a Language pack containing
60-minute CD/cassette and phrase book

HarperCollins*Publishers*
Westerhill Road,
Bishopbriggs, Glasgow G64 2QT

www.collins.co.uk

First published 2004

Reprint 10 9 8 7 6 5 4 3 2 1 0

© HarperCollins*Publishers* 2004

ISBN 0 00-716528-5

Typeset by Davidson Pre-Press Graphics Ltd, Glasgow

Printed in Italy by Amadeus SpA

Introduction

Your *Collins Phrase Book & Dictionary* is a handy, quick-reference guide that will help you make the most of your stay abroad. Its clear layout will save you valuable time when you need that crucial word or phrase. There are four main sections in this book:

Everyday Italy – photoguide

Packed full of photos, this section allows you to see all the practical visual information that will help with using cash machines, driving on motorways, reading signs, etc.

Phrases

Practical topics are arranged thematically with an opening section Key talk containing vital phrases that should stand you in good stead in most situations.

Phrases are short, useful and each one has a pronunciation guide so that there is no problem saying them.

Eating out

This section contains phrases for ordering food and drink (and special requirements) plus a photoguide showing different eating places, menus and practical information to help choose the best options. The menu reader allows you to work out what to choose.

Dictionary

The practical 5000-word English-Italian and Italian-English Dictionary means that you won't be stuck for words.

And finally, there is a short Grammar section explaining how the language works.

So, just flick through the pages to find the information you need. Why not start with a look at Pronouncing Italian on page 6. From there on the going is easy with your *Collins Phrase Book & Dictionary*.

Useful websites

Currency Converters
www.x-rates.com

Foreign Office Advice
www.fco.gov.uk/travel/
countryadvice.asp

Passport Office
www.ukpa.gov.uk

Health advice
www.thetraveldoctor.com
www.doh.gov.uk/traveladvice

Pets
www.defra.gov.uk/animalh/
quarantine/index.htm

Weather
www.bbc.co.uk/weather

Transport
www.trenitalia.com
  (Italian railways)
www.aeroporti.com/aeroporti.
html *(Italian airports)*

Driving
www.autostrade.it
  (Italian motorways)
www.edidomus.it/auto/servizi
(Italian road and traffic info)

Sightseeing
www.enit.it *(official site of
  Italian state tourist board)*
www.initaly.com
www.italytour.com
www.romeguide.it
www.doge.it *(Venice guide)*
www.northernitaly.com
www.uffizi.firenze.it
(Uffizi, Florence)

Internet Cafés
www.netcafes.com

Culture & Activities
www.operabase.com/en/
www.teatroallascala.org/eng/
  homepage.htm *(La Scala)*
www.hostetler.net
  (info on Italian festivals)

Hotels & Accommodation
www.travel.it
www.abouthotel.com
www.italyhotel.com
www.agriturist.it *(staying in
the countryside on a farm)*

Contents

Pronouncing Italian

We've tried to make the pronunciation under phrases as clear as possible. We've split up words to make them easy to read, but don't pause too long between syllables. Italian isn't really hard to pronounce and once you learn a few basic rules, it shouldn't be too long before you can read straight from the Italian.

*Longer words are usually stressed on the next to last syllable, but we show all stressed syllables in **heavy type**, so you won't be caught out by any exceptions.*

*The spellings **c** and **ch** might confuse you, because **c** is sometimes pronounced like English **ch** as in church, while the Italian **ch** is pronounced like the English **k**. (Look at the English for kilo and the Italian **chilo**.) So **c'è** (there is) is pronounced like English check without the final **k** sound, while **che?** (what?) is pronounced **kay**. The rule to remember is that **c** followed by **e** or **i** makes it a soft **ch** sound. But **c** followed by **a**, **o** or **u** has a hard **k** sound. Practise saying and reading the following words:*

chiave *kee-a-vay (key)*   **cibo** *chee-bo (food)*
chiesa *kee-ay-za (church)*   **cena** *chay-na (dinner)*

*The letter **g** behaves in a similar way. When followed by **a**, **o** or **u**, **g** will be hard. When followed by **e** or **i**, **g** will be soft. The word for lake is **lago**, for lakes the word is **laghi**. The **h** has been added to keep the **g** hard. So when you see a **ch** or **gh** combination in Italian, remember to make the **c** and **g** hard.*

*Sometimes Italian has two distinctive vowel sounds next to each other, in other words like **dei**, shown in the pronunciation as day-ee. These sounds merge with each other, so don't separate them with a long pause. Finally, pronounce all **r**'s when you see them in Italian words.*

Basic rules to remember are:

italian	sounds like	example	pronunciation
a	cat	**pasta**	*pas-ta*
e	bet/day	**letto/per**	*let-to/payr*
i	meet	**vino**	*vee-no*
o	got	**botta**	*bot-ta*
u	boot	**luna**	*loo-na*
gli	million	**figlio**	*feel-yo*
sc *(before e/i)*	shop	**sci**	*shee*
sc *(before a/o/u)*	scan	**scarpa**	*skar-pa*

OPEN

Small shops tend to close between 1 & 4pm, but stay open later till about 7.30pm.

OPENING HOURS

Orario = timetable
Apertura = opening

CLOSED

Don't be fooled by the ch, it's pronounced *kee-oo-zo*.

Orario sportello means counter opening hours (i.e. open to public).

ENTRANCE

ENTRATA

Look out for the words *entrata libera* which means free entry.

INGRESSO

EXIT

USCITA

Uscita is also used for exit on motorways.

OUT OF ORDER

FUORI SERVIZIO

IN SERVICE

in servizio

FORBIDDEN

Another word for forbidden is *divieto di...*

divieto di

CASSA

PAY HERE

PUSH

SPINGERE

PULL

TIRARE

DANGER

Everyday Italy

 Symbol for the euro. Italy is in the eurozone.

BANCOMAT Cash machines (**Bancomat**) are common.

 You can carry out the transaction in English and save time queueing in banks.

Italian banks operate a double-door system with metal detectors to check you aren't armed.

To enter you press a button and wait for the green light to let you through.

 Prices are generally written with a comma. The price here is 5 euros:

virgola = comma
punto = full stop

 PRICES The word for price is **prezzo** in the singular and **prezzi** in the plural. **Metà prezzo** means half price.

 Banca Popolare di Sondrio

BANCA Italy has many regional banks such as **Banco Popolare di Sondrio**; nationwide banks include **UniCredit Banca** and **Banca Nazionale del Lavoro**.

The euro is the currency of Italy. It breaks down into 100 euro cents. Notes: 5, 10, 20, 50, 100, 200, 500. Coins: 2 euro, 1 euro, 50 cent, 20 cent, 10 cent, 5 cent, 2 cent, 1 cent.

Although coins are officially **cent**, Italians call them **centesimi** (chen-tez-ee-mee), a more familiar Italian term. Euro is pronounced ay-oo-ro. It stays the same in the plural.

Euro notes are the same throughout Europe. The backs of coins carry different designs from each of the member European countries.

Cash machines operate as at home.
cancella = cancel last part of transaction
annulla = cancel whole of transaction
esegui = proceed

Automatic machines take both coins and notes

RECEIPT *richiesta scontrino* = request for receipt. *Scontrino* is a good word to remember. It is what you get in bars where you pay in advance for your order. *Ricevuta* is a receipt in restaurants, taxis, clothes shops, etc.

banconote
BANKNOTES

monete
COINS

contanti
CASH

resto
CHANGE

Service is usually included in a restaurant bill so tipping is discretionary. However, it is usual to leave a small tip. In busy bars there will often be a saucer to leave loose change.

These are often attached to a bar and sell cigarettes, stamps, bus tickets, etc. They also sell lottery tickets. It is a good place for an early morning cup of

When friends or family meet up, they usually kiss each other on the cheeks. Among friends you hear *ciao* for hi and bye, but for people you come across in the street, use *buongiorno* or *buonasera* (late pm/eve). If you are unsure whether to use *ciao*, *salve* is always a good option.

POLICE In small towns and villages you find *carabinieri*, and in larger towns, *polizia*. You must report any crimes to them.

Everyday Italy

AFFITTASI FOR RENT

vendesi

FOR SALE
'Sold' in Italian is **venduto**
(*ven-doo-to*).

 **AUTONOLEGGIO** CAR HIRE

Noleggio = rental, hire.

in vendita

TOURIST INFORMATION

ufficio turistico **𝒊** ↑

The tourist office is known as the
Ufficio turistico. They have maps
and brochures in English.

FREE

omaggio

(for example a free magazine)

 **agriturist**

Agriturism is popular.
You get away from it all on a farm,
visit *www.agriturist.it*.

annuario
alberghi e
campeggi

lago di Como

The tourist
office has
guides to
hotels and
campsites.

CAMERE

**ROOMS
AVAILABLE**

pensione

GUESTHOUSE

completo

FULL – NO ROOMS/SPACES

CLOSED FOR HOLIDAYS

HOTEL

Chiuso per
ferie
dall'11 al 18
Agosto.

Italians take their
main holiday in the
first 3 weeks in
August. The
weekend of the 15th
August is a public
holiday *Ferragosto*.

←   **albergo**

Hotels are known as *albergo*
(*alberghi* in plural) or *hotel*
(the h is not sounded).

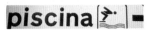

SWIMMING POOL
It's obligatory to wear swimming caps in public pools. You can usually buy or borrow one at the pool.

RUBBISH
Rubbish isn't collected from houses, you must take it to refuse points. There are banks for recycling glass, plastic, etc.

PAPER

toilette **TOILETS**

Some bars (particularly in cities) will lock their toilet and you will have to ask for a key.

doccia **SHOWER**

bagno **BATHROOM**

DONNE

LADIES
Ladies and gents toilets are generally shown with a pictogram.

UOMINI

GENTS
WC is also known as *gabinetto*.

NOT DRINKING WATER
The word for water is *acqua* (ak-wa).

caldo
HOT

freddo
COLD

occupato
ENGAGED

libero
VACANT

Timetables

I GIORNI	THE DAYS
lunedì *loo-ned-ee*	Monday
martedì *mar-ted-ee*	Tuesday
mercoledì *mer-ko-led-ee*	Wednesday
giovedì *jov-ed-ee*	Thursday
venerdì *ven-er-dee*	Friday
sabato *sa-bat-o*	Saturday
domenica *dom-en-ee-ka*	Sunday

In Italian, neither months nor days start with a capital letter as they do in English.

Giornaliere DAILY

Settimanale WEEKLY

oggi TODAY

domani TOMORROW

I MESI	THE MONTHS
gennaio *jen-na-yo*	January
febbraio *feb-ra-yo*	February
marzo *mar-tso*	March
aprile *a-pree-lay*	April
maggio *mad-jo*	May
giugno *joon-yo*	June
luglio *lool-yo*	July
agosto *a-gos-to*	August
settembre *set-tem-bray*	September
ottobre *ot-tob-ray*	October
novembre *nov-em-bray*	November
dicembre *dee-chem-bray*	December

ORARIO ESTIVO
SUMMER TIMETABLE

ORARIO DAL 26 GIUGNO AL 1° OTTOBRE
TIMETABLE
dal = from *al* = to

READING A TIMETABLE

CORSE BATTELLO - SCHIFF - BATEAU - SCHIP   BELLAGIO - LECCO

Annotazioni	❸ feriale	sabato e festivi		festiva	Rapido festiva			❸ feriale	sabato e festivi
N° CORSE	181	283	85	287	SR253	87		189	289
BELLAGIO part.	6.40	8.20	11.45	12.45	14.34	16.50	18.05	18.05
Lierna "		8.38						18.23
Limonta "	6.57	8.46	12.02				18.22	18.31
Vassena "	7.09	8.58	12.14	↓	↓	↓	18.34	18.43

feriale = weekdays (Mon-Fri)
sabato e festivi = Saturday and Sunday holidays

part. ore 19.28   arr. ore 23.45

part. ore = partenza alle ... ore
= departure at ... hours
arr. ore = arrivo alle ... ore
= arrival at ... hours

AFTERNOON

pomeriggio

Biglietteria TICKET OFFICE

MORNING

mattino

adulti ADULTS

ragazzi CHILDREN 5–15

bambini CHILDREN up to 4

terza età SENIORS *(over 60)*

SELF-SERVICE
You can purchase tickets from machines rather than queueing. Note you can also validate train tickets in the yellow slot rather than at the boxes on the platforms.

VILLA VALMARANA «AI NANI»
INGRESSO
alla **PALAZZINA**
ed alla **FORESTERIA**
Ricevuto per l'utente
№ 4499
singoli
€5

ENTRANCE TICKET
is *biglietto d'ingresso*

Getting around

CENTRE Note the pictogram used.

OTHER ROUTES

Pictograms are increasingly used on signs (hospital, post office and police).

150 m a destra **150m ON RIGHT**
a sinistra = on left

pianterreno
GROUND FLOOR

seminterrato
BASEMENT

MUSEI CIVICI
LOCAL MUSEUMS

1º piano
1ST FLOOR

duomo-broletto
CATHEDRAL

PEDESTRIAN AREA

municipio
TOWN HALL

PINACOTECA
ART GALLERY

CHIESA S. CECILIA
CHURCH OF ST. CECILIA

SQUARE (*piazza*)

piazza
Nuova

TAXI You can call for taxis (usually on freephone numbers).

Italian taxis are white. You can find them at stations and ramps. People do not usually hail them in the street. It is always better to use official ones as private operators (blue limousines) might charge more.

City buses are generally orange. You enter from the back and validate your ticket at the machine as you enter. In rural areas shops near the bus stop sell bus tickets and are likely to shut for lunch from 1 to 4pm.

Bus stops often have the time-table and stops en route. Bus stop = *la fermata dell'autobus*.

STATION

ARRIVI ARRIVALS

PARTENZE DEPARTURES

You must validate your ticket before boarding the train.

UNDERGROUND
The symbol for the underground system (*metropolitana*) is M.

DEPARTURE BOARD

CAT. Category of train. The red IC stands for InterCity. On railway timetables the different colours indicate the 'speed' of trains: red being the fastest and usually most expensive. Always check if you need to pay a supplement.

Driving

Pictograms are increasingly used. If you don't see your destination, follow *tutte le direzioni*

(all routes) or *altre direzioni* (other routes). To get to the town centre, follow *centro*.

The word *eccetto* means 'except for'. *Solo* means 'only'.

P AUTOSILO

MULTI-STOREY PARKING

ROUNDABOUTS

Beware! New round-abouts follow the same rules as UK, i.e. you stop and give way to vehicles already on it.

Old roundabouts are the opposite – you can drive straight onto them and cars on it have to give way to you. The problem is telling which system operates! Watch out carefully for signs and don't trust other drivers. Italians aren't yet used to the new system.

rallentare

SLOW DOWN

START OF ROAD WORKS

Inizio = start
Fine = end.

PARKING SIGN

More and more pictograms are being used on signs.

parking disk required

1 hour

cross = Sundays

crossed mallets = work days Mon-Sat

SPACES

Careful! *libero* means spaces not that it's free. *Completo* = full.

Parcheggio gratuito

FREE PARKING

giorni feriali dalle 9.00 alle 20.00

WEEK DAYS
from 9am to 10pm

Motorways are signposted green with **A** for *Autostrada*. Blue signs indicate main routes. White signs indicate local destinations.

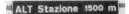

STOP PAYMENT STATION

 **EXITS**
Note colours:
white = local
brown = place of interest
blue = main routes

Prossime uscite = next exits

ACCENDERE I FARI

SWITCH ON HEADLIGHTS
Headlights must be on at all times on motorways and outside towns.

 BENZINA

PETROL Self-service payment machines take 5, 10 and 20 euro notes. Don't choose too much petrol as you don't get money back.

There are different lanes for paying.

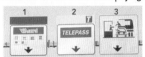

1 *Viacards* can be bought at newsagents. You can also pay by credit card.
2 *Telepass*, the in-car device. Avoid this lane.
3 Cash payment only. The amount is displayed.

RECOMMENDED SPEED 70kph
Speed limits are 130kph on motorways, 110 or 90kph on dual carriageways, 90kph on ordinary roads, 50kph in built-up areas. When raining the limits of 130/110kph are lowered by 20kph.

 PETROL
unleaded *senza piombo*
diesel
24 hours

 PRICE LIST
Servito means that you are served. Prices are slightly higher than self-service.

Shopping

REDUCTIONS

FROM

a partire da

PAY HERE

CASSA

END OF SEASON SALES

saldi fine stagione

You can get bargains at end of season sales (Aug/Sep for summer and Jan/Feb for winter).

Bennet is one of the big chains of supermarkets.

You need euro coins to release the shopping trolley.

STANDA is one of Italy's biggest supermarket chains. *Orario continuato* means that it doesn't close for lunch like most of the smaller shops. Sunday opening is becoming more common in Italy.

gusti

FLAVOURS

al chilo

PER KILO

OFFER
Confezione = packet or pack. Here the offer is for 3 packets of tortellini for 5 euro.

REGALO

GIFT

MERCATO

MARKET

PHARMACY

You can recognise the pharmacy by the green cross. If you're worried about a medical condition, ask the pharmacist for advice. They are medically trained and often able to supply suitable medication. If you need over-the-counter medicine (for headaches, etc), buy them here. They aren't sold in supermarkets.

DUTY PHARMACY

If the address of the duty pharmacy (*farmacia di guardia*) is not displayed, ask at the local police station. Details will also be printed in the local paper.

ALIMENTARI
PANE VINO LIQUORI L.MARCONI

GROCERS An *Alimentari* usually sells bread (*pane*) and wine (*vino*). It generally opens early with fresh bread and shuts from 1 to 4pm.

FRUIT & VEG In the super-market you must get it weighed and stickered. You either do it yourself or an attendant does it.

Pane = bread
Panini = rolls
pane integrale = wholemeal bread
pane di segale = rye bread.
Bread is sold by the weight.

In supermarkets you generally get a ticket at busy counters.

MILK Look for the colour-coding for milk (*latte*). Here, whole milk (*intero*), pink is semi-skimmed (*parzialmente scremato*). Skimmed is *scremato*.

LATTE INTERO
VALORI NUTRITIVI MED
ENERGIA   65
PROTEINE   3.
CARBOIDRATI   5.
GRASSI   3.
CALCIO   120

FATS
grassi = fats

da asporto **TAKE AWAY**

biologico **ORGANIC**

WATER Look out for the colour-coding for *acqua minerale*: sparkling = *frizzante* or *gassata* still = *naturale*

SENZA COLORANTI

NO COLOURING
senza = without   *con* = with

SOLO
ONLY

surgelati
FROZEN FOODS

Keeping in touch

EXPRESS POST For a slightly higher price you can get a quicker service.

The post office *Posta* has a yellow and blue logo. In most places they are open in the mornings until 2pm Mon-Fri and until 12 on Saturdays.

Most phoneboxes take:

monete = coins
schede = phonecards
carte = credit cards

famiglia Galli
via A. Volta, 16
20132 Milano
Italy

Addressing an envelope to family friends : road & house no postcode & town country

Some postboxes have 2 slots, red for ordinary mail. and blue for the priority service
Ultimo ritiro = last collection.
Festivi = Sundays and holidays.

Italian phonecards (**schede telefoniche**) are sold at 5 or 10 €. In order to use them, you must tear off (**strappare**) the perforated corner.

Numero verde = freephone. Numbers begin 800. Landline numbers begin with 0 (the area code) and mobile numbers begin with 3.

The word for 'at' is **chiocciola** (*kee-o-cho-la*).

www.

www dot is *voo voo voo punto.*

Allegato................. Attachment	*Many English terms are used for*
Invio .... Send	*e-mail and the internet.*

Key Talk

- It is customary to use the polite form **lei** and surname with people you've just been introduced to, unless it's clear you're going to establish a friendly relationship. In that case the informal **tu** form and christian name will be used.
- The easiest way to ask for something is to name it and add please, **per favore**.

yes	**no**	**that's fine**
sì	no	va bene
see	*no*	*va ben-ay*
please	**thank you**	**don't mention it**
per favore	grazie	prego
payr fa-vo-ray	***grat**-see-ay*	***pray**-go*
hello	**goodbye**	**good night**
buongiorno	arrivederci	buonanotte
*bwon-**jor**-no*	*ar-ree-ve-**der**-chee*	***bwo**-na-**not**-tay*

good afternoon/evening	**that's very kind**
buonasera	molto gentile
***bwo**-na-**say**-ra*	***mol**-to jen-**tee**-lay*
excuse me/sorry	**excuse me** (to get past people)
scusi	permesso
***skoo**-zee*	*per-**mes**-so*

Here is an easy way to ask for something … just add per favore

a/an…	**an ice cream**	**2 ice creams**
un… ('il' and 'lo' words)	un gelato	due gelati
oon…	*oon jay-**la**-to*	***doo**-ay jay-**la**-tee*
a	**a beer**	**2 beers**
una… ('la' words)	una birra	due birre
***oo**-na…*	***oo**-na **beer**-ra*	***doo**-ay **beer**-ray*

a beer and two ice creams, please
una birra e due gelati, per favore
*oo-na **beer**-ra ay **doo**-ay jay-**la**-tee payr fa-**vo**-ray*

Key Talk

aperto

- *Salve meaning 'hello' is less casual than* ciao.
- *When entering a shop, bar or approaching someone, greet them with* **buongiorno** *(or* **buonasera** *from late afternoon).*
- *There are masculine and feminine endings. 'I'm clever' for a man is* **sono bravo**. *For a lady* **sono brava**.

I'd like...
vorrei...
*vor-**ray**-ee...*

we'd like...
vorremmo...
*vor-**rem**-mo...*

I'd like an ice cream
vorrei un gelato
*vor-**ray**-ee oon jay-**la**-to*

we'd like to go to Pisa
vorremmo andare a Pisa
*vor-**rem**-mo an-**da**-ray a **pee**-za*

do you have...?
avete...?
*a-**vay**-tay...*

do you have any milk?
avete del latte?
*a-**vay**-tay del **lat**-tay*

do you have stamps?
avete dei francobolli?
*a-**vay**-tay **day**-ee fran-ko-**bol**-lee*

do you have a map?
avete una carta?
*a-**vay**-tay **oo**-na **kar**-ta*

do you have fruit?
avete della frutta?
*a-**vay**-tay **del**-la **froot**-ta*

how much is it?
quanto costa?
*kwan-to **kos**-ta*

how much does ... cost?
quanto costa il/la...?
*kwan-to **kos**-ta eel/la...*

how much is the wine?
quanto costa il vino?
*kwan-to **kos**-ta eel **vee**-no*

how much is the ticket?
quanto costa il biglietto?
*kwan-to **kos**-ta eel beel-**yet**-to*

how much is a kilo?
quanto costa al chilo?
*kwan-to **kos**-ta al **kee**-lo*

how much is one?
quanto costa l'uno?
*kwan-to **kos**-ta **loo**-no*

● You can use **ha?** or **avete?** for 'do you have?' Both are equally polite. 'H' isn't sounded in Italian.

● Local dialects are quite different from 'proper' Italian. **Andiamo a casa** (let's go home) in the Como dialect it is **'ndem a ca**. Even if you know Italian, you might have difficulty understanding dialects!

where is...?
dov'è...?
do-ve...

where are...?
dove sono...?
do-vay so-no...

where is the toilet?
dov'è la toilette?
do-ve la twa-let

where are the children?
dove sono i bambini?
do-vay so-no ee bam-bee-nee

is there?
c'è...?
che...

are there...?
ci sono...?
chee so-no...

there is no...
non c'è...
non che...

is there a restaurant?
c'è un ristorante?
che oon ree-sto-ran-tay

where is there a chemist?
dove c'è una farmacia?
do-vay che oo-na far-ma-chee-a

are there any children?
ci sono dei bambini?
che so-no day-ee bam-bee-nee

is there a swimming pool?
c'è una piscina?
che oo-na pee-shee-na

there is no hot water
non c'è acqua calda
non che ak-wa kal-da

there is no bread
non c'è pane
non che pa-nay

I need...
ho bisogno di...
o bee-zon-yo dee...

I need a doctor
ho bisogno di un medico
o bee-zon-yo dee oon med-ee-ko

I need to phone
ho bisogno di telefonare
o bee-zon-yo dee te-le-fo-na-ray

Key Talk

NOTTURN.
ALLO A BO
ZA DA COMO
rile al 30 settembre

- To catch someone's attention, begin your request with *scusi*.
- If you are in a busy street, or market, you can push your way through politely with the word **permesso**.
- You also use **permesso** when entering someone's home. It is a polite custom.

can I...?	can we...?	where can I...?
posso...?	possiamo...?	dove posso...?
pos-so...	pos-see-**a**-mo...	**do**-vay **pos**-so...

can I pay?
posso pagare?
pos-so pa-ga-ray

can we go in?
possiamo entrare?
pos-see-**a**-mo en-**tra**-ray

where can I buy bread?
dove posso comprare del pane?
do-vay **pos**-so kom-**pra**-ray del **pa**-nay

where can I get tickets?
dove posso trovare i biglietti?
do-vay **pos**-so tro-**va**-ray ee beel-**yet**-tee

when?	at what time...?
quando?	a che ora...?
kwan-do	a kay **o**-ra...

when does it leave?
quando parte?
kwan-do **par**-tay

when does it arrive?
quando arriva?
kwan-do ar-**ree**-va

when does it open?
a che ora apre?
a kay **o**-ra **a**-pray

when does it close?
a che ora chiude?
a kay **o**-ra kee-**oo**-day

yesterday	today	tomorrow
ieri	oggi	domani
ye-ree	**od**-jee	do-**ma**-nee

this morning	this afternoon	tonight
stamattina	oggi pomeriggio	stasera
sta-mat-**tee**-na	**od**-jee po-may-**reed**-jo	sta-**say**-ra

is it open?
è aperto?
e a-**payr**-to

is it closed?
è chiuso?
e kee-**oo**-zo

- **Signor** (Mr) is used mainly with name and surname (e.g. **signor Carlo Rossi** or **signor Rossi**), but it can also be used with christian name only (e.g. **signor Carlo**).
- **Signora** (Mrs/Ms) is as above.
- **Signorina** (Miss) is becoming 'politically incorrect'. Women should all be called **signora**, regardless of age or marital status.

how are you?
come sta?
ko-may sta

fine, thanks, and you?
bene, grazie, e Lei?
be-nay **grat**-see-ay ay lay

my name is...
mi chiamo...
*mee kee-**a**-mo...*

what is your name?
come si chiama?
ko-may see kee-**a**-ma

I didn't understand
non ho capito
*non o ka-**pee**-to*

do you speak English?
parla inglese?
***par**-la een-**glay**-zay*

Italy is very beautiful
l'Italia è molto bella
*lee-**tal**-ya e **mol**-to **bel**-la*

I love Italian food
mi piace molto la cucina italiana
*mee pee-**a**-chay **mol**-to la koo-**chee**-na ee-tal-**ya**-na*

Italian people are very kind
gli Italiani sono molto gentili
*lee ee-tal-**ya**-nee **so**-no **mol**-to jen-**tee**-lee*

I'd like to come back
vorrei ritornare
*vor-**ray**-ee ree-**tor**-na-ray*

you're very kind
è molto gentile
*e **mol**-to jen-**tee**-lay*

we will be back next year
mi sono divertito(a) moltissimo
*mee **so**-no dee-ver-**tee**-to(a) mol-**tees**-see-mo*

can I have your address?
potrei avere il suo indirizzo?
*po-**tray**-ee a-**vay**-ray eel **soo**-o een-dee-**reet**-so*

see you next year!
all'anno prossimo!
*al-**lan**-no **pros**-see-mo*

Money – changing

- Italy is in the eurozone. Euro, pronounced ay-**oo**-ro, stays the same in the plural.
- Cent is **centesimo** (chen-**tez**-ee-mo), singular and **centesimi** (chen-**tez**-ee-mee), plural.
- Banks are generally open Mon-Fri, 8.30am-1.30pm, and usually for one hour in the afternoons.

where can I change money?
dove posso cambiare i soldi?
do-vay **pos**-so kam-bee-**a**-ray ee **sol**-dee

where is the bank?
dov'è la banca?
do-**ve** la **ban**-ka

when does the bank open?
quando apre la banca?
kwan-do **a**-pray la **ban**-ka

when does the bank close?
quando chiude la banca?
kwan-do kee-**oo**-day la **ban**-ka

where is the bureau de change?
dov'è il cambio?
do-**ve** eel **kam**-bee-yo

I want to cash these traveller's cheques
vorrei cambiare questi travellers cheque
vor-**ray**-ee kam-bee-**a**-ray **kwes**-tee travellers cheque

what is the rate?
quant'è il cambio?
kwan-**te** eel **kam**-bee-yo

for pounds
per sterline
payr ster-**lee**-nay

for dollars
per dollari
payr **dol**-la-ree

I want to change £50
vorrei cambiare cinquanta sterline
vor-**ray**-ee kam-bee-**a**-ray cheen-**kwan**-ta ster-**lee**-nay

where is there a cash dispenser?
dove c'è un bancomat?
do-ve che oon **ban**-ko-mat

spending – Money

- Credit cards and debit cards are widely accepted.
- Cash machines are widespread and you will be able to use English instructions. It avoids wasting time in bank queues.
- Remember to take your bank's phone number in case you have problems.

how much is it?
quanto costa?
kwan-to kos-ta

where do I pay?
dove devo pagare?
do-vay day-vo pa-ga-ray

I want to pay
vorrei pagare
vor-ray-ee pa-ga-ray

how much do I have to pay?
quanto devo pagare?
kwan-to day-vo pa-ga-ray

can I pay by credit card?
posso pagare con la carta di credito?
pos-so pa-ga-ray kon la kar-ta dee kre-dee-to

I want to pay in euros
vorrei pagare en euro
vor-ray-ee pa-ga-ray en ay-oo-ro

do you accept traveller's cheques?
accettate i travellers cheques?
a-chet-ta-tay ee travellers cheques

how much is it...?	**per person**	**per night**	**per kilo**
quanto costa...?	per persona	per notte	al chilo
kwan-to kos-ta...	*payr per-so-na*	*payr not-tay*	*al kee-lo*

I need a receipt
ho bisogno di una ricevuta
oh bee-zon-yo dee oo-na ree-che-voo-ta

do I need to pay a deposit?
devo lasciare un deposito?
day-vo la-sha-ray oon de-po-zee-to

you pay at the cash desk
si paga alla cassa
see pa-ga al-la kas-sa

Airport

- Signs are generally in Italian and English.
- Research the best way of getting to and from the airport using www.aeroporti.com/aeroporti.html.
- If you are staying in a hotel, they will organise your trip to the airport.
- You can find internet access at airports.

to the airport, please
all'aeroporto, per favore
*a-lay-ro-**por**-to payr fa-**vo**-ray*

how do I get into town?
come si va in città?
ko**-may see va een cheet-**ta

where do I get the bus to the town centre?
da dove prendo l'autobus per il centro città?
*da **do**-vay **pren**-do **low**-to-boos payr eel **chen**-tro cheet-**ta***

how much is it...?
quanto costa...?
***kwan**-to **kos**-ta...*

to the centre
per il centro
*payr eel **chen**-tro*

to the airport
per l'aeroporto
*payr lay-ro-**por**-to*

where do I check in for...?
dov'è il check-in per...?
*do-**ve** eel check-in payr...*

which gate is it for the flight to...?
qual è l'uscita per il volo per...?
*kwal e loo-**shee**-ta payr eel **vo**-lo payr...*

boarding will take place at gate number...
l'imbarco sarà all'uscita numero...
*leem-**bar**-ko sa-**ra** al-loo-**shee**-ta **noo**-may-ro...*

the last call
l'ultima chiamata
***lool**-tee-ma kee-a-**ma**-ta*

the flight is delayed
il volo è in ritardo
*eel **vo**-lo e een ree-**tar**-do*

Customs & Passports

- *EU citizens with nothing to declare can use the blue customs channels.*
- *There's no restriction by quantity or value on goods purchased by travellers in another EU country, provided they are for their own personal use (this covers gifts). Check guidelines on www.hmce.gov.uk.*

I have nothing to declare
non ho niente da dichiarare
*non o nee-**en**-tay da dee-kee-a-**ra**-ray*

here is...
ecco...
ek-ko...

my passport
il mio passaporto
*eel **mee**-o pas-sa-**por**-to*

my green card
la mia carta verde
*la **mee**-a **kar**-ta **ver**-day*

do I have to pay duty on this?
devo pagare la dogana per questo?
*day-vo pa-**ga**-ray la do-**ga**-na payr **kwes**-to*

it's for my own personal use
è per il mio uso personale
*e payr eel **mee**-o **oo**-zo per-so-**na**-lay*

we're going to...
andiamo a...
*an-dee-**a**-mo a...*

the children are on this passport
i bambini sono su questo passaporto
*ee bam-**bee**-nee **so**-no soo **kwes**-to pas-sa-**por**-to*

I'm...
sono...
so-no...

British *(m/f)*
inglese
*een-**glay**-zay*

Australian *(m/f)*
australiano(a)
*ow-stra-lee-**a**-no(a)*

I bought it in...
l'ho comprato in...
*lo kom-**pra**-to een...*

here's the receipt
ecco la ricevuta
*ek-ko la ree-**chay**-voo-ta*

Asking the Way - questions

- You can ask the way simply by asking **scusi, per andare a...?** (how do I get to...?)
- Tourist offices have free maps and leaflets in English.
- Learn the words for 'near', **vicino** (vee-**chee**-no) and 'far' **lontano** (lon-**ta**-no).

excuse me	**where is...?**	**how do I get to...?**
scusi	dov'è...?	per andare a...?
skoo-zee	*do-ve...*	*payr an-da-ray a...*

where is the nearest...?
dov'è il/la ... più vicino(a)?
do-ve eel/la ... pee-yoo vee-chee-no(a)

is this the right way to...?
questa è la strada giusta per...?
kwes-ta e la stra-da joos-ta payr...

the...	**is it far?**
il/la...	è lontano?
eel/la...	*e lon-ta-no*

can I walk there?
si può andare a piedi?
see pwo an-da-ray a pee-ay-dee

is there a bus that goes there?
c'è un autobus che ci va?
che oon ow-to-boos kay chee va

we're looking for...	**we're lost**
stiamo cercando...	ci siamo persi
stee-a-mo cher-kan-do...	*chee see-a-mo per-see*

can you show me on the map?
mi può indicare sulla cartina?
mee pwo een-dee-ka-ray sool-la kar-tee-na

- Key words – 'right' **destra** (**des**-tra), 'left' **sinistra** (see-**nees**-tra).
- Learn 'crossroads' **l'incrocio** (leen-**kroch**-o), 'square' **piazza** (pee-**at**-sa), 'centre of town' **centro** (**chen**-tro), 'exit' **uscita** (oo-**shee**-ta) and 'follow' **seguire** (seg-**wee**-ray).
- If you're not sure of the reply, say **non ho capito** (non o ka-**pee**-to), 'I didn't understand'.

keep going straight ahead
continui sempre dritto
kon-**tee**-noo-ee **sem**-pray **dreet**-to

you have to turn round
deve tornare indietro
dev-ay tor-**na**-ray een-dee-**ay**-tro

turn...
giri...
gee-ree...

right
a destra
a **des**-tra

left
a sinistra
a see-**nee**-stra

go...
vada...
va-da...

towards...
verso...
ver-so...

keep going...
continui...
kon-**tee**-noo-ee...

as far as...
fino a...
fee-no a...

take...
prenda...
pren-da...

the first road on the right
la prima strada a destra
la **pree**-ma **stra**-da a **des**-tra

the second road on the left
la seconda strada a sinistra
la se-**kon**-da **stra**-da a see-**nee**-stra

cross...
attraversi...
at-tra-**ver**-see...

the square
la piazza
la pee-**at**-sa

it's after the traffic lights
è dopo il semaforo
e **do**-po eel se-**ma**-fo-ro

Bus

- Tickets must be stamped on board in a machine which is usually beside the front or rear doors on buses.
  - Tickets can be bought at newsstands, tobacconists and bars displaying the bus company logo.
  - In Milan tickets can be used on bus and underground and are valid for 75 minutes.

where is the bus station?
dov'è la stazione degli autobus?
*do-**ve** la stats-**yo**-nay **del**-yee **ow**-to-boos*

I want to go...
voglio andare...
***vol**-yo an-**da**-ray...*

to the station
alla stazione
***al**-la stats-**yo**-nay*

to the museum
al museo
***al** moo-**zay**-o*

to Piazza Cavour
a Piazza Cavour
*a pee-**at**-sa ka-**voor***

to the Vatican
al Vaticano
*al va-tee-**ka**-no*

does this bus go to...?
questo autobus va a...?
***kwes**-to **ow**-to-boos va a...*

which bus do I take?
quale autobus devo prendere?
***kwa**-lay **ow**-to-boos **day**-vo **pren**-day-ray*

where does the bus go from?
da dove parte l'autobus?
*da **do**-vay **par**-tay **low**-to-boos*

how often are the buses?
ogni quanto ci sono gli autobus?
***on**-yee **kwan**-to chee **so**-no lyee **ow**-to-boos*

can you please tell me when to get off?
può dirmi quando devo scendere?
*pwo **deer**-mee **kwan**-do **day**-vo **shen**-day-ray*

Underground

- Only Milan and Rome have underground systems.
- You can get 24- and 48-hour tickets as well as a book (**carnet**) of 10 tickets.
- In the underground system, tickets can be stamped only once, so you couldn't come out and go on a bus then go back onto the underground with the same ticket.

where is the metro station?
dov'è la stazione della metropolitana?
*do-**ve** la stats-**yo**-nay **del**-la met-ro-po-lee-**ta**-na*

a block of tickets, please
un carnet di biglietti, per favore
*oon kar-**nay** dee beel-**yet**-tee payr fa-vo-ray*

do you have an underground map?
avete una piantina della metro?
*a-**vay**-tay **oo**-na pee-an-**tee**-na **del**-la **met**-ro*

I want to go to...
voglio andare a...
***vol**-yo an-**da**-ray a...*

can I go by underground?
si può andare con la metro?
*see pwo an-**da**-ray kon la **met**-ro*

do I have to change?
devo cambiare?
***day**-vo kam-bee-**a**-ray*

where?
dove?
***do**-vay*

which line do I take?
quale linea prendo?
***kwa**-lay **lee**-nay-a **pren**-do*

which is the station for the cathedral?
qual è la stazione per il duomo?
*kwal e la stats-**yo**-nay payr eel **dwo**-mo*

Train

missione servizio a Telefonica

7 - 14 - 15 →

Accoglie

- Italy has a highly efficient national rail network. Check offers and info on **www.trenitalia.com**.
- The highspeed tilting train (**pendolino**) must be booked in advance.
- Tickets must be validated before boarding the train. Machines are yellow and located at the beginning of the platform.

where is the station?
dov'è la stazione?
*do-**ve** la stats-**yo**-nay*

to the main station, please
alla stazione centrale, per favore
*al-la stats-**yo**-nay chen-**tra**-lay payr fa-**vo**-ray*

a single to...	**2 singles to...**
un andata per...	due andate per...
*oon an-**da**-ta payr...*	***doo**-ay an-da-tay payr...*

a return to...	**2 returns to...**
un andata e ritorno per...	due andata e ritorno per...
*oon an-**da**-ta ay ree-**tor**-no payr...*	***doo**-ay an-**da**-ta ay ree-**tor**-no payr...*

a child's return to...
un andata e ritorno ridotto per...
*oon an-**da**-ta ay ree-**tor**-no ree-**dot**-to payr...*

Ist/2nd class	smoking	non smoking
prima/seconda classe	fumatori	non fumatori
***pree**-ma/se-**kon**-da **klas**-say*	*foo-ma-**to**-ree*	*non foo-ma-**to**-ree*

do I have to pay a supplement?
devo pagare un supplemento?
***day**-vo pa-**ga**-ray oon soop-play-**men**-to*

is my pass valid for this journey?
è valida la tessera per questo viaggio?
*e **va**-lee-da la **tes**-say-ra payr **kwes**-to vee-**ad**-jo*

● Some trains require a supplement. Buy it before boarding as it costs more on the train. The overhead board indicates if a **supplemento** is required.
● A Swiss Pass must be bought before arriving in Switzerland. Check **www.raileurope.com**.
● Remember to validate tickets for both outward and return trips.

I want to book...
voglio prenotare...
vol-yo pray-no-**ta**-ray...

a seat
un posto
oon **pos**-to

a couchette
una cuccetta
oo-na koo-**chet**-ta

where is the timetable?
dov'è l'orario dei treni?
do-**ve** lo-**rar**-yo **day**-ee **tray**-nee

do I need to change?
devo cambiare?
day-vo kam-bee-a-ray

where?
dove?
do-vay

which platform does it leave from?
da quale binario parte?
da **kwa**-lay bee-**nar**-yo **par**-tay

does the train to ... leave from this platform?
il treno per ... parte da questo binario?
eel **tray**-no payr ... **par**-tay da **kwes**-to bee-**nar**-yo

is this the train for...?
è questo il treno per...?
e **kwes**-to eel **tray**-no payr...

where is the left-luggage?
dov'è il deposito bagagli?
do-**ve** eel de-**po**-zee-to ba-**gal**-yee

is this seat taken?
è occupato?
e ok-koo-**pa**-to

Taxi

● Get a taxi from a taxi stand – *generally located at stations or call a radio taxi.*
● *Taxis are white and it's better to use these as other private operators (blue limousines) might charge more.*
● *To go from Fiumicino airport to the centre of Rome or from Malpensa to Milan the price should be around 80 euros.*

to the airport, please
all'aeroporto, per favore
*al-lay-ro-**por**-to payr fa-**vo**-ray*

please take me to this address
per favore mi porti a questo indirizzo
*payr fa-**vo**-ray mee **por**-tee a **kwes**-to een-dee-**reet**-so*

how much will it cost?
quanto verrà a costare?
***kwan**-to ver-**ra** a kost-**ta**-ray*

it's too much
è troppo
*e **trop**-po*

how much is it to the centre?
quanto costa per il centro?
***kwan**-to **kos**-ta payr eel **chen**-tro*

where can I get a taxi?
dove posso trovare un taxi?
***do**-vay **pos**-so tro-**va**-ray oon **tak**-see*

please order me a taxi
per favore mi chiami un taxi
*payr fa-**vo**-ray mee kee-**a**-mee oon **tak**-see*

can I have a receipt?
posso avere una ricevuta?
***pos**-so a-**vay**-ray **oo**-na ree-che-**voo**-ta*

I've nothing smaller
non ho moneta
*non o mon-**ay**-ta*

keep the change
tenga il resto
***ten**-ga eel **res**-to*

Boat

- In the city of Venice, public transport is by waterbus (**vaporetto**). Tickets may be purchased in advance at landing stages or from some tobacconists, shops and bars.
- Tickets must be punched before boarding.
- In Switzerland the Swiss Pass includes travel on some lake steamers.

1 ticket	**2 tickets**	**single**	**round trip**
un biglietto	due biglietti	andata	andata e ritorno
*oon beel-**yet**-to*	***doo**-ay beel-**yet**-tee*	*an-**da**-ta*	*an-**da**-ta ay ree-**tor**-no*

a Venice card for one day
una carta Venezia per un giorno
*oo-na **kar**-ta ven-**et**-see-a payr oon **jor**-no*

is there a tourist ticket?
c'è un biglietto turistico?
*che oon beel-**yet**-to too-**rees**-tee-ko*

are there any boat trips?
ci sono delle gite in battello?
*chee **so**-no **del**-lay **jee**-tay een bat-**tel**-lo*

when does the boat leave?
quando parte il battello?
***kwan**-do **par**-tay eel bat-**tel**-lo*

do you have a time table?
ha l'orario?
*a lo-**rar**-yo*

is there a restaurant on board?
c'è un ristorante sul battello?
*che oon rees-to-**ran**-tay sool bat-**tel**-lo*

can we hire a boat?
possiamo noleggiare una barca?
*pos-see-**a**-mo no-led-**ja**-ray **oo**-na **bar**-ka*

Car – driving

● Headlights must be kept on during the day on motorways and on roads outside towns.
● When raining (i.e. when windscreen wipers in use), limits of 130 and 110kph are lowered by 20kph.
● Fines are high if you drive 11kph or more over the limit.
● Carry your passport at all times, even if you're a passenger.

can I park here?
posso parcheggiare qui?
pos-so par-ked-*ja*-ray kwee

do I need a parking disk?
è necessario il disco orario?
*e ne-ches-**sar**-yo eel **dee**-sko o-**ra**-ree-o*

where can I park?
dove posso parcheggiare?
***do**-vay **pos**-so par-ked-**ja**-ray*

is there a car park?
c'è un parcheggio?
*che oon par-**ked**-jo*

where can I get a parking disk?
dove posso trovare un disco orario?
***do**-vay **pos**-so tro-**va**-ray oon **dee**-sko o-**rar**-yo*

how long can I park here?
per quanto tempo posso stare qui?
*payr **kwan**-to **tem**-po **pos**-so **sta**-ray kwee*

we're going to....
andiamo a...
*an-dee-**a**-mo a...*

what's the best route?
qual è la strada migliore?
*kwal e la **stra**-da meel-**yo**-ray*

is the pass open?
il passo è aperto?
*eel **pas**-so e a-**payr**-to*

how do I get to the motorway?
scusi, per andare sull'autostrada?
***skoo**-zee payr an-**da**-ray sool-**low**-to-stra-da*

which exit is it for...?
quale uscita è per...?
***kwa**-lay oo-**shee**-ta e payr...*

● *Petrol stations have both manned and self-service pumps. Prices are lower for self-service pumps.*
● *If you choose a manned pump, don't accept oil checks, etc – you might be charged for ones that aren't required.*
● *Most petrol stations have self-service pumps. Make sure you have 5, 10 and 20 euro notes on you. No change is given so be careful how much fuel you put in.*

is there a petrol station near here?
c'è una stazione di servizio qui vicino?
*che **oo**-na stats-**yo**-nay dee ser-**veets**-yo kwee vee-**chee**-no*

fill it up, please
il pieno, per favore
*eel pee-**ay**-no payr fa-**vo**-ray*

unleaded
senza piombo
***sent**-sa pee-**om**-bo*

diesel
gasolio
*ga-**zol**-ee-o*

20 euro-worth of petrol
venti euro di benzina
***ven**-tee ay-**oo**-ro dee ben-**tsee**-na*

where is the air line?
dov'è l'aria compressa?
***do**-vay **la**-ree-a kom-**pres**-sa*

please check...
per favore controlli...
*payr fa-**vo**-ray kon-**trol**-lee...*

the tyre pressure
la pressione delle gomme
*la pres-**yo**-nay del-lay gom-may*

the oil
l'olio
***lol**-yo*

the water
l'acqua
***lak**-wa*

can I pay by credit card?
posso pagare con la carta di credito?
***pos**-so pa-**ga**-ray kon la **kar**-ta dee **kre**-dee-to*

everything is ok
tutto a posto
***toot**-to a **pos**-to*

which pump?
quale pompa?
***kwa**-lay **pom**-pa*

Car – problems/breakdown

● Motorways have emergency phones every 2km. The police will automatically know your location if you use them.
● If you break down on the motorway and have to get out for a puncture, etc, you must put on a fluorescent waistcoat that should be carried in all vehicles.
● If you need the police dial 113 (motorways) and 112 (elsewhere).

I've broken down
mi si è rotta la macchina
mee see e **rot**-ta la **ma**-kee-na

I'm on my own (female)
sono da sola
so-no da **so**-la

there are children in the car
ci sono bambini nella macchina
chee **so**-no bam-**bee**-nee **nel**-la **ma**-kee-na

where is the nearest garage?
dov'è il garage più vicino?
do-**ve** eel ga-**raj** pee-**yoo** vee-**chee**-no

is it serious?
è una cosa seria?
e **oo**-na **ko**-za **say**-ree-a

can you repair it?
può ripararlo?
pwo ree-pa-**rar**-lo

when will it be ready?
quando sarà pronta?
kwan-do sa-**ra pron**-ta

how much will it cost?
quanto costerà?
kwan-to kos-tay-**ra**

the car won't start
la macchina non parte
la **ma**-kee-na non **par**-tay

I have a flat tyre
ho una gomma a terra
o **oo**-na **gom**-ma a **ter**-ra

the engine is overheating
il motore si surriscalda
eel mo-**to**-ray see soor-rees-**kal**-da

the battery is flat
la batteria è scarica
la bat-te-**ree**-a e **ska**-ree-ka

can you replace the windscreen?
può cambiare il parabrezza?
pwo kam-bee-**a**-ray eel pa-ra-**bret**-sa

- To avoid problems, book a car in advance. If you buy your air ticket on the internet, many airlines offer car hire.
- All hire cars have air conditioning.
- Check that there are an emergency fluorescent waistcoat and parking disk in the car.
- The word for 'hire' is **noleggio** (no-**led**-jo).

I want to hire a car
vorrei noleggiare una macchina
vor-**ray**-ee no-led-**ja**-ray oo-na ma-**kee**-na

for one day
per un giorno
payr oon **jor**-no

for ... days
per ... giorni
payr ... **jor**-nee

does the price include fully comprehensive insurance?
il prezzo è inclusivo della polizza kasko?
eel **pret**-so e een-kloo-**see**-vo **del**-la po-**leet**-sa **kas**-ko

I want...
vorrei...
vor-**ray**-ee...

a large car
una macchina grande
oo-na ma-**kee**-na **gran**-day

a small car
una macchina piccola
oo-na ma-**kee**-na **peek**-kol-la

an automatic
una automatica
oo-na ow-to-**ma**-tee-ka

what do we do if we break down?
che cosa facciamo se ci capita un guasto?
kay **ko**-za fa-chee-**a**-mo say chee **ka**-pee-ta oon **gwas**-to

must I return the car here?
devo riportare la macchina qui?
day-vo ree-por-**ta**-ray la ma-**kee**-na kwee

by what time?
per che ora?
payr kay **o**-ra

I'd like to leave it in...
vorrei lasciarla a...
vor-**ray**-ee la-**shar**-la a...

where are the documents?
dove sono i documenti?
do-vay **so**-no ee do-koo-**men**-tee

Shopping – holiday

ORNALI
CARTO
OCATTOLI
ARTICOLI

- Shops close from 1–4pm, but stay open till about 7.30pm.
- If you want to go shopping, you are better to avoid tourist areas.
- Street markets are good places for clothes, food and antiques.
- Smaller shops close on Monday mornings.

do you sell...?
vendete...?
ven-**day**-tay...

stamps
francobolli
fran-ko-**bol**-lee

batteries for this
pile per questo
pee-lay payr **kwes**-to

where can I buy...?
dove posso comprare...?
do-vay **pos**-so kom-**pra**-ray...

a colour film
una pellicola a colori
oo-na pel-**lee**-ko-la a ko-**lo**-ree

10 stamps
dieci francobolli
dee-**ay**-chee fran-ko-**bol**-lee

for postcards
per cartoline
payr kar-to-**lee**-nay

to Britain
per la Gran Bretagna
payr la gran bre-**tan**-ya

a tape for this video camera, please
una cassetta per questa videocamera, per favore
oo-na kas-set-ta payr **kwes**-ta vee-**day**-o-ka-**may**-ra payr fa-**vo**-ray

I'm looking for a present
cerco un regalo
cher-ko oon ray-**ga**-lo

have you something cheaper?
ha qualcosa di meno caro?
a kwal-**ko**-za dee **may**-no **ka**-ro

it's a gift
è un regalo
e oon ray-**ga**-lo

please wrap it up
può incartarlo, per favore
pwo een-kar-**tar**-lo payr fa-**vo**-ray

is there a market?
c'è un mercato?
che oon mer-**ka**-to

which day?
quale giorno?
kwa-lay **joor**-no

clothes – Shopping

- *There are some good Italian department stores:*
  Upim, Coin *and* **Standa**. *In Milan there is* **La Rinascente**.
- *Big malls are open all day until late (about 10 or 11pm).*
- *If you are interested in designer clothes then you have to stay in the centre of towns. But good deals can be found in factory outlets. Ask at tourist info centres.*

can I try this on?
posso provarlo?
pos-so pro-var-lo

it's too big
è troppo grande
e trop-po gran-day

it's too small
è troppo piccolo
e trop-po peek-ko-lo

it's too expensive
è troppo caro
e trop-po ka-ro

I'll take this one
prendo questo
pren-do kwes-to

can you give me a discount?
mi può fare uno sconto?
mee pwo fa-ray oo-no skon-to

I take a size ... shoe
porto il numero...
por-to eel noo-may-ro...

what size are you?
che taglia porta?
kay tal-ya por-ta

I like it
mi piace
mee pee-a-chay

have you a smaller one?
ha uno più piccolo?
a oo-no pee-yoo peek-ko-lo

have you a larger one?
ha uno più grande?
a oo-no pee-yoo gran-day

what shoe size do you take?
che numero di scarpe porta?
kay noo-may-ro dee skar-pay por-ta

Shopping – food

- Smaller shops generally close between 1 and 4pm.
- Supermarkets are generally open all day Mon–Sat, with late-night shopping on Thurs and Fri. Sunday opening is not as common as in the UK.
- Supermarkets include **Standa** and **Bennet**.
- You will need euro coins to release the shopping trolley.

where can I buy...?
dove posso comprare...?
*do-vay **pos**-so kom-**pra**-ray...*

fruit	**bread**	**milk**
della frutta	del pane	del latte
del-la froot-ta	*del pa-nay*	*del lat-tay*

where is the supermarket?
dov'è il supermercato?
*doh-**ve** eel **soo**-per-mer-**ka**-to*

where is the market?
dov'è il mercato?
*doh-**ve** eel mer-**ka**-to*

when is the market?
quando c'è il mercato?
***kwan**-do che eel mer-**ka**-to*

it's me next
tocca a me
***tok**-ka a me*

that's enough
basta così
bas**-ta ko-**zee

6 bread rolls
sei panini
*say pa-**nee**-nee*

a ciabatta
una ciabatta
***oo**-na cha-**bat**-ta*

a litre of...	**milk**	**beer**	**mineral water**
un litro di...	latte	birra	acqua minerale
*oon **lee**-tro dee...*	***lat**-tay*	***beer**-ra*	***ak**-wa mee-nay-**ra**-lay*

a bottle of...	**wine**	**still water**	**sparkling water**
una bottiglia di...	vino	acqua naturale	acqua gassata
***oo**-na bot-**teel**-ya dee...*	***vee**-no*	***ak**-wa na-too-**ra**-lay*	***ak**-wa gas-**za**-ta*

a can of...	**coke**	**tonic water**	**beer**
una lattina di...	coca	acqua tonica	birra
***oo**-na lat-**tee**-na dee...*	***ko**-ka*	***ak**-wa **to**-nee-ka*	***beer**-ra*

food – Shopping

● Fruit and veg must be weighed and stickered before taking it to the check-out. In some places you do it yourself, in others an assistant does it.
● Bread is generally bought daily.
● You need to pay for plastic bags. They are usually found next to the checkout.

100 grams of...
un etto di...
oon et-to dee...

salami
salame
sa-la-may

grated parmesan
parmigiano grattugiato
par-mee-ja-no grat-too-ja-to

cooked ham
prosciutto cotto
pro-shoot-to kot-to

Parma ham
prosciutto crudo
pro-shoot-to kroo-do

250 grams of...
due etti e mezzo di...
doo-ay et-tee ay med-zo dee...

butter
burro
boor-ro

cheese
formaggio
for-mad-jo

a kilo of...
un chilo di...
oon kee-lo dee...

potatoes
patate
pa-ta-tay

apples
mele
may-lay

two slices of pizza
due fette di pizza
doo-ay fet-tay dee peet-sa

three slices of focaccia
tre fette di focaccia
tray fet-tay dee fo-ka-cha

a portion of...
una porzione di...
oo-na ports-yo-nay dee...

Russian salad
insalata russa
een-sa-la-ta roos-sa

lasagne
lasagne
la-zan-yay

a packet of...
un pacchetto di...
oon pak-ket-to dee...

biscuits
biscotti
bee-skot-tee

sugar
zucchero
tsook-ke-ro

a tin of tomatoes
una scatola di pelati
oo-na ska-to-la dee pay-la-tee

a jar of honey
un vaso di miele
oon va-zo dee mee-ay-lay

can I help you?
mi dica?
mee dee-ka

anything else?
altro?
al-tro

is that everything?
è tutto?
e toot-to

45

Sightseeing

- The Italian Tourist Office website is **www.enit.it**.
- It is sometimes necessary to book tickets in advance (e.g. for the **Musei Vaticani** in Rome or to see **Il Cenacolo**, the Last Supper, in Milan).
- If visiting churches or religious sites, remember that these are primarily places of worship, so no shorts or bare shoulders.

where is the tourist office?
dov'è l'ufficio turistico?
*do-**ve** loof-**fee**-cho too-**rees**-tee-ko*

we want to visit...
vogliamo visitare...
*vol-**ya**-mo vee-zee-**ta**-ray...*

do you have a town guide?
ha una guida della città?
*a **oo**-na **gwee**-da **del**-la cheet-**ta***

we want to go to...
vogliamo andare a...
*vol-**ya**-mo an-**da**-ray a...*

are there any excursions?
ci sono delle gite?
*chee **so**-no **del**-lay **jee**-tay*

when does it leave?
quando parte?
***kwan**-do **par**-tay*

how much is it to get in?
quanto costa l'ingresso?
***kwan**-to **kos**-ta leen-**gres**-so*

is it open to the public?
è aperto al pubblico?
*e a-**payr**-to al poob-**blee**-ko*

have you any leaflets?
ha degli opuscoli?
*a **del**-yee o-**poos**-ko-lee*

in English
in inglese
*een een-**glay**-zay*

where does it leave from?
da dove parte?
*da **do**-vay **par**-tay*

Beach

- *Beaches are crowded in July, August and summer weekends.*
- *Every resort must have at least one free beach where you can go without paying.*
- *If you want an umbrella, chairs, changing cabins, lifeguard, bars, etc, then go to a **bagno**. These can be really nice, but fees can be quite high.*

can you recommend a quiet beach?
ci può consigliare una spiaggia tranquilla?
*chee pwo kon-seel-**ya**-ray **oo**-na spee-**ad**-ja tran-**kweel**-la*

is there a swimming pool?
c'è una piscina?
*che **oo**-na pee-**shee**-na*

can we swim in the lake?
si può fare il bagno nel lago?
*see pwo **fa**-ray eel **ban**-yo nel la-go*

is the water clean?
l'acqua è pulita?
***lak**-wa e poo-**lee**-ta*

is the water deep?
l'acqua è profonda?
***lak**-wa e pro-**fon**-da*

is the water cold?
l'acqua è fredda?
***lak**-wa e **fred**-da*

is it dangerous?
c'è pericolo?
*che pe-**ree**-ko-lo*

are there currents?
ci sono delle correnti?
*chee **so**-no **del**-lay kor-**ren**-tee*

where can we...?
dove si può...?
***do**-vay see pwo...*

windsurf
fare il surfing
***fa**-ray eel surfing*

waterski
fare lo sci nautico
***fa**-ray lo shee **now**-tee-ko*

hire a beach umbrella
noleggiare un ombrellone
*no-led-**ja**-ray oon om-brel-**lo**-nay*

Sport

● Tourist offices are the places to ask about sport.
● Football matches usually start at 3pm on Sundays, but in winter
they start at 2.30 or even 2pm. Visit www.calcioFans.com.
● It is compulsory to wear a swimming cap in pools, even
outdoor ones. It is usually possible to buy or borrow a cap
from the reception if you don't have one.

where can we...?
dove si può...?
do-vay see pwo...

play tennis
giocare a tennis
jo-ka-ray a ten-nees

play golf
giocare a golf
jo-ka-ray a golf

hire bikes
noleggiare le biciclette
no-led-ja-ray lay bee-chee-kle-tay

go fishing
pescare
pes-ka-ray

go riding
andare a cavallo
an-da-ray a ka-val-lo

how much is it...?
quanto costa...?
kwan-to kos-ta...

per hour
all'ora
al-lo-ra

per day
al giorno
al jor-no

how do I book a court?
come si prenota il campo da tennis?
ko-may see pray-no-ta eel kam-po da ten-nees

can I hire...?
posso noleggiare...?
pos-so no-led-ja-ray...

racquets
le racchette
lay rak-ket-tay

golf clubs
le mazze da golf
lay mat-say da golf

is there a football match?
c'è una partita di calcio?
che oo-na par-tee-ta dee kal-cho

where is there a sports shop?
dove c'è un negozio di articoli sportivi?
da-vay che oon nay-gots-yo dee ar-tee-ko-lee spor-tee-vee

● Take some passport-sized photos with you. It will save time when getting your ski pass organized.
● Ski resorts and runs get very busy. It is vital that skiers and snowboarders behave in such a manner so as not to cause any danger to others. Italy has begun to impose codes of conduct with fines for breaking them.

can I hire skis?
posso noleggiare gli sci?
pos-so no-led-*ja*-ray lyee shee

how much is a pass?
quanto costa lo skipass?
kwan-to *kos*-ta lo skee-pass

I'm a beginner
sono un principiante
so-no oon preen-chee-pee-*an*-tay

which is an easy run?
qual è una pista facile?
kwal e *oo*-na *pees*-ta *fa*-chee-lay

what is the snow like today?
com'è la neve oggi?
ko-*me* la *nay*-vay *od*-jee

is there a map of the ski runs?
avete una piantina delle piste?
a-*vay*-tay *oo*-na pee-an-*tee*-na *day*-lay *pees*-tay

my skis are...
i miei sci sono...
ee mee-*ay*-ee shee *so*-no...

too long
troppo lunghi
trop-po *loon*-gee

too short
troppo corti
trop-po *kor*-tee

my bindings are...
i miei attacchi sono...
ee mee-*ay*-ee at-*tak*-kee *so*-no...

too loose
troppo larghi
trop-po *lar*-gee

too tight
troppo stretti
trop-po *stret*-tee

where can we go cross-country skiing?
dove si può andare a fare lo sci di fondo?
do-vay see pwo an-*da*-ray a *fa*-ray lo shee dee *fon*-do

there is danger of avalanches
c'è pericolo di valanghe
che pe-*ree*-ko-lo dee va-*lan*-gay

Nightlife – popular

● *The best bars, restaurants and nightclubs are usually in town centres, whereas large discos can be outside towns along main roads. Check the local paper.*
● *To see what locals do, simply go to the trendy areas of a town and watch.*
● *When you go to a disco, the entrance fee usually includes one drink.*

what is there to do at night?
che cosa c'è da fare di sera?
*kay **ko**-za che da **fa**-ray dee **say**-ra*

can you recommend a good place/bar?
mi può consigliare un buon locale/bar?
*me pwo-kon-seel-**ya**-ray oon bwon lo-**ka**-lay/bar*

can you recommend a good disco?
mi può consigliare una buona discoteca?
*mee pwo kon-seel-**ya**-ray **oo**-na **bwo**-na dee-sko-**te**-ka*

is it expensive?
è caro?
*e **ka**-ro*

where do local people go at night?
dove va la gente del posto di sera?
*do-vay va la **jen**-tay del **pos**-to dee **say**-ra*

is it in a safe area?
è in una zona sicura?
*e een oona **zo**-na see-**koo**-ra*

are there any concerts?
ci sono dei concerti?
*chee **so**-no **day**-ee kon-**cher**-tee*

do you like dancing?
ti piace ballare?
*tee pee-**a**-chay bal-**la**-ray*

I like dancing
mi piace ballare
*mee pee-**a**-chay bal-**la**-ray*

do you want to dance?
vuoi ballare?
***vwo**-ee bal-**la**-ray*

what's your name?
come ti chiami?
***ko**-may tee kee-**a**-mee*

I'm Marco
mi chiamo Marco
*mee kee-**a**-mo **mar**-ko*

- *Always check the local newspaper to find what's on.*
- *There is usually one cheap night for films, but it varies from town to town (in Milan it is Wednesdays).*
- *The opera season runs Oct–June (though **La Scala** starts in December). Visit **www.teatroallascala.org**.*
- *Check out Italian festivals on **www.hostetler.net**.*

is there a list of cultural events?
c'è un programma degli spettacoli?
*che oon pro-**gram**-ma **del**-yee spet-**ta**-ko-lee*

are there any local festivals?
ci sono delle feste locali?
*chee **so**-no **del**-lay **fes**-tay lo-**ka**-lee*

we'd like to go...
vogliamo andare...
*vol-**ya**-mo an-**da**-ray...*

to the theatre
a teatro
*a tay-**a**-tro*

to the opera
all'opera
*al-**lo**-pay-ra*

to the ballet
al balletto
*al bal-**let**-to*

to a concert
a un concerto
*a oon kon-**cher**-to*

what's on?
che cosa c'è?
*kay **ko**-za che*

do I need to book?
devo prenotare?
***day**-vo pray-no-**ta**-ray*

how much are the tickets?
quanto costano i biglietti?
***kwan**-to **kos**-ta-no ee beel-**yet**-tee*

2 tickets...
due biglietti...
***doo**-ay beel-**yet**-tee...*

for tonight
per stasera
*payr sta-**say**-ra*

for tomorrow night
per domani sera
*payr do-**ma**-nee **say**-ra*

when does the performance end?
a che ora finisce lo spettacolo?
*a kay **o**-ra fee-**nee**-shay lo spet-**ta**-ko-lo*

Hotel

Information on local hotels can be found at the tourist office.

Hotels are star-rated. One star is generally quite basic with shared facilities. Two star might have ensuite facilities.

Only the more modern hotels have air conditioning.

have you a room for tonight?
avete una camera per stanotte?
a-**vay**-tay **oo**-na **ka**-may-ra payr sta-**not**-tay

a single room
una camera singola
oo-na **ka**-may-ra seen-**go**-la

a double room
una camera doppia
oo-na **ka**-may-ra **dop**-ya

a family room
una camera per una famiglia
oo-na **ka**-may-ra payr **oo**-na fa-**meel**-ya

with bathroom
con bagno
kon **ban**-yo

with shower
con doccia
kon **do**-cha

how much is it?
quanto costa?
kwan-to **kos**-ta

is breakfast included?
comprende la colazione?
kom-**pren**-day la ko-lats-**yo**-nay

I booked a room
ho prenotato una camera
o pray-no-**ta**-to **oo**-na **ka**-may-ra

my name is...
mi chiamo...
mee kee-**a**-mo...

I'd like to see the room
vorrei vedere la camera
vor-**ray**-ee ve-**day**-ray la **ka**-may-ra

is there anything cheaper?
c'è qualcosa di meno caro?
che kwal-**ko**-za dee **may**-no **ka**-ro

what time is...?
a che ora c'è...?
a kay **o**-ra che...

breakfast
la colazione
la ko-lats-**yo**-nay

dinner
la cena
la **chey**-na

we'll be back late tonight
ritorniamo tardi stasera
ree-tor-nee-**a**-mo **tar**-dee sta-**say**-ra

the key, please
la chiave, per favore
*la kee-**a**-vay payr fa-**vo**-ray*

can you keep these in the safe?
può tenere questi nella cassaforte?
*pwo te-**ne**-ray **kwes**-tee **nel**-la kas-sa-**for**-tay*

come in!
avanti!
*a-**van**-tee*

please come back later
ritorni più tardi per favore
*ree-**tor**-nee pee-**yoo** tar-dee payr fa-**vo**-ray*

can we have breakfast in our room?
possiamo fare la colazione in camera?
*pos-see-**a**-mo **fa**-ray la ko-lats-**yo**-nay een **ka**-may-ra*

please bring...
per favore mi porti...
*payr fa-**vo**-ray mee **por**-tee...*

ashtray
un portacenere
*oon por-ta-**chay**-nay-ray*

soap
il sapone
*eel sa-**po**-nay*

towels
degli asciugamani
***del**-yee a-shoo-ga-**ma**-nee*

a glass
un bicchiere
*oon beek-**ye**-ray*

please clean...
può pulire per favore...
*pwo poo-**lee**-ray payr fa-**vo**-ray...*

my room
la camera
*la **ka**-may-ra*

the bathroom
il bagno
*eel **ban**-yo*

I would like a wake-up call...
vorrei la sveglia...
*vor-**ray**-ee la **svel**-ya...*

at 7 o'clock
alle sette
***al**-lay **set**-tay*

is there a laundry service?
c'è il servizio lavanderia?
*che eel ser-**veets**-yo la-van-day-**ree**-a*

I'm leaving tomorrow
parto domani
***par**-to do-**ma**-nee*

please prepare the bill
ci prepari il conto
*chee pray-**pa**-ree eel **kon**-to*

Self-catering

- *Voltage in Italy is 220 with 2-pronged plugs.*
- *Take an adaptor for any electrical appliances you pack.*
- *Rubbish must be taken to the local collection point. These are mainly lidded skips which are widespread. There are recycling banks for glass, plastic and paper.*
- *The word for neighbours is i vicini (ee vee-chee-nee).*

which is the key for this door?
qual è la chiave di questa porta?
kwal e la kee-a-vay dee kwes-ta por-ta

where are the fuses?
dove sono i fusibili?
do-vay so-no ee foo-zee-bee-lee

can you show us how this works?
può farci vedere come funziona questo?
pwo far-chee ve-day-ray ko-may foonts-yo-na kwes-to

how does ... work?	**the dishwasher**	**the waterheater**
come funziona...?	la lavastoviglie	lo scaldabagno
ko-may foonts-yo-na...	*la la-va-sto-veel-yay*	*lo skal-da-ban-yo*
	the washing machine	**the cooker**
	la lavatrice	la cucina
	la la-va-tree-chay	*la koo-chee-na*

whom do I speak to if there are any problems?
con chi devo parlare se ci sono dei problemi?
kon kee day-vo par-la-ray say chee so-no day-ee prob-lay-mee

where do I put the rubbish?
dove lascio la spazzatura?
do-vay la-sho la spat-sa-too-ra

the gas has run out	**what do I do?**
è finito il gas	che cosa devo fare?
e fee-nee-to eel gaz	*kay ko-za day-vo fa-ray*

Camping & Caravanning

- *Campsites are not as widespread as one may think; in certain areas you won't find one at all.*
- *If you drive a camper, don't expect to be able to camp on the road; it is forbidden almost everywhere.*
- *Speed limits for cars towing caravans are lower than normal speed limits.*

we're looking for a campsite
cerchiamo un campeggio
*cher-kee-**a**-mo oon kam-**ped**-jo*

have you any vacancies?
avete dei posti?
*a-**vay**-tee **day**-ee **pos**-tee*

we'd like to stay for ... nights
vorremmo restare per ... notti
*vor-**rem**-mo res-**ta**-ray payr ... **not**-tee*

is the campsite sheltered?
il campeggio è riparato?
*eel kam-**ped**-jo e ree-pa-**ra**-to*

can we have a more sheltered site?
possiamo avere un posto più riparato?
*pos-see-**a**-mo a-**vay**-ray oon **pos**-to pee-**yoo** ree-pa-**ra**-to*

this site is very muddy
questo posto è molto fangoso
***kwes**-to **pos**-to e **mol**-to fan-**go**-zo*

can we park our caravan here overnight?
possiamo mettere la nostra roulotte qui per la notte?
*pos-see-**a**-mo **met**-te-ray la **nos**-tra roo-**lot** kwee payr la **not**-tay*

can we put our tent here?
possiamo mettere la tenda qui?
*pos-see-**a**-mo **met**-te-ray la **ten**-da kwee*

have you a list of campsites?
ha una lista dei campeggi?
*a **oo**-na **lees**-ta **day**-ee kam-**ped**-jee*

how much is it per night?
quanto costa per notte?
***kwan**-to **kos**-ta payr **not**-tay*

is there another site?
c'è un altro posto?
*che oon **al**-tro **pos**-to*

Children

● *A small child is* **bambino(a)**. *An older child is* **ragazzo(a)**.
● *Children are welcome everywhere. Italian parents often take their children out with them in the evenings to restaurants, etc.*
● *On most public transport children under 5 travel free. Between 5 and 12 years of age they can get 50% discount.*

a child's ticket
un biglietto ridotto
*oon beel-**yet**-to ree-**dot**-to*

he/she is … years old
ha … anni
*a … **an**-nee*

is there a reduction for children?
c'è una riduzione per bambini?
*che **oo**-na ree-doots-**yo**-nay payr bam-**bee**-nee*

is there a children's menu?
c'è un menù per bambini?
*che oon me-**noo** payr bam-**bee**-nee*

do you have…?
avete…?
*a-**vay**-tay…*

a high chair
un seggiolone
*oon sed-jo-**lo**-nay*

a cot
un lettino
*oon let-**tee**-no*

is it ok to bring children?
si possono portare i bambini?
*see **pos**-so-no por-**ta**-ray ee bam-**bee**-nee*

what is there for children to do?
che cosa c'è da fare per i bambini?
*kay **ko**-za che da **fa**-ray payr ee bam-**bee**-nee*

is it safe for children?
va bene per bambini?
*va **be**-nay payr bam-**bee**-nee*

is it dangerous
c'è pericolo?
*che pe-**ree**-ko-lo*

I have two children
ho due figli
*o **doo**-ay **feel**-yee*

do you have children?
ha dei figli?
*a **day**-ee **feel**-yee*

Special Needs

- *Words for disabled are **disabili** and **handicappati** ('h' not pronounced). There are often discounts for entrance fees, etc.*
- *Many intercity trains have facilities for the disabled. They are marked with the blue disabled badge.*
- *Disabled parking is usually available and indicated with an orange wheelchair badge.*

is it possible to visit ... with a wheelchair?
si può visitare ... con la sedia a rotelle?
*see pwo vee-zee-**ta**-ray kon la **sed**-ya a ro-**tel**-lay*

do you have toilets for the disabled?
ci sono le toilette per i disabili?
*chee **so**-no lay twa-**let** payr ee dee-**za**-bee-lee*

I need a bedroom on the ground floor
ho bisogno di una camera al pian terreno
*o bee-**zon**-yo dee **oo**-na ka-**may**-ra al **pee**-an ter-**ray**-no*

is there a lift?
c'è l'ascensore?
*che la-shen-**so**-ray*

where is the lift?
dov'è l'ascensore?
*do-**ve** la-shen-**so**-ray*

are there many steps?
ci sono tanti gradini?
*chee **so**-no tan-tee gra-**dee**-nee*

is there an entrance for wheelchairs?
c'è l'accesso per la sedia a rotelle?
*che la-**ches**-so payr la **sed**-ya a ro-**tel**-lay*

is there a place on this train for a wheelchair?
c'è un posto su questo treno per una sedia a rotelle?
*che oon **pos**-to soo **kwes**-to **tray**-no payr **oo**-na **sed**-ya a ro-**tel**-lay*

is there a reduction for the disabled?
c'è una riduzione per i disabili?
*che **oo**-na ree-doots-**yo**-nay payr ee dee-**za**-bee-lee*

Exchange Visitors

● These phrases are intended for families hosting Italian-speaking visitors. We've used the more familiar **tu** (rather than the more formal **lei**) form.
● Italians generally eat dinner 7.30/8pm (later the further south you go) – Italian visitors might not be used to eating early.

did you sleep well?
hai dormito bene?
*a-ee dor-**mee**-to **be**-nay*

would you like to take a shower?
vuoi fare la doccia?
***vwo**-ee fa-ray la **do**-cha*

what would you like for breakfast?
che cosa prendi per colazione?
*kay **ko**-za **pren**-dee payr ko-lats-**yo**-nay*

do you eat...?
mangi...?
***man**-jee...*

what would you like to eat/drink?
che cosa vuoi da mangiare/bere?
*kay **ko**-za **vwo**-ee da man-**ja**-ray/**be**-ray*

do you drink...?
bevi...?
***be**-vee...*

what would you like to do today?
che cosa vuoi fare oggi?
*kay **ko**-za **vwo**-ee **fa**-ray od-jee*

would you like to go shopping?
vuoi andare a fare lo shopping?
***vwo**-ee an-**da**-ray a **fa**-ray lo **shop**-ping*

I will pick you up at...
vengo a prenderti alle...
***ven**-go a **pren**-der-tee **al**-lay...*

take care
sta' attento(a)
*sta at-**ten**-to(a)*

did you enjoy yourself?
ti sei divertito(a)?
*tee **say**-ee dee-ver-**tee**-to(a)*

please be back by...
devi essere a casa per le...
***day**-vee **es**-say-ray a **ka**-za payr lay...*

we'll be in bed when you get back
saremo a letto quando ritorni
*sa-**ray**-mo a **let**-to **kwan**-do ree-**tor**-nee*

Exchange Visitors

- If you are invited to an Italian home for a meal, you wouldn't be expected to bring a bottle of wine or gift. However, it might be an idea to take some British specialities on holiday with you (shortbread, fudge, etc).
- When you enter someone's home, it is polite to say **permesso** (per-**mes**-so).

I like...
mi piace...
me pee-a-chay...

I don't like...
non mi piace...
non mee pee-a-chay

that was delicious
era buonissimo
ay-ra bwo-nees-see-mo

may I phone home?
posso telefonare a casa?
***pos**-so te-le-fo-**na**-ray a **ka**-za*

may I make a local call?
posso fare una telefonata?
***pos**-so **fa**-ray **oo**-na te-le-fo-**na**-ta*

can I have a key?
posso avere la chiave di casa?
***pos**-so a-**vay**-ray la kee-**a**-vay dee **ka**-za*

can you take me by car?
mi può portare in macchina?
*mee pw**o** por-**ta**-ray een **ma**-kee-na*

can I borrow...?
mi può prestare...?
*mee pw**o** pres-**ta**-ray...*

an iron
un ferro da stiro
*oon **fer**-ro da **stee**-ro*

a hairdryer
un fon
oon fon

what time do I have to get up?
a che ora devo alzarmi?
*a kay **o**-ra **day**-vo alt-**sar**-mee*

please call me at...?
per favore mi chiama alle...?
*payr fa-**vo**-ray mee kee-**a**-ma **al**-lay...*

how long are you staying?
quanto tempo resta?
***kwan**-to **tem**-po **res**-tah*

I'm leaving in a week
parto tra una settimana
***par**-to tra **oo**-na set-tee-**ma**-na*

thanks for everything
grazie di tutto
*grat-**see**-ay dee **toot**-to*

I've had a great time
mi sono proprio divertito(a)
*mee **so**-no **pro**-pree-o dee-ver-**tee**-to(a)*

Problems

● *People are usually quite helpful and if you are lucky you'll also find someone who can speak English.*
● *Traffic wardens are an invaluable source of information and help, although their English might not be great.*
● *Try to stay calm. Not understanding each other can often aggravate the situation.*

can you help me?
può aiutarmi?
*pwo a-yoo-**tar**-mee*

I don't speak Italian
non parlo italiano
*non **par**-lo ee-tal-lee-**a**-no*

do you speak English?
parla inglese?
***par**-la een-**glay**-zay*

does anyone speak English?
c'è qualcuno che parla inglese?
*che kwal-**koo**-no kay **par**-la een-**glay**-zay*

I'm lost
mi sono smarrito(a)
*mee **so**-no smar-**ree**-to(a)*

how do I get to...?
come si fa per andare a...?
***ko**-may see fa payr an-**da**-ray a...*

I've missed...	**my plane**		**my connection**
ho perso...	l'aereo		la coincidenza
*o **per**-so...*	*la-**e**-ray-o*		*la ko-een-chee-**dent**-sa*

I've lost...	**my money**		**my passport**
ho perso...	i soldi		il passaporto
*o **per**-so...*	*ee-**sol**-dee*		*eel pas-sa-**por**-to*

my suitcase isn't here
non c'è la mia valigia
*non che la **mee**-a va-**lee**-ja*

I have no money
non ho soldi
*non o **sol**-dee*

I've left my bag in...
ho lasciato la mia borsa nel/nella...
*o lash-**a**-to la **mee**-a **bor**-sa nel/**nel**-la...*

on the coach
sul pullman
*sool **pool**-man*

leave me alone!
mi lasci in pace!
*mee **la**-shee een **pa**-chay*

go away!
se ne vada!
*say nay **va**-da*

Complaints

- *If you want to complain, it's always best to ask for the person in charge – il responsabile (eel res-pon-sa-bee-lay) or il direttore (eel dee-ret-tor-ay).*
- *You might be surprised at the way people queue in Italy – it's usually every man (or woman) for himself! Arm yourself with the phrase 'it's my turn!' tocca a me (tok-ka a me).*

the light
la luce
la **loo**-chay

the telephone
il telefono
eel te-**le**-fo-no

...doesn't work
...non funziona
...non foonts-**yo**-na

the toilet
il water
eel **va**-ter

the heating
il riscaldamento
eel ree-skal-da-**men**-to

the room is dirty
la camera è sporca
la ka-**may**-ra e **spor**-ka

the bath is dirty
il bagno è sporco
eel **ban**-yo e **spor**-ko

I don't like the room
non mi piace la camera
non mee pee-**a**-chay la ka-**may**-ra

it's too noisy
c'è troppo rumore
che **trop**-po roo-**mo**-ray

I didn't order this
non ho ordinato questo
non o or-dee-**na**-to **kwes**-to

I want to complain
voglio fare un reclamo
vol-yo **fa**-ray oon rek-**la**-mo

I want a refund
voglio un rimborso
vol-yo oon reem-**bor**-so

we're in a hurry
abbiamo fretta
ab-bee-**a**-mo **fret**-ta

there is a mistake
c'è un errore
che oon er-**ro**-ray

this is broken
questo è rotto
kwes-to e **rot**-to

can you repair it?
può ripararlo?
pwo ree-pa-**rar**-lo

Emergencies

● All the emergency services can be called on 113 although each has its own number: **Carabinieri** 112, **Police** 113, A&E 118, Fire brigade 115.
● Police officers can be very helpful (especially on motorways).
● If you've been robbed or attacked, go to the police station to report it and fill in a form. A copy is needed for insurance.

help!
aiuto!
a-**yoo**-to

can you help me?
può aiutarmi?
pwo a-yoo-**tar**-mee

there's been an accident
c'è stato un incidente
che **sta**-to oon een-chee-**den**-tay

someone is injured
qualcuno si è fatto male
kwal-**koo**-no see e **fat**-to **ma**-lay

please call...
per favore chiamate...
payr fa-**vo**-ray kee-a-**ma**-tay...

the police
la polizia
la po-leet-**see**-a

an ambulance
un'ambulanza
oon am-boo-**lant**-sa

he was going too fast
andava troppo forte
an-**da**-va **trop**-po **for**-tay

that man keeps following me
quell'uomo mi segue
kwel **wo**-mo mee **seg**-way

where's the police station?
dov'è la questura?
do-vay la kwes-**too**-ra

I want to report a theft
voglio denunciare un furto
vol-yo den-oon-**cha**-ray oon **foor**-to

I've been robbed
mi hanno derubato
*mee **an**-no de-roo-**ba**-to*

I've been attacked
mi hanno assalito
*mee **an**-no as-sa-**lee**-to*

my car has been broken into
hanno svaligiato la mia macchina
***an**-no sva-lee-**ja**-to la **mee**-a **ma**-kee-na*

my car has been stolen
mi hanno rubato la macchina
*mee **an**-no roo-**ba**-to la **ma**-kee-na*

I've been raped
mi hanno violentata
*mee **an**-no vee-o-len-**ta**-ta*

I need a report for my insurance
ho bisogno di un verbale per la mia assicurazione
*o bee-**zon**-yo dee oon ver-**ba**-lay payr la **mee**-a as-see-koo-rats-**yo**-nay*

how much is the fine?
quant'è la multa?
*kwan-**te** la **mool**-ta*

where do I pay it?
dove devo pagarla?
***do**-vay **day**-vo pa-**gar**-la*

I would like to phone the British Consulate
vorrei telefonare il Consolato Britannico
*vo-**ray**-ee te-le-fo-**na**-ray eel kon-so-**la**-to bree-**tan**-nee-ko*

I have no money
sono senza soldi
***so**-no **sent**-sa **sol**-dee*

we're on our way
arriviamo
*ar-ree-vee-**a**-mo*

Health

● Take a stamped E111 form (from post offices). You can keep it for future trips (unless you change address).
 ● If ill, ask the chemist which is the nearest doctor.
 ● You can go directly to the A&E of the nearest hospital. Be prepared to pay 35 euros for the visit (it's free only for serious emergencies) and 50 euros if you need an X-ray or blood test.

have you something for...?
può darmi qualcosa per...
*pwo **dar**-mee kwal-**ko**-za payr...*

car sickness
il mal d'auto
*eel mal **dow**-to*

diarrhoea
la diarrea
*la dee-ar-**ray**-a*

is it safe to give children?
va bene per i bambini?
*va **be**-nay payr ee bam-**bee**-nee*

I feel ill
mi sento male
*mee **sen**-to **ma**-lay*

I need a doctor
ho bisogno di un medico
*o bee-**zon**-yo dee oon **me**-dee-ko*

my son/my daughter is ill
mio figlio/mia figlia non sta bene
***mee**-o **feel**-yo/**mee**-a **feel**-ya non sta **be**-nay*

(s)he has a temperature
ha la febbre
*a la **feb**-bray*

I'm on this medication
sto prendendo queste medicine
*sto pren-**den**-do **kwes**-tay me-dee-**chee**-nay*

I have high blood pressure
ho la pressione alta
*o la pres-**yo**-nay **al**-ta*

I'm diabetic
sono diabetico(a)
***so**-no dee-a-**be**-tee-ko(a)*

I'm pregnant
sono incinta
***so**-no een-**cheen**-ta*

I'm on the pill
prendo la pillola
***pren**-do la **peel**-lo-la*

I'm allergic to penicillin
sono allergico(a) alla penicillina
***so**-no al-**ler**-jee-ko(a) **al**-la pe-nee-cheel-**lee**-na*

my blood group is...
il mio gruppo sanguigno è...
*eel **mee**-o **groop**-po san-**gween**-yo e...*

I'm breastfeeding
sto allattando al seno
*sto al-lat-**tan**-do al **say**-no*

is it safe for me to take?
posso prenderlo senza pericolo?
***pos**-so pren-**der**-lo **sen**-tsa per-**ee**-ko-lo*

will he/she have to go to hospital?
deve andare in opsedale?
***day**-vay an-**da**-ray een o-spe-**da**-lay*

I need to go to casualty
devo andare al pronto soccorso
***day**-vo an-**da**-ray al pron-to sok-**kor**-so*

where is the hospital?
dov'è l'ospedale?
*do-**ve** los-pe-**da**-lay*

when are visiting hours?
qual è l'orario di visita?
*kwal e lo-**rar**-yo dee **vee**-zee-ta*

which ward?
quale reparto?
***kwal**-lay re-**par**-to*

I need a dentist
ho bisogno di un dentista
*o bee-**zon**-yo dee oon den-**tee**-sta*

I have toothache
ho mal di denti
*o mal dee **den**-tee*

the filling has come out
è uscita l'otturazione
*e oo-**shee**-ta lot-too-rats-**yo**-nay*

I have an abscess
ho un ascesso
*o oon a-**shes**-so*

it hurts
fa male
*fa **ma**-lay*

can you repair my dentures?
può riparare la mi dentiera?
*pwo ree-pa-**ra**-ray la mee den-tee-**e**-ra*

do I have to pay now?
devo pagare subito?
***day**-vo pa-**ga**-ray **soo**-bee-to*

Business

● You will encounter bureaucracy for anything concerning the state (local government, etc). Things you think should take a short time may drag on.
● Italian company websites end *.it*.
● If an Italian bank holiday falls on a Thursday, Friday also becomes a holiday, making it into a long weekend.

ORARIO SPORTEL
da LUNEDÍ a VENERD
8.20 - 13.20
14.35 - 15.35

I am...
sono...
so-no...

here's my card
ecco il mio biglietto da visita
ek-ko eel mee-o beel-yet-to da vee-zee-ta

I'm from the Smith Company
sono della ditta Smith
so-no del-la deet-ta Smith

I'd like to arrange an appointment
vorrei fissare un appuntamento
vor-ray-ee fees-sa-ray oon ap-poon-ta-men-to

with Mr/Ms...
con il Signor/la Signora...
kon eel seen-yor/la seen-yo-ra...

for April 4th at 11 o'clock
per il quattro aprile alle undici
payr eel kwat-tro a-pree-lay al-lay oon-dee-chee

can we meet at a restaurant?
possiamo incontrarci in un ristorante?
pos-see-a-mo een-kon-trar-chee een oon rees-to-ran-tay

I will send a fax to confirm
manderó un fax di conferma
man-der-o oon fax dee kon-fayr-ma

I'm staying at Hotel...
sono all'Hotel...
so-no al-lo-tel...

how do I get to your office?
come si arriva al suo ufficio?
ko-may see ar-ree-va al soo-o oo-fee-cho

here is some information about my company
ecco alcune informazioni sulla mia ditta
ek-ko al-*koo*-nay een-for-mats-*yo*-nay *sool*-la *mee*-a *deet*-ta

I have an appointment with... at ... o'clock
ho un appuntamento con...   alle...
*o oon ap-poon-ta-**men**-to kon...   *al*-lay...

delighted to meet you!
molto piacere!
mol-to pee-a-*chay*-ray

my Italian isn't very good
parlo poco l'italiano
par-lo *po*-ko lee-tal-ee-*a*-no

what is the name of the managing director
come si chiama il direttore?
ko-may see kee-*a*-ma eel dee-ret-*to*-ray

I would like some information about your company
vorrei delle informazioni sulla sua ditta
vor-*ray*-ee *del*-lay een-for-mats-*yo*-nee *sool*-la *soo*-a *deet*-ta

do you have a press office?
avete l'ufficio stampa?
a-*vay*-tay loof-*fee*-cho *stam*-pa

I need an interpreter
ho bisogno di un interprete
o bee-*zon*-yo dee oon een-*ter*-pray-tay

can you photocopy this for me?
mi può fare una fotocopia?
mee pwo *fa*-ray *oo*-na fo-to-*ko*-pee-a

do you have an appointment?   **at what time?**
ha un appuntamento?   a che ora?
a oon ap-poon-ta-*men*-to   a kay *o*-ra

Phoning

● *International dialling codes: UK 0044; USA/Canada 001; Australia 0061. Take an adaptor for rechargers.*
  ● ***Numero verde*** *means freephone. They begin with 800.*
  ● *You can buy phonecards at 5 or 10 euros.*
  ● *Italian phone numbers include the area code, even for local calls.*

a phonecard
una scheda telefonica
*oo-na **skay**-da te-le-**fo**-nee-ka*

I want to make a phone call
vorrei fare una telefonata
*vor-**ray**-ee **fa**-ray oo-na te-le-**fon**-na-ta*

Mr Ponti, please
il signor Ponti, per favore
*eel seen-**yor** Ponti payr fa-**vo**-ray*

extension ..., please
interno ..., per favore
*een-**ter**-no ... payr fa-**vo**-ray*

can I speak to...?
posso parlare con...?
***pos**-so par-**la**-ray kon...*

this is Jim Brown
sono Jim Brown
***so**-no Jim Brown*

I'll call back later
richiamo più tardi
*ree-kee-**a**-mo pee-**yoo tar**-dee*

I'll call back tomorrow
richiamo domani
*ree-kee-**a**-mo do-**ma**-nee*

can I have an outside line, please
posso avere la linea, per favore
***pos**-so a-**vay**-ray la **lee**-nay-a payr fa-**vo**-ray*

hello
pronto
***pron**-to*

who is calling?
chi parla?
*kee **par**-la*

it's engaged
la linea è occupata
*la **lee**-nay-a e ok-koo-**pa**-ta*

can you call back later?
può richiamare più tardi?
*pwo ree-kee-a-**ma**-ray pee-**yoo tar**-dee*

do you want to leave a message?
vuole lasciare un messaggio?
***vwo**-lay la-**sha**-ray oon mes-**sad**-jo*

E-mail/Fax

- Internet cafés are on the increase. Visit **www.cybercafes.com**.
- www. is **voo voo voo punto**. @ is **chiocciola** (kee-**och**-o-la), but 'at' is also understood.
- The ending for Italian websites is **.it**.
- You can find internet points at larger post offices and at stations, etc.

I want to send an e-mail
vorrei mandare una mail
*vor-**ray**-ee man-**da**-ray **oo**-na mail*

what's your e-mail address?
qual è il suo indirizzo di posta elettronica?
*kwal e eel **soo**-o een-dee-**reet**-so dee **pos**-ta el-et-**tron**-ee-ka*

did you get my e-mail?
ha ricevuto la mia mail?
*a ree-**chay**-voo-to la **mee**-a mail*

my e-mail address is…
il mio indirizzo di posta elettronica è…
*eel **mee**-o een-dee-**reet**-so dee **pos**-ta el-et-**tron**-ee-ka e…*

caro.smith@anycompany.co.uk
carl punto smith @ anycompany punto co punto uk
*caro **poon**-to smith kee-**och**-o-la anycompany **poon**-to ko **poon**-to oo **kap**-pa*

I want to send a fax
vorrei mandare un fax
*vor-**ray**-ee man-**da**-ray oon fax*

what's your fax number?
qual è il suo numero di fax?
*kwal e eel **soo**-o **noo**-may-ro dee fax*

I cna't read it
non riesco a leggerlo
*non ree-**es**-ko a **led**-jer-lo*

do you have a fax?
avete il fax?
*a-**vay**-tay eel fax*

did you get my fax?
ha ricevuto il mio fax?
*a ree-chay-**voo**-to eel **mee**-o fax*

Numbers

0	zero *tsay*-ro			
1	uno *oo*-no	1st/1°	primo	*pree*-mo
2	due *doo*-ay			
3	tre *tray*	2nd/2°	secondo	se-**kon**-do
4	quattro **kwat**-tro			
5	cinque **cheen**-kway	3rd/3°	terzo	**tert**-so
6	sei *say*-ee			
7	sette *set*-tay	4th/4°	quarto	**kwar**-to
8	otto *ot*-to			
9	nove *no*-vay	5th/5°	quinto	**kween**-to
10	dieci dee-**ay**-chee			
11	undici **oon**-dee-chee	6th/6°	sesto	**ses**-to
12	dodici *do*-dee-chee			
13	tredici **tray**-dee-chee	7th/7°	settimo	**set**-tee-mo
14	quattordici kwat-**tor**-dee-chee			
15	quindici **kween**-dee-chee	8th/8°	ottavo	ot-**ta**-vo
16	sedici **say**-dee-chee			
17	diciassette dee-chas-**set**-tay	9th/9°	nono	**no**-no
18	diciotto dee-**chot**-to			
19	diciannove dee-chan-**no**-vay	10th/10°	decimo	**de**-chee-mo
20	venti **ven**-tee			
21	ventuno ven-**too**-no			
22	ventidue ven-tee-**doo**-ay			
30	trenta **tren**-ta			
40	quaranta kwa-**ran**-ta			
50	cinquanta cheen-**kwan**-ta			
60	sessanta ses-**san**-ta			
70	settanta set-**tan**-ta			
80	ottanta ot-**tan**-ta			
90	novanta no-**van**-ta			
100	cento **chen**-to			
110	cento dieci chent-to-dee-**ay**-chee			
200	cinquecento cheen-kway-**chen**-to			
1,000	mille *meel*-lay			
2,000	duemila doo-ay-**mee**-la			
1,000,000	un millione oon meel-**yo**-nay			

Days & Months

Monday	lunedì *loo-ned-**ee***
Tuesday	martedì *mar-ted-**ee***
Wednesday	mercoledì *mer-ko-led-**ee***
Thursday	giovedì *jov-ed-**ee***
Friday	venerdì *ven-er-**dee***
Saturday	sabato ***sa**-bat-o*
Sunday	domenica *do-**men**-ee-ka*

January	gennaio *je-**na**-yo*
February	febbraio *feb-**ra**-yo*
March	marzo ***mar**-tso*
April	aprile *a-**pree**-lay*
May	maggio ***mad**-jo*
June	giugno ***joon**-yo*
July	luglio ***lool**-yo*
August	agosto *a-**gos**-to*
September	settembre *set-**tem**-bray*
October	ottobre *ot-**tob**-ray*
November	novembre *nov-**emb**-ray*
December	dicembre *dee-**chemb**-ray*

what's the date today?
quanti ne abbiamo oggi?
***kwan**-tee nay ab-bee-**a**-mo **od**-jee*

which day?
quale giorno?
***kwal**-lay **jor**-no*

which month?
quale mese?
***kwal**-lay **me**-zay*

it's the 5th of October 2004
è il cinque ottobre dumilaequattro
*e eel **cheen**-kway ot-**tob**-ray doo-ay-**mee**-la-**kwat**-tro*

on Saturday
sabato
***sa**-ba-to*

on Saturdays
il sabato/di sabato
*eel **sa**-ba-to/dee **sa**-ba-to*

every Saturday
ogni sabato
***on**-yee **sa**-ba-to*

this Saturday
questo sabato
***kwes**-to **sa**-ba-to*

next Saturday
sabato prossimo
***sa**-ba-to **pros**-see-mo*

last Saturday
sabato scorso
***sa**-ba-to **skor**-so*

Time

- am = *di mattina* (dee mat-**tee**-na)
- pm = *di pomeriggio* (dee pom-er-**eed**-jo)
- The 24-hour clock is used a lot more in Europe than in Britain.
- With the 24-hour clock the words **quarto** (quarter) and **mezzo** (half) aren't used. 15 and 30 are used.

giorni feriau.
dalle 9.00
alle 20.00

excuse me, what time is it?
scusi, che ore sono?
skoo-zee kay **o**-ray **so**-no

am
di mattina
dee mat-**tee**-na

pm
di pomeriggio/sera
dee po-may-**reed**-jo/**say**-ra

at midday
a mezzogiorno
a med-zo-**jor**-no

at midnight
a mezzanotte
a med-za-**not**-tay

it's 1 o'clock
è l'una
e **loo**-na

it's six o'clock
sono le sei
so-no lay **say**-ee

it's half past 8
sono le otto e mezza
so-no lay **ot**-to ay **med**-za

an hour
un'ora
oon **o**-ra

half an hour
una mezz'ora
oo-na med-**zo**-ra

until 8 o'clock
fino alle otto
fee-no **al**-lay **ot**-to

it is half past 10
sono le dieci e mezza
so-no lay dee-**ay**-chee ay **med**-za

at 10 o'clock
alle dieci
al-lay dee-**ay**-chee

at 2200
alle ore ventidue
al-lay **o**-ray ven-tee-doo-ay

soon
fra poco
fra **po**-ko

later
più tardi
pee-yoo **tar**-dee

La cucina italiana

Italian cooking is among the best-loved in the world. It has travelled the globe along with the Italians who took their recipes with them. The emphasis has always been on good ingredients and what is available locally and in season, rather than quantity.

In the north of the country Italian cooking reveals the influences of its neighbours: France, Austria, Switzerland and Slovenia. The further south you go the lighter and more colourful the food becomes.

In Milan and Lombardy you find veal and **risotto** dishes. The rice fields of the Po valley produce pudding-like rice which can be cooked with butter, parmesan and saffron.

Liguria with its long coastline boasts numerous fish dishes as well as wonderful aromatic basil found in its **pesto**.

Another of Italy's great exports is Parma ham and Bolognese sauce. These come from the Emilia-Romagna with its cities of Parma and Bologna.

As you reach Italy's calf and ankle, you find the mountainous areas of Puglia, Campania and Basilicata where lamb becomes one of the main ingredients of its dishes.

With the Mediterranean on all sides, its influences can be tasted everywhere: olives, fresh fish, pasta dishes, fresh fruit and vegetables.

And Sicily, surrounded by sea, yields dishes of prehistoric-looking fish, with influences of neighbouring Africa such as couscous.

Breakfast (**prima colazione**) is light: coffee (**caffè** or **caffelatte** or **cappuccino**) with bread and jam, biscuits or croissant. Lunch (**pranzo**) for people who work can be a snack or canteen meal (usually between 12.30 and 2pm). The evening meal (**cena**) is normally the main meal of the day, usually eaten between 7.30 and 9pm. The further south, the later it can be, often after 9pm.

Ordering drinks

● It's cheaper to have a drink at the bar. If you're in a hurry and want a quick coffee, do as the locals do and stand.
● In city bars and caffè you pay first at the **cassa** and then present the receipt (**scontrino**) at the bar to whoever is serving you. You need to be able to explain what you want at the **cassa** and again to the barman.

an espresso un caffè *oon kaf-***fe**	**a cappuccino** un cappuccino *oon kap-poo-***chee**-*no*	**2 cappuccinos** due cappuccini *doo-ay kap-poo-***chee**-*nee*
a tea un tè *oon te*	**with milk** al latte *al ***lat**-*tay*	**with lemon** al limone *al lee-***mo**-*nay*

a lager una birra *oo-na ***beer**-*ra*	**small** piccola *pee-kol-la*	**medium** media *med-***ee**-*a*	**large** grande *gran-day*

a bottle of mineral water una bottiglia di acqua minerale *oo-na bot-***teel**-*ya dee ***ak**-*wa mee-nay-***ra**-*lay*	**sparkling** gassata *gas-***za**-*ta*	**still** naturale *na-too-***ra**-*lay*

would you like a drink?
prende qualcosa da bere?
pren**-day kwal-ko**-za da ***be**-ray*

what will you have?
che cosa prende?
*kay ***ko**-za ***pren**-day*

the wine list, please
la lista dei vini, per favore
*la ***lee**-sta ***day**-ee ***vee**-nee payr fa-***vo**-ray*

a bottle of house wine
una bottiglia di vino della casa
*oo-na bot-***teel**-ya dee ***vee**-no ***del**-la ***ka**-za*

a glass of wine
un bicchiere di vino
*oon bee-kee-***e**-ray dee ***vee**-no*

a bottle of wine una bottiglia di vino *oo-na bot-***teel**-ya dee ***vee**-no*	**red** rosso *ros-so*	**white** bianco *bee-***an**-ko*

- You don't have to have all the courses in a restaurant, pick and choose.
- 'Cheers' is **salute** or **cin cin** (sa-**loo**-tay, cheen cheen).
- It's polite to wish **buon appetito** (bwon ap-pay-**tee**-to). The reply is 'thanks and you, too', **grazie e altrettanto** (**grat**-see-ay e al-tret-**tan**-to).

I'd like to book a table
vorrei prenotare un tavolo
vor-ray-ee pray-no-**ta**-ray oon **ta**-vo-lo

for ... people
per ... persone
payr ... per-**so**-nay

do you have a table?
avete un tavolo?
a-**vay**-tay oon **ta**-vo-lo

for tonight
per stasera
payr sta-**say**-ra

at 8 pm
alle otto
al-lay **ot**-to

the menu, please
il menù, per favore
eel me-**noo** payr fa-**vo**-ray

is there a dish of the day?
c'è un piatto del giorno?
che oon pee-**at**-to del **jor**-no

have you a set-price menu?
c'è un menù turistico?
che oon me-**noo** too-**rees**-tee-ko

I'll have this
prendo questo
pren-do **kwes**-to

I'll just have the first course
prendo solo il primo
pren-do **so**-lo eel **pree**-mo

I'll just have the main course
prendo solo il secondo
pren-do **so**-lo eel se-**kon**-do

what do you recommend?
che cosa ci consiglia?
kay **ko**-za chee kon-**seel**-ya

I don't eat meat
non mangio carne
non **man**-jo **kar**-nay

do you have any vegetarian dishes?
avete dei piatti per vegetariani?
a-**vay**-tay **day**-ee pee-**at**-tee payr ve-jay-ta-ree-**a**-nee

excuse me!
scusi!
skoo-zee

please bring...
ci porti...
chee **por**-tee...

more bread
altro pane
al-tro **pa**-nay

another bottle
un'altra bottiglia
oon **al**-tra bot-**teel**-ya

some butter
del burro
del **boor**-ro

the bill, please
il conto, per favore
eel **kon**-to payr fa-**vo**-ray

Special requirements

- Gluten-free is **senza glutine** (**sent**-sa **gloo**-tee-nay). These products are available in most supermarkets, but there are also special shops that sell only these products (**NaturaSì**).
  - **Integrale** means wholemeal.
  - **Biologico** or **bio** means organic.
- On labels, **grassi** means fats.

what's in this?
cosa c'è dentro?
*ko-za che **den**-tro*

I'm vegetarian
sono vegetariano(a)
***so**-no ve-jay-ta-ree-**a**-no(a)*

I don't eat meat/pork
non mangio carne/carne di maiale
*non **man**-jo **kar**-nay/**kar**-nay dee ma-**ya**-lay*

I don't eat fish/shellfish
non mangio pesce/i frutti di mare
*non **man**-jo **pay**-shay/ee **froot**-tee dee **ma**-ray*

I'm allergic to shellfish
sono allergico(a) ai frutti di mare
*so-no al-**ler**-jee-ko/a **a**-ee **froot**-tee dee **ma**-ray*

I am allergic to peanuts
sono allergico(a) alle arachidi
***so**-no al-**ler**-jee-ko(a) **al**-lay a-**ra**-kee-dee*

is it raw?
è crudo?
*e **kroo**-do*

I have a gluten intolerance
sono ciliaco(a)
*so-no chee-lee-**a**-ko(a)*

I can only eat gluten-free foods
posso mangiare soltanto cibi senza glutine
***pos**-so man-**ja**-ray sol-**tan**-to **chee**-bee **sent**-sa **gloo**-tee-nay*

I am on a diet
sono a dieta
*so-no a dee-**ay**-ta*

I don't drink alcohol
non bevo l'alcool
*non **bay**-vo **lal**-kol*

MARKET

For lunch, buy produce in one of the morning markets.

There is a staggering array of bread, fruit, olives, cheese, etc.

Be prepared to stand your ground in the queues at busy

stalls. *Tocca a me!* = it's my turn!

A *rosticceria* sells spit-roasted chicken and food to be eaten there (generally standing) or to take away. The food should be good and well-worth sampling.

TABACCAIO

As well as a tobacconist, a *tabaccaio* is often a bar and may serve meals. There are no frills, but the food will be good.

GROCER'S If you fancy a picnic, ask for a *panino* to be made up. It will be pretty basic, but the bread will be fresh and the ham or cheese freshly sliced.

DELI COUNTER The types of cold meats you find in the starter, *antipasto misto*.

bresaola = cured beef
p. = *prosciutto* = ham
p. crudo = cured ham (Parma ham)
p. cotto = cooked ham

Many bars and *caffè* serve food: mainly salads, sandwiches, pasta dishes and pizzas.

SANDWICH BAR

Paninoteca

It would be a mistake to translate *panini* simply as sandwiches, they can be a feast in themselves, full of delicious fresh ingredients. Try a *panzerotto* (fried bread dough filled with tomato and mozzarella).

Restaurants are generally well sign-posted with the knife and fork symbol.

CROTTO

A rustic-style eating place where you can get cold meats (*salami*, *prosciutto*, etc) and dishes like *polenta*. They are gradually becoming more gentrified.

CLOSED MONDAYS

Bars and restaurants generally close one day a week. This one is shut *lunedì* (Mondays)

LOCAL CUISINE

A *gelateria* is a bar selling ice cream where you can also get drinks.

ICE CREAMS

Gelati

FLAVOURS *gusti*

cono = cone
coppa = tub
grande = big
piccola = small
media = medium
frappè = milkshakes
frullati = smoothies

CIOCCOLATO	chocolate
VANIGLIA	vanilla
NOCCIOLA	hazelnut
LIMONE	lemon
FRAGOLA	strawberry
BANANA	banana
ALBICOCCA	apricot

FOOD TO GO

rice salad — RISO FREDDO

cold pizza — PIZZA FREDDA

cheese focaccia — FOCACCIA DI RECCO

filled sandwiches — PANINI IMBOTTITI

Menù a prezzo fisso (solo pranzo)
€9,50

FIXED-PRICE MENU
(lunch only)
This will usually be a 2-course meal, pasta and a meat dish.

MENU' TURISTICO € 13,00

TOURIST MENU
Many restaurants offer tourist menus (sometimes including wine). Although generally good value, the food is aimed mainly at the tourist market.

TRATTORIA
Traditionally, family-run and usually with less choice than a *ristorante*. However, it will have local dishes. Here the speciality is fish (*pesce*). It also has a terrace on the lake.

Tavola Calda

HOT MEALS
Generally self-service type cafeteria.

PIZZA
Pizza is served in pizzerias (rather than in normal restaurants), and these aren't as common as you might think.

TOASTED SANDWICHES
with extra filling

TOAST FARCITI

CHIPS

PATATINE FRITTE

Restaurants must display their menu outside.

MENU *menu*

ANTIPASTI *starters*

PRIMI *first courses*

pasta *different types of pasta dishes*
  al pomodoro *with a tomato sauce*
  al ragù *with a Bolognese meat sauce*
  all'arrabbiata *with a tomato and chilli pepper sauce*
  alla carbonara *with a bacon and egg sauce*
  alla puttanesca *with a tomato, chilli pepper and anchovy sauce*
  al pesto *with a basil, pine nut and pecorino sauce*
  in brodo *in broth (generally ravioli or other stuffed pasta)*
risotto *rice cooked in stock*

SECONDI *main dishes*
carne *meat*
  vitello *veal*
  manzo *beef*
  maiale *pork*
  pollo *chicken*
  agnello *lamb*
pesce *fish*

CONTORNI *vegetables*

FORMAGGI *cheeses*

DOLCI *sweets*

FRUTTA *fruit*

pane – coperto

BREAD AND COVER CHARGE
In a restaurant they always charge for *pane* (bread) or *grissini* (breadsticks). If you eat it all you may ask for more.

bibite

SOFT DRINKS

HOT

caldo

freddo

COLD

TAKE-AWAY

da asporto

bevande escluse

DRINKS NOT INCLUDED

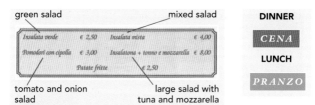

green salad   mixed salad

Insalata verde	€ 2,50	Insalata mista	€ 4,00
Pomodori con cipolla	€ 3,00	Insalatona + tonno e mozzarella	€ 8,00
	Patate fritte	€ 2,50	

tomato and onion salad   large salad with tuna and mozzarella

DINNER

CENA

LUNCH

PRANZO

a scelta

CHOICE OF
There may be a couple of options to choose from.

nostrano

LOCAL

stagione

IN SEASON

cucina casalinga

HOME COOKING

DISH OF THE DAY
With **polenta** – Beef stew or Rabbit or Veal stew

IL PIATTO DEL GIORNO
CON
POLENTA
Brasato o Coniglio
o Ossobuco

€ 13,00

CHEESE BOARD

Il tagliere
del
formaggio
€ 6,00

Watch out for the little words –
o means 'or', **con** means 'with',
e means 'and'.

Half a bottle of wine included.

1/2 bottiglia vino
compreso

Drinks & bills

COFFEE If you ask for **un caffè** you'll get an **espresso**, very small, strong and black. For a white coffee, ask for **un caffelatte** or **un cappuccino**. You generally get a standard cup, not a choice of regular or large.

It is cheaper to have a drink standing at the bar. You pay high prices for sitting outside in top tourist areas like St Mark's Square in Venice.

locale con aria condizionata

ROOM WITH AIR CONDITIONING

BIRRA When you ask for **birra** in Italy, you'll be served lager. If you want ale or bitter, ask for **birra scura** or **birra rossa**. Draught beer (**alla spina**) will come either **piccola** (half pint approx.) or **media** (just under a pint). If you want to drink beer, look out for bars which call themselves pubs. However, they may be quite expensive.

pagare alla cassa

When you enter a bar, check for the sign **pagare alla cassa** (pay at the cash desk). If there is a cashier, place your order with them and then go to the counter and give the barman your receipt, repeating your order. **CASSA**

Your **ricevuta** (receipt) lists what you have consumed. It is advisable to check the prices. The word for the bill is **il conto**.

Service is generally 10% and included. If not, a tip of 10% is acceptable.

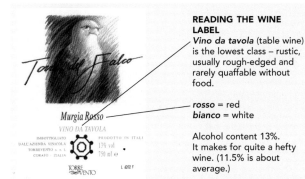

READING THE WINE LABEL

Vino da tavola (table wine) is the lowest class – rustic, usually rough-edged and rarely quaffable without food.

rosso = red
bianco = white

Alcohol content 13%. It makes for quite a hefty wine. (11.5% is about average.)

SANNIO BENEVENTANO
INDICAZIONE GEOGRAFICA TIPICA

Indicazione Geograficha Tipica is the equivalent of French *vin de pays*; it can either be rustic or superb.

Carta dei vini

WINE LIST

Aperitive

HAPPY HOUR

In cities, the 'happy hour' aperitif from 6.30 to 9pm is very common. Bars do fantastic things! When you order your cocktail or *crodino* (a non-alcoholic aperitif) you can have lots of nibbles: crisps, olives, slices of *focaccia*. You might even have to skip dinner afterwards.

DOC (Denominazione di Origine Controllata) operates like *AC* in France, with tight controls on wine production. The higher classification of *DOCG* does not necessarily promise a better wine, despite its adding of *Garantita* (guaranteed).

A

abbacchio suckling or milk-fed lamb, usually eaten at Easter. Roasted with garlic and rosemary
abbacchio alla cacciatora lamb cooked in olive oil, garlic and rosemary

acciughe anchovies: fresh, salted or in olive oil
acciughe ripiene fresh anchovies filled with salted anchovy fillets and cream cheese and fried in oil

aceto vinegar
aceto balsamico balsamic vinegar

acqua brillante tonic water

acqua cotta traditional Tuscan soup made from onions, peppers, celery and tomato. Beaten eggs and parmesan are added just before serving

acqua minerale mineral water; this can be still (**naturale**), with gas (**effervescente**), or with artificial gas (**gassata**)

affettato misto selection of cold meats: ham, salami, mortadella, etc

affogato poached
affogato al caffè vanilla ice cream with hot espresso coffee poured over it

affumicato smoked

aglio garlic
aglio, olio e peperoncino garlic, olive oil and hot chilli sauce

agnello lamb
agnello al forno roast lamb with vegetables

agnello all'arrabbiata lamb cooked in a tomato and chilli sauce
agnello arrosto roast lamb

agnolotti pasta squares filled with white meat and cheese, usually served with bolognese sauce

agoni small fish, usually marinated in vinegar and herbs

agrodolce sweet and sour sauce made from sugar, water, vinegar, wine, pine-nuts and sultanas; served with vegetables or meat such as rabbit or duck

ai ferri grilled

al, alla etc means with, or in the style of: e.g. **pasta al sugo** is pasta with tomato sauce, and **pollo alla cacciatora** is chicken hunter-style

albicocche apricots
albicocche ripiene stuffed apricots

alici fresh anchovies, often served dipped in flour and fried

alloro bayleaf

amarene dark morello cherries

amaretti macaroons, biscuits with a strong almond flavour

Amaretto di Saronno almond liqueur

amaro bitter liqueur drunk as a digestivo (to aid digestion)

amatriciana, ...all' bacon, tomato and onion sauce

analcolico non-alcoholic, slightly bitter drink served as an aperitif

ananas pineapple

anatra *duck*
  anatra di Palmina *duck cooked in wine*
  anatra in porchetta *roast duck stuffed with its liver and ham*

anelletti *baked squid or cuttlefish rings*

anguille *eel*
  anguille alla comácchio *stewed eel*
  anguille carpionate *fried eels*
  anguille in umido *eel stewed in tomato sauce*

anguria *watermelon*

anice *aniseed liqueur*

anisetta *powerful aniseed liqueur*

antipasto *starters/appetizers*
  antipasto misto *selection of cold starters such as ham, salami, russian salad and pickles*

aperitivo *aperitif*

Aperol *aperitif made with the essence of various plants*

aragosta *crayfish*
  aragosta allo spiedo *crayfish cooked kebab-style*

arance *oranges*

aranciata *orangeade*

arancini di riso *rice croquettes filled with minced veal and peas*

arrabbiata, ...all' *tomato sauce with bacon, onion, tomatoes and hot chillies*

arrosto *roast meat, usually cooked in casserole with wine and herbs*
  arrosto di maiale *roast pork*
  arrosto di manzo *roast beef*
  arrosto di vitello *roast veal*

asparagi *asparagus*
  asparagi alla parmigiana *lightly boiled asparagus baked with parmesan*

astice *lobster*

B

baccalà *salt cod*
  baccalà alla fiorentina *salt cod cooked in tomato sauce*
  baccalà alla vicentina *salt cod cooked in milk with anchovies, onion, garlic, parsley and herbs*
  baccalà alla livornese *salt cod cooked in a tomato sauce*
  baccalà alla milanese *Milanese salt cod fritters, served with lemon*

bagna cauda *hot garlic and anchovy dip*

banana *banana*

basilico *basil*

Bel Paese *soft, creamy mild cheese*

ben cotto *well done*

besciamella *béchamel sauce*

bianco, in *literally it means white, pasta or rice served with butter or olive oil and parmesan cheese*

bietola *beetroot*

birra *lager-type beer; draught beer is* **birra alla spina**

biscotti *biscuits*

bistecca *steak*
  bistecca alla fiorentina *thickly cut, charcoal-grilled steak*
  bistecca alla pizzaiola *fried steak in a tomato and herb sauce*

bistecchini di cinghiale *wild boar steaks in a sweet and sour sauce*

bitter *non-alcoholic, bitter drink served as an aperitif*

bocconcini di vitello *pieces of veal cooked in wine and butter*

bollito *boiled*
  bollito misto *different kinds of meat and vegetables cooked together*

bolognese, ...alla *tomato and minced meat sauce, served with parmesan*

bomba *doughnut with custard filling*

bonet *chocolate pudding with caramel*

borlotti *dried red haricot beans*

boscaiola, ...alla *with mushroom and ham sauce*

bottarga *preserved tuna or mullet roes, served in thin slices as a starter (Sardinian speciality)*

brace, ...alla *grilled*

braciola *rib steak/chop*
  braciole al ragù *chops cooked in tomato sauce*

brasato *beef stew*

bresaola *dried cured beef, cut finely and served with black pepper and olive oil*

broccoletti *leafy green vegetable similar to turnip tops*

broccoli *broccoli*

brodetto di pesce *fish soup made with different kinds of fish*

brodo *bouillon or broth often served with meat-stuffed pasta such as ravioli (**in brodo**)*

bruschetta *thickly-sliced bread rubbed with garlic and olive oil, often served topped with tomato*

bucatini *thick spaghetti-like pasta with hole running through it*

budino *a blancmange-type pudding*
  budino di ricotta *pudding made from ricotta cheese*

buridda *famous Genoese fish soup using a variety of fish*

burrini *a creamy cheese from Basilicata*

burro *butter*
  burro, ...al *fried in butter, usually wih garlic and sage*
  burro e salvia *butter and sage sauce*

busecca *rich tripe and cheese soup*

C

cacciatora, ...alla *meat or game, hunter-style – cooked with tomato, herbs, garlic and wine*

cachi *persimmons*

caciocavallo *cow's cheese, quite strong when mature*

caffè *coffee – if you ask for* **un caffè** *you'll be served* **un espresso** *(small, strong and black)*
  caffè americano *black filter coffee*
  caffè corretto *coffee laced with* **grappa** *or any strong spirit*
  caffè doppio *a large coffee (twice normal size)*
  caffèllatte *milky coffee*

calamaretti imbottiti *baby squid stuffed with breadcrumbs and anchovies*

calamari *squid*
  calamari fritti *squid rings dipped in batter and fried*

calzone *folded over pizza with filling. There are lots of local variations*

camomilla *camomile tea*

Campari *bitter-tasting aperitif made with herbs and fruit*

canederli tirolesi *Tyrolean dumplings made with bacon and sausage*

cannella *cinnamon*

cannellini *small white beans*

cannelloni *meat-filled pasta tubes covered with béchamel sauce and baked. Vegetarian options are filled with spinach and ricotta*

cannoli *fried pastries stuffed with ricotta, candied fruit and bitter chocolate from Sicily*

cantucci *nutty biscuits*

capocello *smoked salami preserved in olive oil*

caponata *Sicilian dish of aubergines cooked in a sweet and sour sauce*

cappelletti *literally 'little hats' filled with ricotta cheese, can be served with bolognese meat sauce*

capperi *capers*

cappon magro *an elaborate cold seafood and cooked vegetable salad*

cappuccino *frothy white coffee*

caprese *tomato and mozzarella salad with basil*

capretto *baby goat (kid)*
capretto arrosto *oven-roasted kid with vegetables and wine*

caprino *soft goat's cheese, usually eaten with a sprinkling*

of olive oil and freshly ground black pepper

caramelle *sweets*

carbonade *beef cooked in wine; polenta is the classic accompaniment*

carbonara, ...alla *smoked bacon, egg, cream and parmesan*

carciofi *globe artichokes*
carciofi alla Giudia *young globe artichokes, flattened and deep-fried*
carciofi alla romana *globe artichokes stuffed with breadcrumbs, parsley and anchovies*
carciofi ripieni *artichokes stuffed with mozzarella, parmesan and anchovies*

carciofini *artichoke hearts*

cardi *cardoons (similar to fennel)*

carne *meat*

carote *carrots*

carpaccio *raw sliced lean beef eaten with lemon juice, olive oil and thickly grated parmesan cheese*

carpione *carp*

carpione, in *pickled in vinegar, wine and lemon juice. Fish is often served this way and fried*

casalinga, ...alla *home-made*

cassata *layers of ice cream with candied fruits*
cassata siciliana *sponge dessert with ricotta and candied fruits*

cassola *pork, cabbage and vegetable casserole*

castagnaccio *chestnut cake*

castagne *chestnuts*

cavolatte *rich custard pudding*

cavolfiore *cauliflower*

cavolo *cabbage*

ceci *chickpeas*

céfalo *grey mullet*

cena *dinner*

Centerbe *herbal liqueur*

cervelle *calves' brains usually fried*

cetriolo *cucumber*

China *bitter liqueur*

chinotto *fizzy, bitter-orange soft drink*

cialzons alla carnia *pasta squares filled with spinach, chocolate and cinnamon*

ciambella *ring-shaped fruit cake*

ciambellini *ring-shaped aniseed biscuits*

cicoria *chicory*

ciliege *cherries*

cinghiale *wild boar*

Cinzano *popular aperitif*

cioccolata calda *rich hot chocolate, often served with cream*

cioccolatini *chocolates*

cioccolato *chocolate*

ciociara, ...alla *mushroom, cream and ham sauce*

cipolle *onions*
  cipolle ripiene *stuffed onions*

coccio *a yeast cake with dried fruit*

cocco *coconut*

cocomero *watermelon*

coda di bue *oxtail*
  coda alla vaccinara *famous Roman dish of oxtail stewed with tomatoes and herbs*

conchiglie *shell-shaped pasta*

confetti *sugared almonds*

congelato *frozen*

coniglio *rabbit*
  coniglio all'ischiana *rabbit stewed in wine*
  coniglio in umido *rabbit stew*

contorni *vegetable side dishes*

cornetto *ice-cream cone; a croissant filled with jam, custard or chocolate*

cosciotto d'agnello all'abruzzese *braised lamb with garlic, tomatoes, rosemary and wine*

cotechino *spicy pork sausage usually cooked with lentils*

cotoletta *cutlet/chop*
  cotoletta al prosciutto *veal cutlet with a slice of Parma ham*
  cotoletta alla bolognese *veal cutlet topped with ham and cheese*
  cotoletta alla milanese *veal cutlet dipped in egg and breadcrumbs then fried*
  cotoletta alla valdostana *breaded veal chop stuffed with cheese*
  cotoletta di vitello *veal cutlet*
  cotolette di abbacchio *lamb chops*
  cotolette di agnello alla brace *marinated, grilled lamb chops*

cotto *cooked*

cozze *mussels*
  cozze arraganate *grilled mussels*

crema di... *cream soup or sauce/custard*

crêpe *pancake*

crespolina *stuffed pancake*

crocchette di patate *potato croquettes*

crodino slightly bitter, non-alcoholic aperitif

crostata tart, usually filled with fruit and glazed
  crostata di frutta fruit tart

crostini di fegatini chicken liver pâté on toast

crudo raw

Cynar bitter aperitif (made from artichokes)

D

dente, ...al pasta cooked so it is still quite firm

dèntice sea bream

digestivo slightly bitter, herb-flavoured liqueur to aid digestion

dolce dessert

dolcelatte soft, creamy blue cheese

dragoncello tarragon

E

entrecote steak

F

fagiano pheasant
  fagiano con funghi pheasant with porcini mushrooms
  fagiano in salmì pheasant stewed in wine

fagioli type of bean
  fagioli al tonno haricot beans with tuna fish in olive oil
  fagioli con cotiche bean stew with pork
  fagioli nel fiasco haricot beans cooked in a flask

fagiolini runner beans

faraona guinea fowl

farcito stuffed

farfalle butterfly-shaped pasta

farsu magru veal stuffed and rolled up, cooked in wine (Sicilian speciality)

fave broad beans
  fave al guanciale broad beans cooked with bacon and onion

fegatini di pollo chicken livers

fegato liver (mainly calves')
  fegato alla veneziana calves' liver fried in butter and onion

ferri, ...ai grilled without oil

fettuccine fresh ribbon pasta

ficatu all'agru e duci calves' liver in sweet and sour sauce (Sicilian)

fichi figs
  fichi d'India prickly pears

filetto fillet steak
  filetto di tacchino alla bolognese turkey breast served with a slice of ham and cheese

Filu Ferru very strong grappa from Sardinia

finanziera, ...alla chicken livers, mushrooms and wine sauce

finocchio fennel

fiori di zucchini courgette flowers fried in batter

focaccia flat bread brushed with garlic, salt and olive oil, sprinkled with herbs or onions

fonduta al parmigiano cheese fondue made with Fontina cheese, eggs, butter and truffles. Eaten with crusty bread

fontina mild to strong cow's milk cheese

formaggio cheese

forno, ...al cooked in the oven

fragole strawberries

frittata omelette, usually with different ingredients

fritto fried
  fritto misto platter of deep-fried food including different kinds of meat and vegetables
  fritto misto di mare fried/grilled selection of seafood

frullato di frutta milk shake made with fruits

frutta fruit

frutti di mare shellfish/seafood

funghi mushrooms – very popular and varied in Italy. In autumn many Italians take to the woods in search of the prized **porcini**
  funghi trifolati sliced mushrooms fried with garlic and parsley

Fuoco dell'Etna very strong liqueur from Sicily

fusilli spiral-shaped pasta

G

gamberi prawns

gamberoni giant prawns

gazzosa fizzy bottled lemonade

gelato ice cream
  gelato misto a selection of different flavoured ice creams

gioddu yoghurt

girasole sunflower

gnocchi small dumplings made from potato and flour, can be made with spinach. Boiled and served with tomato sauce or ragù

gnocchi alla romana dumplings made from semolina, butter and parmesan, oven-baked

gnocchi verdi spinach and cheeese dumplings, usually cooked in butter, garlic and sage

Gorgonzola a strong blue cows'-milk cheese

granchio crab

grana hard cows'-milk cheese; generic name given to Parmesan cheese

granita flavoured crushed ice drink
  granita al caffè coffee drink with crushed ice and cream
  granita al limone lemon drink with crushed ice

granseola large crab

grappa strong spirit from grape pressings, often added to coffee

grattugiato grated

griglia, ...alla grilled

grigliata di cervo grilled venison steaks

grigliata mista mixed grill consisting of various barbecued meats

grissini breadsticks

guanciale streaky bacon made from pig's cheek

gulasch spicy beef stew

I

impepata di cozze peppery mussels

insalata salad
  insalata caprese tomato, basil and mozarella salad

90

insalata di mare *mixed seafood salad*
insalata di pomodori *tomato salad*
insalata di riso *rice salad*
insalata mista *mixed salad*
insalata russa *russian salad*
insalata verde *green salad*
involtini *rolls of veal or pork stuffed with chicken liver, pork sausage and parmesan*
italiana, ...alla *platters with mixed cured meats/cheeses, olives and savouries*

L

lamponi *raspberries*
lasagne *layers of pasta with bolognese and béchamel sauces, baked*
lasagne verdi *layers of green pasta filled with bolognese (or ricotta) and béchamel sauces.*
latte *milk*
lattuga *lettuce*
lemonsoda *fizzy lemon drink*
lenticchie *lentils usually cooked with pork sausage*
lepre *hare*
lepre in salmì *hare stewed in wine*
latte *milk*
lesso *boiled*
limonata *bottled lemon drink*
limone *lemon*
limoncello *lemon liqueur*
lingua *tongue*
linguine *thin strips of pasta*
lombata di maiale *pork chop*
lonza *type of salami*

luccio *pike*
lumache *snails*

M

maccheroni *macaroni*
maccheroni ai quattro formaggi *pasta with four cheeses*
maccheroni alla chitarra *square-shaped pasta often served with lamb in chilli and tomato sauce*
macedonia (con panna) *fresh fruit salad (with cream)*
macinata *mince*
magro, di *a meatless dish (often a fish alternative)*
maiale *pork*
maionese *mayonnaise*
mandorle *almonds*
manzo *beef*
marmellata *jam*
Marsala *dark dessert wine from Sicily*
Martini *famous Italian aperitif*
mascarpone *rich cream cheese used in desserts such as tiramisù*
mela *apple*
melanzane *aubergines*
melanzane alla Parmigiana *layers of aubergine baked with tomato sauce, parma ham, parmesan and mozzarella*
melanzane ripiene *stuffed aubergines*
melagrana *pomegranate*
melone *melon*
menta *mint*
meringata *meringue and ice cream dessert*
merluzzo *cod*

miele *honey*

milanese, ...alla *normally applied to veal cutlets dipped in egg and breadcrumbs before frying*

minestra *soup*
minestra calanchina *vegetable and rice soup served with cheese*

minestrone *vegetable, bean and pasta soup*
minestrone al pesto *minestrone flavoured with pesto sauce*

missultin *grilled dried fish, often eaten with* polenta

misto di funghi *mushroom stew*

more *blackberries*

mortadella *type of salami*

mostarda *pickled fruit. Served with* bollito *(boiled meats)*

mozzarella *buffalo-milk cheese*
mozzarella in carozza *mozarella sandwiched in bread, dipped in egg and breadcrumbs and fried*

mugnaia, ...alla *usually fish dusted in flour then fried in butter*

N

nocciole *hazelnuts*

nocciole d'agnello *noisette of lamb*

nocepesca *nectarine*

noci *walnuts*

norma, ...alla *tomato and fried aubergine Sicilian sauce*

O

olio *oil*
olio d'oliva *olive oil*

olive *olives*

orecchiette *ear-shaped pasta*
orecchiette ai broccoli *pasta with broccoli*

origano *oregano*

orzata *cool, milky drink made from barley*

ossobuco *marrow-bone veal steak cooked in tomato and wine sauce*

ostriche *oysters*

P

paglia e fieno *green and plain ribbon pasta cooked with mushrooms, sausage and cream*

pan pepato *sweet loaf with mixed nuts*

pancetta *streaky bacon*

pandoro *yeast cake, traditionally eaten at Christmas*

pane *bread*
pane e coperto *cover charge*
pane integrale *wholemeal bread*

panettone *cork-shaped yeast cake with dried fruit, traditionally eaten at Christmas*

panforte *a hard, dried-fruit and nut cake*

panino *bread roll or sandwich*

panna *cream*

pansôti (di Rapallo) *pasta squares filled with spinach and egg and served in a walnut and parmesan sauce*

panzerotti *ravioli stuffed with mozzarella, salami and ham, usually fried*

paparelle e fegatini *chicken livers with pasta*

pappardelle *wide ribbon-shaped pasta*
pappardelle al sugo di lepre *wide ribbon pasta with hare, wine and tomato sauce*

parmigiana, ...alla *with parmesan cheese*

parmigiana di melanzane *aubergine layers, oven-baked with tomato sauce and parmesan cheese*

parmigiano *parmesan cheese. A hard cow's milk cheese used extensively in Italian cooking.*

pasta *the dry variety takes 10–15 minutes to cook, the fresh just 3 or 4*
pasta al forno *pasta baked with minced meat, eggs, tomato and cheese*
pasta all'uovo *fresh pasta made from flour and eggs*
pasta asciutta *pasta served with a sauce, such as* **spaghetti al sugo***, and not in a soup form, such as* **ravioli in brodo** *(ravioli in bouillon)*
pasta con le sarde *a baked dish of layers of pasta and fried sardines*
pasta e fagioli *pasta with beans*
pasta fresca *fresh pasta*

pasticcio *pie*

pastina in brodo *pasta pieces in clear broth*

patate *potatoes*
patate fritte *chips*

patatine *crisps*
patatine fritte *chips*

pecorino *hard tangy cheese made from ewe's milk, used in* **pesto**

penne *quill-shaped pasta*
penne rigate *ribbed quill-shaped pasta*

pepe *pepper*

peperonata *sweet peppers cooked with tomatoes and olive oil*

peperoncino *hot chilli pepper*

peperoni *peppers*
peperoni ripieni *stuffed peppers*

pere *pears*

pesca *peach*

pesce *fish*
pesce arrosto *baked fish*
pesce persico *perch*
pesce spada *swordfish, often grilled or served in a tomato sauce*
pesce spada alla siciliana *swordfish cooked with orange and lemon juice*

pesto *sauce of pounded basil, garlic, pine-nuts, olive oil and pecorino*

petto di pollo *chicken breast*

pezzenta *variety of salad*

piatto *dish*
piatto del giorno *dish of the day*
piatti tipici *regional dishes*

piccatine al limone *tender thinly sliced veal in butter and lemon*

pietanze *main courses*

pinoli *pine nuts*

piselli *peas*

pistacchio *pistachio*

pizza *originally from Naples, cooked in wood-burning ovens*
pizza ai funghi *mushroom pizza*
pizza alla Siciliana *pizza with tomato, anchovy, black olives and capers*
pizza capricciosa *pizza with baby artichoke, ham and egg*
pizza cardinale *pizza with ham and olives*
pizza frutti di mare *pizza with seafood*
pizza margherita *named after the first queen of a united Italy; symbolising the Italian flag's colours: red (tomatoes), green (basil) and white (mozarella)*
pizza marinara *tomato and garlic pizza*
pizza Napoli/Napoletana *pizza with tomato, cheese, anchovy, olive oil and oregano*
pizza quattro formaggi *a pizza divided into four sections, each with a different cheese topping*
pizza quattro stagioni *pizza divided into four sections with a selection of toppings on each*

pizzaiola, ...alla *cooked with tomatoes, garlic and herbs*

pizzetta *small cheese and tomato pizza*

pizzoccheri *buckwheat pasta noodles, oven-baked with cabbage, potatoes and cheese*

polenta *coarse corn or maize meal solidified porridge. A perfect accompaniment to stews. Can be dipped in egg, breadcrumbs, grated parmesan and then fried*
polenta e osei *polenta with song birds*

polenta uncia *polenta cooked with butter, garlic and Fontina cheese*

pollame *poultry/fowl*

pollo *chicken*
pollo alla diavola *chicken grilled with herbs and chilli pepper*
pollo alla marengo *chicken cooked in wine, served with eggs and prawns*
pollo alla romana *chicken with tomatoes and peppers*
pollo arrosto *roast chicken*

polpette *beef meatballs made with parmesan and parsley*

polpo *octopus, served in salad (cold) or tomato sauce*
polpo affogato *octopus cooked in tomato sauce*

pomodoro *tomato*
pomodoro, ...al *tomato sauce (same as sugo)*
pomodori da sugo *plum tomatoes*
pomodori ripieni *stuffed tomatoes*

pompelmo *grapefruit*

porceddu *suckling pig*

porchetta *roast suckling pig*

porcini *prized cep mushrooms, often dried*

porri *leeks*

pranzo *lunch*

prezzemolo *parsley*

prima colazione *breakfast*

primo *first course*

prosciutto *ham*
prosciutto cotto *boiled ham*
prosciutto crudo *cured Parma ham which is sliced off the bone*

prosciutto di cinghiale *cured ham made from wild boar*
prosciutto e melone *Parma ham and melon slices*

Prosecco *sparkling dry white wine*

provolone *creamy cow's milk cheese, mild to strong*

prugne *plums*

puttanesca, ...alla *tomato, garlic, hot chilli, anchovies and capers*

Q

quaglie *quails*

R

radicchio *red-leaf lettuce*

ragù, ...al *minced meat, tomato and garlic (same as **bolognese**)*

rana pescatrice *monkfish*

rane *frogs' legs*

ravioli *pasta cushions filled with meat or cheese and spinach*

ribes *blackcurrants*

riccio di mare *sea urchin*

ricotta *soft white cheese used as filling for pasta as well as in desserts*

rigatoni *ribbed tubes of pasta*

ripieno *stuffed*

risi e bisati *rice cooked with eel, a traditional Venetian dish*

risi e bisi *thick rice and pea soup (almost liquid risotto) cooked with bacon*

riso *rice*
riso alla pilota *rice cooked with sausage, nutmeg and cinnamon*

risotto *rice cooked in broth with different ingredients added*
risotto ai funghi *risotto with porcini mushrooms*
risotto al nero di seppia *risotto made with squid and its ink*
risotto alla milanese *rich yellow risotto flavoured with saffron, parmesan and butter, and cooked in meat broth*
risotto alla pescatora *seafood rice*
risotto alle seppie *risotto cooked with squid (Venetian speciality). Its ink turns the rice black*
risotto con le quaglie *quails with risotto*

robiola *creamy cheese with a mild taste*

rognone *kidney*

rosmarino *rosemary*

rospo *monkfish*

S

salame *salami (there are many types)*

sale *salt*

salmone *salmon*

salsa *sauce*
salsa verde *sauce made of olive oil, breadcrumbs, anchovies, hard boiled egg and parsley, usually served with boiled meat or fish*

salsicce *sausages: there are many regional variations but they are mainly thick pork sausages which can be boiled or grilled*

saltimbocca alla romana *veal cooked in white wine with parma ham*

salvia sage

Sambuca aniseed liqueur, served with coffee beans and set alight

sampiero John Dory (type of fish)

sangue, ...al rare

sarde sardines
sarde e beccafico sardines stuffed with breadcrumbs, anchovies, sultanas and pine-nuts
sarde in saour sardines marinated in vinegar, sultanas and pine nuts

sartù di riso rice and meat timbale (rather like a pie)

scaloppine veal escalopes
scaloppine al limone veal escalopes cooked in lemon juice
scaloppine al marsala veal escalopes cooked in marsala
scaloppine alla milanese veal escalopes dipped in egg, breadcrumbs and fried in butter, served with wedges of lemon

scamorza a cheese similar to mozzarella but smoked

scampi scampi

secondo main dish, usually meat or fish

sedano celery

selz soda water

semifreddo chilled dessert made with ice cream

senape mustard

seppia coi piselli squid cooked with peas

servizio compreso service included

sfogliatelle frolle puff pastry cakes filled with ricotta cheese

sgavecio fried fish served cold with vinegar and seasonings

sgombro mackerel

soffritto sliced onion and/or garlic fried in olive oil, generally used to prepare sauces or meat dishes

sogliola sole

sopa cauda soup made from bread and pigeon

soppressata type of salami, with pistachio

sott'olio in olive oil

spaghetti spaghetti
spaghetti aglio, olio e peperoncino spaghetti with garlic, chilli pepper and olive oil sauce
spaghetti all'amatriciana spaghetti with bacon, onion and tomato sauce
spaghetti alle vongole spaghetti with clams
spaghettini aromatici fine spaghetti in a sauce of anchovies, garlic, black olives and capers

speck type of smoked cured ham from mountain regions

spezzatino stew, usually with tomato sauce

spiedini meat kebabs

spiedo, ...allo spit-roasted, or on skewer

spinaci spinach
spinaci alla piemontese spinach cooked with anchovies and garlic

spremuta freshly squeezed fruit juice
spremuta di pompelmo fresh grapefruit juice

spumante *sparkling wine*

stoccafisso *dried stockfish which requires lots of soaking before cooking*

stracciatella *consommé with egg stirred in and grated parmesan*

stracotto *braised beef slow-cooked with vegetables. Often served with polenta*

Strega *strong herb-flavoured liqueur*

succo di frutta *bottled fruit juice*

sugo *sauce, often refers to the basic tomato, basil and garlic sauce (same as al pomodoro)*

surgelato *frozen*

T

tacchino *turkey*

tagliatelle *ribbon-like pasta often served in cream sauce*

Taleggio *soft, creamy cheese similar to Camembert*

tartine *canapés*

tartufo *truffles: black (nero) and white (bianco) are used extensively in risotto and game dishes*
  tartufo di cioccolato *rich chocolate ice cream shaped like a truffle*

tè *tea. Normally served with lemon (al limone). If you want it with milk you must ask for tè al latte*

teglia *earthenware casserole dish*

tiella di sardine *baked sardines with cheese*

timballo *a baked dish*

timballo di melanzane *baked aubergines, egg, cheese and parma ham*

timo *thyme*

tinche *tench*

tiramisù *dessert made with mascarpone, sponge, coffee and marsala*

tónica *tonic water*

tonno *tuna fish*
  tonno, ...al *sauce made of tuna fish and tomatoes*
  tonno e fagioli *tuna and bean salad*

torrone *nougat, traditionally eaten at Christmas*

torta *cake/flan/tart*

tortellini *meat-filled pasta cushions*
  tortellini panna e prosciutto *tortellini cooked with cream and ham*

tortine al tartufo *little savoury tarts with truffles*

tramezzini *sliced white bread with mixed fillings*

trenette *long thin strips of pasta, traditionally served with pesto sauce*

triglie *red mullet*
  triglie alla livornese *red mullet fried with chillies in tomato sauce*
  triglie alla siciliana *a Sicilian dish of red mullet cooked in white wine and orange peel*

trippa *tripe, often cooked with tomatoes and onions*

trota *trout*
  trote alla panna acida *trout in soured cream*

U

uccelli scappati *pork kebabs*

umido, in *stewed*

uova *eggs*
  uova alla fiorentina *poached eggs on spinach tarts*

uva *grapes*

uva passa *raisins*

V

vaniglia *vanilla*

Vecchia Romagna *Italian cognac*

verdure *vegetables*

vermicelli *very thin pasta*

Vermut *very popular aperitif made from herbs and wine*

verza *Savoy (green) cabbage*

vino *wine*
  vin brûlé *mulled wine*
  vino bianco *white wine*
  vino dolce *sweet wine*
  vino frizzante *sparkling wine*
  vino rosato *rosé wine*
  vino rosso *red wine*
  vino secco *dry wine*

vitello *veal*

vongole *clams*
  vongole, ...alle *clam, parsley, garlic and olive oil*

W

wurstel *Frankfurter sausages*

Y

yogurt *yoghurt*

Z

zabaglione *frothy dessert made with egg yolks and sugar beaten with marsala over heat*

zafferano *saffron, used in risotto alla milanese*

zampone *spicy sausage in the shape of a pig's trotter, sliced and served hot*

zucca *marrow*

zucchero *sugar*

zucchini *courgettes*

zuccotto *rich cream and nut pudding in a pumpkin shape*

zuppa *soup*
  zuppa di cozze *mussel and tomato soup*
  zuppa di fagioli *bean soup*
  zuppa di pesce *seafood soup with many delicious regional variations*
  zuppa inglese *dessert similar to trifle laced with whisky or Vermut*
  zuppa pavese *a bread soup with broth and poached eggs, topped with grated cheese*

DICTIONARY
English-Italian
Italian-English

A

a(n) un/una/uno
abbey l'abbazia (f)
able: *to be able (to)* essere capace (di)
abortion l'aborto (m)
about su ; circa
  a book about... un libro su...
  about ten o'clock circa le dieci
above sopra
abroad all'estero (m)
  to go abroad andare all'estero
abscess l'ascesso (m)
accelerator l'acceleratore (m)
accent l'accento (m)
to accept accettare
access l'accesso (m)
  wheelchair access l'accesso per disabili
accident l'incidente (m)
accident & emergency department il pronto soccorso
accommodation l'alloggio (m)
to accompany accompagnare
account (bill) il conto
  (in bank) il conto in banca
account number il numero del conto
to ache fare male
  it aches fa male
acid l'acido (m)
actor (m/f) l'attore/l'attrice
adaptor (electrical appliance) il riduttore
address l'indirizzo (m)
  what is the address? qual è l'indirizzo?
address book la rubrica
admission charge/fee il biglietto d'ingresso
to admit (to hospital) ricoverare
adult l'adulto(a)
  for adults per adulti
advance: *in advance* in anticipo
advertisement la pubblicità
  (in newspaper) l'annuncio (m)

to advise consigliare
A&E il pronto soccorso
aeroplane l'aeroplano (m)
aerosol l'aerosol (m)
afraid: *to be afraid* avere paura
after dopo
afternoon il pomeriggio
  this afternoon oggi pomeriggio
  tomorrow afternoon domani pomeriggio
  in the afternoon di pomeriggio
aftershave il dopobarba
again ancora ; di nuovo
against contro
age l'età (f)
agency l'agenzia (f)
ago fa
  a week ago una settimana fa
to agree essere d'accordo
agreement l'accordo (m)
AIDS l'AIDS (m)
airbag l'airbag (m)
airbed il materassino gonfiabile
air-conditioning l'aria condizionata (f)
air freshener il deodorante per l'ambiente
airline la linea aerea
air mail: *by air mail* per via aerea
airplane l'aeroplano (m)
airport l'aeroporto (m)
airport bus l'autobus per l'aeroporto (m)
air ticket il biglietto d'aereo
aisle il corridoio
alarm l'allarme (m)
alarm clock la sveglia
alcohol l'alcool (m)
alcohol-free analcolico(a)
alcoholic alcolico(a)
all tutto(a)
allergic to allergico(a) a
  I'm allergic to... sono allergico(a) a...
allergy l'allergia (f)
to allow permettere

all right *(agreed)* va bene
  are you all right? sta bene?
almost quasi
alone solo(a)
Alps le Alpi
already già
also anche
altar l'altare *(m)*
aluminium foil la carta stagnola
always sempre
a.m. del mattino
am: *I am* sono
amber *(light)* il giallo
ambulance l'ambulanza *(f)*
America l'America *(f)*
American americano(a)
anaesthetic l'anestetico *(m)*
  local anaesthetic l'anestetico locale
  general anaesthetic l'anestetico generale
anchor l'ancora *(f)*
ancient antico(a)
and e
angina l'angina pectoris *(f)*
angry arrabbiato(a)
animal l'animale *(m)*
ankle la caviglia
anniversary l'anniversario *(m)*
to announce annunciare
announcement l'annuncio *(m)*
annual annuale
another un altro/un'altra
  another beer un'altra birra
  another coffee un altro caffè
answer la risposta
to answer rispondere
answerphone la segreteria telefonica
antacid l'antiacido *(m)*
antibiotic l'antibiotico *(m)*
antifreeze l'antigelo *(m)*
antihistamine l'antistaminico
antiques i pezzi d'antiquariato
antique shop il negozio d'antiquariato
antiseptic l'antisettico *(m)*

any dei/delle/degli (di)
  I haven't any money non ho soldi
  have you any apples? ha delle mele?
anyone qualcuno ; chiunque
anything qualcosa ; qualsiasi cosa
apartment l'appartamento *(m)*
appendicitis l'appendicite *(f)*
apple la mela
application form il modulo di domanda
appointment l'appuntamento *(m)*
  I have an appointment ho un appuntamento
approximately circa
apricots le albicocche
April aprile
architect *m/f* l'architetto
architecture l'architettura *(f)*
are sono
arm il braccio
armbands *(swimming)* i braccioli
armchair la poltrona
to arrange sistemare
to arrest arrestare
arrivals *(plane, train)* gli arrivi
to arrive arrivare
art l'arte *(f)*
art gallery la galleria d'arte ; la pinacoteca
arthritis l'artrite *(f)*
artificial finto(a) ; artificiale
artist *m/f* l'artista
ashtray il portacenere
to ask *(question)* domandare *(for something)* chiedere
asleep: *he/she is asleep* dorme
asparagus gli asparagi
aspirin l'aspirina *(f)*
asthma l'asma *(f)*
  I have asthma ho l'asma
at a
  at home a casa
  at 8 o'clock alle otto
  at once subito
  at night di notte

to attack aggredire
attractive attraente
aubergine la melanzana
auction l'asta (f)
audience il pubblico
August agosto
aunt la zia
au pair la ragazza alla pari
Australia l'Australia (f)
Australian australiano(a)
author m/f l'autore/l'autrice
automatic automatico(a)
automatic car la macchina con cambio automatico
auto-teller il Bancomat®
autumn l'autunno (m)
available disponibile
avalanche la valanga
avenue il viale
average medio(a)
to avoid evitare
awake: to be awake essere sveglio(a)
away via
awful terribile
axle (car) l'asse (m)

B

baby il/la bambino(a)
baby food gli alimenti per bambini
baby milk il latte per bambini
baby wipes le salviettine per bambini
baby's bottle il biberon
babyseat (in car) il seggiolino per bambini
babysitter il/la babysitter
back (of body) la schiena
backpack lo zaino
bacon la pancetta
bad (food) andato(a) a male
(weather, news) brutto(a)
badminton il badminton
bag la borsa
baggage i bagagli

baggage allowance il peso consentito di bagaglio
baggage reclaim il ritiro bagagli
bait (for fishing) l'esca (m)
baked al forno
baker's la panetteria ; il panificio
balcony il balcone
bald (person) calvo(a)
(tyre) liscio(a)
ball (large) il pallone
(small) la pallina
ballet il balletto
balloon il palloncino
banana la banana
band (musical) la banda
bandage la benda
bank la banca
(river) la riva
bank account il conto in banca
banknote la banconota
bankrupt fallito(a)
bar il bar
bar of chocolate la tavoletta di cioccolato
barbecue il barbecue
to have a barbecue fare il barbecue
barber il barbiere
to bark abbaiare
barn il granaio
barrel (wine/beer) il barile
basement il seminterrato
basil il basilico
basket il cestino
basketball la pallacanestro
bat (baseball, etc) la mazza
bath il bagno
to have a bath fare un bagno
bathing cap la cuffia
bathroom il bagno
with bathroom con bagno
battery (radio, etc) la pila
(car) la batteria
(rechargeable) la batteria ricaricabile
bay (along coast) la baia
B&B la pensione familiare

to be essere
beach la spiaggia
 private beach la spiaggia privata
 sandy beach la spiaggia con sabbia
 nudist beach la spiaggia di nudisti
beach hut la cabina
bean il fagiolo
beard la barba
beautiful bello(a)
beauty salon l'istituto di bellezza *(m)*
because perché
to become diventare
bed il letto
 double bed il letto matrimoniale
 single bed il letto a una piazza
 sofa bed il divano letto
 twin beds i letti gemelli
bed and breakfast la pensione
 familiare
bed clothes le coperte e lenzuola
bedroom la camera da letto
bee l'ape *(f)*
beef il manzo
beer la birra
 draught beer la birra alla spina
before prima di
 before breakfast prima di colazione
to begin cominciare
behind dietro di
beige beige
to believe credere
bell *(church)* la campana
 (doorbell) il campanello
to belong to appartenere a
 it belongs to... appartiene a...
below sotto
belt la cintura
bend *(in road)* la curva
berth *(train, ship)* la cuccetta
beside *(next to)* accanto a
 beside the bank accanto alla banca
best: *the best* il/la migliore
bet la scommessa
to bet scommettere
better (than) meglio (di)

between fra
to beware of stare attento(a) a
beyond oltre
bib *(baby's)* il bavaglino
bicycle la bicicletta ; la bici
 by bicycle in bicicletta
bicycle repair kit il kit per riparare
 la bici
bidet il bidet
big grande
 bigger (than) più grande (di)
bike *(pushbike)* la bici
 (motorbike) la moto
bike lock il lucchetto della bici
bikini il bikini
bill *(hotel, restaurant)* il conto
 (for work done) la fattura
 (gas, telephone) la bolletta
bin *(dustbin)* il bidone
bin liner il sacco della spazzatura
binoculars il binocolo
bird l'uccello *(m)*
biro la biro
birth la nascita
birth certificate il certificato di
 nascita
birthday il compleanno
 happy birthday! auguri! buon
 compleanno
 my birthday is on... il mio
 compleanno è il...
birthday card il biglietto d'auguri
 di compleanno
birthday present il regalo di
 compleanno
biscuits i biscotti
bit il pezzo
 a bit un po'
bite *(of insect)* la puntura
 (of dog) la morsicatura
 a bite to eat qualcosa da mangiare
to bite *(animal)* mordere
 (insect) morsicare
bitten morso(a)
 (by insect) punto(a)
bitter *(taste)* amaro(a)

black nero(a)

black ice il ghiaccio sulla strada

blanket la coperta

bleach la candeggina

to bleed sanguinare

blender il frullatore

blind (person) cieco(a)

blind (window) la veneziana ;
la tapparella

blister la vescica

block of flats il palazzo ;
il condominio

blocked (pipe, sink) tappato(a)
(road) bloccato(a)

blond (person) biondo(a)

blood il sangue

blood group il gruppo sanguigno

blood pressure la pressione
sanguigna

blood test l'analisi del sangue (f)

blouse la camicetta

to blow-dry asciugare con il fon

blue (light) azzurro(a)
dark blue blu scuro
light blue azzurro(a)

blunt (knife, blade) non taglia

boar il cinghiale

to board (plain, train, etc) imbarcarsi su

boarding card/pass la carta
d'imbarco

boarding house la pensione

boat la barca ; il battello
(rowing) la barca a remi

boat trip la gita in battello

body il corpo
(dead) il cadavere

to boil bollire

boiler la caldaia

boiled bollito(a)

bomb la bomba

bone l'osso (m)
fish bone la spina di pesce

bonfire il falò

bonnet (car) il cofano

book il libro
book of tickets il blocchetto di
biglietti

to book prenotare

booking la prenotazione

booking office (train) la biglietteria

bookshop la libreria

boot (of car) il bagagliaio

boots (long) gli stivali
(ankle) gli stivaletti

border (of country) la frontiera

boring noioso(a)

born: to be born essere nato(a)

to borrow prendere in prestito

boss il capo

both tutti e due

bottle la bottiglia
a bottle of wine una bottiglia
di vino
a half-bottle una mezza bottiglia

bottle opener l'apribottiglie

bowl (cereal, soup) la scodella

bow tie la cravatta a farfalla

box la scatola

box office il botteghino

boxer shorts i boxer

boy (young child) il bambino
(teenage) il ragazzo

boyfriend il ragazzo

bra il reggiseno

bracelet il braccialetto

brain il cervello

to brake frenare

brake fluid il liquido dei freni

brake light il fanalino dello stop

brake pads le pastiglie dei freni

brakes i freni

branch (of tree) il ramo
(of bank, etc) la succursale

brand (make) la marca

brass l'ottone (m)

brave coraggioso(a)

bread il pane
brown bread il pane integrale
French bread il filoncino
sliced bread il pancarré

bread roll il panino
to break rompere
breakable fragile
breakdown (car) il guasto
   (nervous) l'esaurimento nervoso (m)
breakdown van il carro attrezzi
breakfast la (prima) colazione
breast il seno
to breast-feed allattare
to breathe respirare
brick il mattone
bride la sposa
bridegroom lo sposo
bridge il ponte
briefcase la cartella
Brillo-pad la paglietta
to bring portare
Britain la Gran Bretagna
British britannico(a)
broccoli i broccoli
brochure l'opuscolo (m)
broken rotto(a)
broken down (car, etc) guasto(a)
bronchitis la bronchite
bronze il bronzo
brooch la spilla
broom (brush) la scopa
brother il fratello
brother-in-law il cognato
brown marrone
bruise il livido
brush la spazzola
bubble bath il bagnoschiuma
bucket il secchiello
buffet car il vagone ristorante
to build costruire
building l'edificio (m)
bulb (lightbulb) la lampadina
bumbag il marsupio
bumper (on car) il paraurti
bunch (of flowers) il mazzo di fiori
   (of grapes) il grappolo d'uva
bungee jumping il bungee jumping
bureau de change l'agenzia di
   cambio (f)

burger l'hamburger (m)
burglar il/la ladro(a)
burglar alarm l'antifurto (m)
to burn bruciare
   (CD) masterizzare
bus l'autobus (m)
bus pass la tessera dell'autobus
bus station la stazione delle
   autolinee
bus stop la fermata (dell'autobus)
bus ticket il biglietto d'autobus
business gli affari
   on business per affari
business card il biglietto da visita
business class la business class
businessman/woman l'uomo/
   la donna d'affari
business trip il viaggio d'affari
busy occupato(a) ; impegnato(a)
but ma ; però
butcher's il macellaio
butter il burro
button il bottone
to buy comprare
by (next to) accanto a
   (via) via
   by bus in autobus
   by car in macchina
   by train in treno
   by ship in battello
bypass (road) la circonvallazione

C

cab (taxi) il taxi
cabaret il cabaret
cabin (on boat) la cabina
cabin crew l'equipaggio di bordo (m)
cablecar la funivia
café il bar
   internet café il cyber-café
cafetière la caffettiera
cake (big) la torta
   (small) il pasticcino
cake shop la pasticceria

calculator la calcolatrice
calendar il calendario
call *(phone call)* la chiamata
to call chiamare
  (phone) chiamare per telefono
calm calmo(a)
camcorder la videocamera
camera la macchina fotografica
  digital camera la fotocamera
  digitale
camera case la custodia della
  macchina fotografica
to camp campeggiare
camping gas il camping gas
camping stove il fornellino da
  campeggio
campsite il campeggio
can il barattolo ; la scatola
to can *(to be able)* potere
  I can posso
  we can possiamo
  I cannot non posso
  we cannot non possiamo
  can I...? posso...?
  can we...? possiamo...?
Canada il Canada
Canadian canadese
canal il canale
to cancel cancellare ; annullare
cancellation la cancellazione
cancer il cancro
candle la candela
canoe la canoa
to canoe andare in canoa
can opener l'apriscatole *(m)*
cap *(hat)* il berretto
  (diaphragm) il diaframma
capital *(city)* la capitale
car la macchina ; l'auto *(m)*
car alarm l'antifurto *(m)*
car ferry il traghetto
car hire l'autonoleggio *(m)*
car insurance l'assicurazione della
  macchina *(f)*
car keys le chiavi della macchina

car park il parcheggio
car parts i pezzi di ricambio
car radio l'autoradio *(f)*
car seat *(for children)* il seggiolino
  per bambini
carrots le carote
carwash l'autolavaggio *(m)*
carafe la caraffa
caravan la roulotte
carburettor il carburatore
card *(greetings)* il biglietto d'auguri
  (business) il biglietto da visita
  (playing cards) le carte da gioco
cardboard il cartone
cardigan il cardigan
careful attento(a)
  to be careful fare attenzione
carpet *(fitted)* la moquette
  (rug) il tappeto
carriage *(railway)* il vagone
carrots le carote
to carry portare
carton il cartone
case *(suitcase)* la valigia
cash i contanti
to cash *(cheque)* incassare
cash desk la cassa
cash dispenser il Bancomat®
cashier il/la cassiere(a)
cashpoint il Bancomat®
casino il casinò
casserole dish la casseruola
cassette la cassetta
cassette player il registratore
castle il castello
casualty department il pronto
  soccorso
cat il gatto
cat food il cibo per gatti
catacombs le catacombe
catalogue il catalogo
to catch *(train, etc)* prendere
cathedral il duomo
Catholic cattolico(a)

cauliflower il cavolfiore
cave la grotta
cavity (in tooth) la carie
CD il CD
  (blank) il CD vuoto
CD player il lettore CD
ceiling il soffitto
celery il sedano
cellar la cantina
cellphone il cellulare
cemetery il cimitero
cent (euro) il centesimo
centimetre il centimetro
central centrale
central heating il riscaldamento
central locking (car) la chiusura
  centralizzata
centre il centro
century il secolo
ceramics la ceramica
cereal (for breakfast) i cereali
certificate il certificato
chain la catena
chair la sedia
chairlift la seggiovia
chalet lo chalet
challenge la sfida
chambermaid la cameriera
Champagne lo Champagne
change il cambio
  (small coins) gli spiccioli
  (money returned) il resto
to change: to change money
  cambiare soldi
  to change clothes cambiarsi
  to change train cambiare treno
changing room lo spogliatoio
Channel (English) la Manica
chapel la cappella
charcoal il carbone
charge (fee) la tariffa
to charge addebitare
  charge it to my account lo metta
  sul mio conto
charger (for battery) il caricabatterie

charter flight il volo charter
cheap economico(a)
  cheaper più economico(a)
cheap rate (phone) la tariffa
  economica
to check controllare
to check in (airport) fare il check-in
  (at hotel) firmare il registro
check-in il check-in
cheek la guancia
cheers! salute! ; cin-cin!
cheese il formaggio
chef il cuoco
chemist's la farmacia
cheque l'assegno (m)
cheque book il libretto degli assegni
cheque card la carta assegni
cherries le ciliegie
chess gli scacchi
chest (of body) il petto
chewing gum la gomma da
  masticare
chicken il pollo
chicken breast il petto di pollo
chickenpox la varicella
child il/la bambino(a)
children (small) i bambini
  (older children) i ragazzi
  for chidren per bambini
child safety seat (car) il seggiolino
  di sicurezza per bambini
chimney il camino
chin il mento
china la porcellana
chips (french fries) le patatine fritte
chocolate la cioccolata
chocolates i cioccolatini
choir il coro
choice la scelta
to choose scegliere
chop (meat) la costoletta
chopping board il tagliere
christening il battesimo
Christian name il nome di battesimo
Christmas il Natale

Merry Christmas! Buon Natale!

Christmas card il biglietto d'auguri natalizi

Christmas Eve la vigilia di Natale

church la chiesa

cigar il sigaro

cigarette la sigaretta

cigarette lighter l'accendino

cigarette papers le cartine

cinema il cinema

circle *(theatre)* la galleria

circuit breaker il salvavita

circus il circo

cistern la cisterna
(of toilet) il serbatoio dell'acqua

city la città

city centre il centro città

class: first class prima classe
second class seconda classe

clean pulito(a)

to clean pulire

cleaner *(person)* l'addetto(a) alle pulizie

cleanser il detergente

clear chiaro(a)

client il/la cliente

cliff *(on coast)* la scogliera
(mountain) la rupe

to climb scalare

climbing l'alpinismo *(m)*

climbing boots gli scarponi da montagna

Clingfilm® la pellicola per alimenti

clinic la clinica

cloakroom il guardaroba

clock l'orologio *(m)*

to close chiudere

closed *(shop, etc)* chiuso(a)

cloth il panno

clothes i vestiti

clothes peg la molletta

clothes shop il negozio d'abbigliamento

cloudy nuvoloso(a)

club il club

clutch *(car)* la frizione

coach il pullman

coach station la stazione dei pullman

coach trip la gita in pullman

coal il carbone

coast la costa

coastguard il guardacoste

coat il cappotto

coat hanger la gruccia

cockroach lo scarafaggio

cocktail il cocktail

cocoa il cacao

code il codice

coffee *(espresso)* il caffè
black coffee il caffè americano
white coffee il caffellatte
instant coffee il caffè solubile
cappuccino il cappuccino
decaffeinated coffee il decaffeinato

coil *(IUD)* la spirale

coin la moneta

Coke® la Coca®

colander lo scolapasta

cold freddo(a)
I'm cold ho freddo
it's cold fa freddo

cold *(illness)* il raffreddore
I have a cold ho il raffreddore

cold sore l'herpes *(m)*

Coliseum il Colosseo

collar il colletto

collar bone la clavicola

colleague il/la collega

to collect raccogliere
(to collect someone) andare a prendere

collection *(of stamps)* la collezione
(of letters) la levata
(of rubbish) la rimozione

colour il colore

colour-blind daltonico(a)

colour film *(for camera)* la pellicola a colori

comb il pettine

to come venire
(to arrive) arrivare
to come back tornare
to come in entrare
come in! avanti!
comedy la commedia
comfortable comodo(a)
company *(firm)* la ditta
compartment lo scompartimento
compass la bussola
to complain fare un reclamo
complaint il reclamo
complete completo(a)
to complete *(finish)* finire
(form) riempire
compulsory obbligatorio(a)
computer il computer
computer disk il dischetto
computer game il videogioco
computer program il programma di computer
concert il concerto
concert hall la sala da concerti
concession la riduzione
concussion la commozione cerebrale
condensed milk il latte condensato
conditioner il balsamo
condoms i preservativi
conductor *(on bus)* il bigliettaio
cone il cono
conference il congresso
to confirm confermare
confirmation *(of flight, etc)* la conferma
confused confuso(a)
congratulations le congratulazioni
connection *(train, etc)* la coincidenza
constipated stitico(a)
consulate il consolato
to consult consultare
to contact mettersi in contatto con
contact lens cleaner il liquido per lenti a contatto
contact lenses le lenti a contatto

to continue continuare
contraceptive l'anticoncezionale
contract il contratto
convenient: *is it convenient?* va bene?
convulsions le convulsioni
to cook cucinare
cooked cotto(a)
cooker la cucina
cookies i biscotti
cool fresco(a)
cool-box *(picnic)* la borsa termica
copper il rame
copy la copia
to copy copiare
cork il tappo
corkscrew il cavatappi
corner l'angolo *(m)*
cornflakes i cornflakes
corridor il corridoio
cosmetics i cosmetici
to cost costare
how much does it cost? quanto costa?
costume *(swimming)* il costume da bagno
cot il lettino
cottage il cottage
cotton il cotone
cotton bud il cotton fioc®
cotton wool il cotone idrofilo
couchette la cuccetta
cough la tosse
to cough tossire
cough mixture lo sciroppo per la tosse
cough sweets le pasticche per la tosse
counter *(in shop, etc)* il banco
country *(not town)* la campagna
(nation) il paese
countryside la campagna
couple *(two people)* la coppia
a couple of... un paio di...
courgettes gli zucchini
courier service il corriere

course *(of meal)* il piatto
  (of study) il corso
cousin il/la cugino(a)
cover charge il coperto
cow la mucca
crafts l'artigianato *(m)*
craftsperson l'artigiano(a)
cramps i crampi
crash *(car)* lo scontro
to crash *(car)* avere un incidente
crash helmet il casco
cream *(lotion)* la crema
  (dairy) la panna
    soured cream la panna acida
    whipped cream la panna montata
credit card la carta di credito
crime il reato
crisps le patatine
croissant la brioche
to cross *(road)* attraversare
cross la croce
cross-country skiing lo sci di fondo
crossing *(sea, lake)* la traversata
crossroads l'incrocio *(m)*
crossword puzzle il cruciverba
crowd la folla
crowded affollato(a)
crown la corona
cruise la crociera
crutches le grucce
to cry *(weep)* piangere
crystal *(made of)* di cristallo
cucumber il cetriolo
cufflinks i gemelli
cul-de-sac il vicolo cieco
cup la tazza
cupboard l'armadio *(m)*
curlers i bigodini
currant la sultanina
currency: *(foreign) currency* la valuta
  (estera)
current la corrente
curtain la tenda
cushion il cuscino

custom *(tradition)* il costume
customer il/la cliente
customs *(duty)* la dogana
cut il taglio
to cut tagliare
cutlery le posate
to cycle andare in bicicletta
cycle track la pista ciclabile
cycling il ciclismo
cyst la cisti
cystitis la cistite

D

daily *(each day)* ogni giorno ;
  quotidiano(a)
dairy produce i latticini
dam la diga
damage il danno
damp umido(a)
dance il ballo
to dance ballare
danger il pericolo
dangerous pericoloso(a)
dark *(colour)* scuro(a)
  (night) buio(a)
    after dark a notte fatta
date la data
date of birth la data di nascita
daughter la figlia
daughter-in-law la nuora
dawn l'alba *(f)*
day il giorno
  per day al giorno
  every day ogni giorno
  (span of time) la giornata
dead morto(a)
deaf sordo(a)
dear caro(a)
debts i debiti
decaffeinated decaffeinato(a)
  have you decaff coffee? ha del
  decaffeinato?
December dicembre
deckchair la sedia a sdraio

to declare dichiarare
  nothing to declare niente da dichiarare
deep profondo(a)
deep freeze il surgelatore
deer il cervo
to defrost scongelare
to de-ice sbrinare
delay il ritardo
  how long is the delay? di quant'è il ritardo?
delayed: *to be delayed* (flight) subire un ritardo
delicatessen il negozio di specialità gastronomiche
delicious delizioso(a)
demonstration la manifestazione
dental floss il filo interdentale
dentist il/la dentista
dentures la dentiera
deodorant il deodorante
to depart partire
department il reparto
department store il grande magazzino
departure la partenza
departure lounge la sala partenze
deposit il deposito
to describe descrivere
description la descrizione
desk la scrivania
  (information, etc) il banco
dessert il dolce
details i dettagli
detergent il detersivo
detour la deviazione
to develop (photos) sviluppare
diabetes il diabete
diabetic diabetico(a)
  I'm diabetic sono diabetico(a)
to dial fare il numero
dialect il dialetto
dialling code il prefisso telefonico
dialling tone il segnale di libero
diamond il diamante

diapers i pannolini
diaphragm il diaframma
diarrhoea la diarrea
diary l'agenda (f)
dice il dado
dictionary il dizionario ;
  il vocabolario
to die morire
diesel il gasolio
diet la dieta
  I'm on a diet sono a dieta
  special diet una dieta specifica
different diverso(a)
difficult difficile
digital camera la fotocamera digitale
to dilute diluire
dinghy (rubber) il canotto
dining room la sala da pranzo
dinner (evening meal) la cena
  to have dinner cenare
dinner jacket lo smoking
direct (train, etc) diretto(a)
directions le indicazioni
  to ask for directions chiedere la strada
directory (telephone) l'elenco telefonico (m)
directory enquiries il servizio informazioni
dirty sporco(a)
disability l'handicap (m)
disabled (person) disabile ;
  handicappato(a)
to disagree non essere d'accordo
to disappear scomparire
disaster il disastro
disco la discoteca
discount lo sconto
to discover scoprire
disease la malattia
dishtowel lo strofinaccio dei piatti
dishwasher la lavastoviglie
disinfectant il disinfettante
disk (floppy disk) il disco

to dislocate *(joint)* lussarsi
disposable *(camera)* usa e getta
distance la distanza
distilled water l'acqua distillata *(f)*
district *(of town)* il quartiere
to disturb disturbare
to dive tuffarsi
diversion la deviazione
diving i tuffi
divorced divorziato(a)
DIY shop il negozio di bricolage
dizzy: *to be dizzy* avere il capogiro
to do fare
doctor il medico/la dottoressa
documents i documenti
dog il cane
dog food il cibo per cani
dog lead il guinzaglio
doll la bambola
dollars i dollari
domestic *(flight)* nazionale
donor card la tessera dell'A.I.D.O.
door la porta
doorbell il campanello
double doppio(a)
double bed il letto matrimoniale
double room la camera doppia
down: *to go down* scendere
downstairs giù ; dabbasso
drain lo scarico
draught *(of air)* la corrente (d'aria)
   there's a draught c'è corrente
draught lager la birra alla spina
drawer il cassetto
drawing il disegno
dress il vestito
to dress *(oneself)* vestirsi
dressing *(for food)* il condimento
   (for wound) la fasciatura
dressing gown la vestaglia
drill *(tool)* il trapano
drink *(soft)* la bibita
to drink bere
drinking water l'acqua potabile *(f)*

to drive guidare
driver *(of car)* l'autista *(m/f)*
driving licence la patente
drought la siccità
to drown affogare
drug *(medicine)* il farmaco
   (narcotics) la droga
drunk ubriaco(a)
dry secco(a) ; asciutto(a)
to dry asciugare
dry-cleaner's la tintoria ; il lavasecco
dummy *(for baby)* la tettarella
during durante
dust la polvere
duster lo straccio
dustpan and brush lo scopino e
   la paletta
duty-free esente da dogana
duvet il piumino
duvet cover il copripiumone
dye la tinta
dynamo la dinamo

E

each ogni
ear l'orecchio *(m)*
earache il mal d'orecchi
earlier più presto
early presto
to earn guadagnare
earphones le cuffie
earplugs i tappi per le orecchie
earrings gli orecchini
earth la terra
earthquake il terremoto
east l'est *(m)*
Easter la Pasqua
   Happy Easter! Buona Pasqua!
easy facile
to eat mangiare
economy *(class)* la classe turistica
egg l'uovo *(m)*
   eggs le uova
   fried egg l'uovo fritto

hard-boiled egg l'uovo sodo
scrambled eggs le uova strapazzate
soft-boiled egg l'uovo alla coque
either ... or o ... o
elastic band l'elastico *(m)*
Elastoplast il cerotto
elbow il gomito
electric elettrico(a)
electric blanket la coperta elettrica
electrician l'elettricista *(m/f)*
electricity l'elettricità *(f)*
electricity meter il contatore dell'elettricità
electric razor il rasoio elettrico
electric shock la scossa
elevator l'ascensore *(m)*
e-mail la posta elettronica ; l'e-mail *(f)*
to e-mail s.o. mandare un'e-mail a qualcuno
e-mail address l'indirizzo di posta elettronica *(m)*
embassy l'ambasciata *(f)*
emergency l'emergenza *(f)*
emergency exit l'uscita d'emergenza *(f)*
emery board la limetta per le unghie
empty vuoto(a)
end la fine
engaged *(to be married)* fidanzato(a)
(phone, toilet, etc) occupato(a)
engine il motore
England l'Inghilterra *(f)*
English inglese
(language) l'inglese *(m)*
to enjoy divertirsi
(to like) piacere
I enjoyed the trip la gita mi è piaciuta
I enjoy swimming mi piace nuotare
enjoy your meal! buon appetito!
enough abbastanza
that's enough basta così
enquiry desk il banco informazioni
to enter entrare
entertainment il divertimento

entrance l'entrata *(f)* ; l'ingresso *(m)*
entrance fee il biglietto d'ingresso
envelope la busta
epileptic epilettico(a)
epileptic fit la crisi epilettica
equal uguale ; pari
equipment l'attrezzatura *(f)*
eraser la gomma da cancellare
error l'errore *(m)*
eruption l'eruzione *(f)*
escalator la scala mobile
to escape fuggire
essential essenziale
estate agent's l'agenzia immobiliare *(f)*
euro l'euro *(m)*
euro cent il centesimo
eurocheque l'eurocheque *(m)*
Europe l'Europa *(f)*
European europeo(a)
European Union l'Unione Europea *(f)*
eve la vigilia
evening la sera
this evening stasera
tomorrow evening domani sera
in the evening la sera
evening dress l'abito da sera *(m)*
evening meal la cena
every ogni ; ciascuno ; tutti
everyone tutti
everything tutto
everywhere dappertutto
examination l'esame *(m)*
example: *for example* per esempio
excellent ottimo(a)
except salvo
excess baggage il bagaglio in eccedenza
to exchange cambiare
exchange rate il cambio
exciting emozionante
excursion l'escursione *(f)*
to excuse scusare
excuse me! *(sorry)* mi scusi!
(when passing) permesso!

exercise l'esercizio (m)

exhaust pipe il tubo di scappamento

exhibition la mostra

exit l'uscita (f)

expenses le spese

expensive costoso(a) ; caro(a)

expert l'esperto(a)

to expire (ticket, etc) scadere

to explain spiegare

explosion l'esplosione (f)

to export esportare

express (train) l'espresso (m)

express (parcel, etc) espresso(a)

extension (electrical) la prolunga

extra (spare) in più
  (more) supplementare
  an extra bed un letto in più

eye l'occhio (m)

eyebrows le sopracciglia

eye drops il collirio

eyelashes le ciglia

eye shadow l'ombretto (m)

F

fabric la stoffa

face la faccia

face cloth il guanto di spugna

facial la pulizia del viso

facilities (leisure facilities)
  le attrezzature

factory la fabbrica

to fail fallire

to faint svenire

fainted svenuto(a)

fair (just) giusto(a)
  (blond) biondo(a)

fair (trade) la fiera
  (funfair) il luna park

fake falso(a)

fall (autumn) l'autunno (m)

to fall cadere
  he/she has fallen è caduto(a)

false teeth la dentiera

family la famiglia

famous famoso(a)

fan (hand-held) il ventaglio
  (electric) il ventilatore
  (football) il/la tifoso(a)

fan belt la cinghia della ventola

fancy dress il costume ; la maschera

far lontano(a)
  is it far? è lontano?

fare la tariffa

farm la fattoria

farmer l'agricoltore (m)

farmhouse la fattoria

fashionable alla moda

fast veloce
  too fast troppo veloce

to fasten (seatbelt, etc) allacciare

fat grasso(a)
  (noun) il grasso
  saturated fats i grassi saturi
  unsaturated fats i grassi insaturi

father il padre

father-in-law il suocero

fault (defect) il difetto
  it's not my fault non è colpa mia

favour il favore

favourite preferito(a)

fax il fax
  by fax per fax

to fax mandare un fax

February febbraio

to feed dare da mangiare

to feel sentire ; sentirsi
  I don't feel well non mi sento bene
  I feel sick ho la nausea

feet i piedi

felt-tip pen il pennarello

female femmina ; femminile

ferry il traghetto

festival la festa

to fetch (bring) portare
  (to go and get) andare a prendere

fever la febbre

few pochi
  a few alcuni

fiancé(e) il/la fidanzato(a)

field il campo
to fight combattere ; lottare
file *(folder)* il raccoglitore
  (computer) l'archivio *(m)*
to fill riempire
to fill in *(form)* compilare
fill it up! *(petrol)* il pieno!
fillet il filetto
filling *(dental)* l'otturazione *(f)*
film *(at cinema)* il film
  (for camera) la pellicola
Filofax® l'agenda *(f)*
filter il filtro
to find trovare
fine *(to be paid)* la multa
finger il dito
to finish finire
finished finito(a)
fire il fuoco ; l'incendio *(m)*
  fire! al fuoco!
fire alarm l'allarme antincendio *(m)*
fire brigade i vigili del fuoco
fire engine l'autopompa *(f)*
fire escape la scala antincendio
fire extinguisher l'estintore
fireplace il caminetto
fireworks i fuochi d'artificio
firm *(company)* l'azienda *(f)* ; la ditta
first primo(a)
first aid il pronto soccorso
first aid kit la cassetta di pronto soccorso
first class la prima classe
first name il nome di battesimo
fish il pesce
to fish pescare
fisherman il pescatore
fishing permit la licenza di pesca
fishing rod la canna da pesca
fishmonger's la pescheria
to fit *(clothes)* andare bene
  it doesn't fit non va bene
fit *(seizure)* l'attacco *(m)*
to fix riparare ; sistemare
  can you fix it? può ripararlo?

fizzy gassato(a)
flag la bandiera
flame la fiamma
flash *(for camera)* il flash
flashlight la pila
flask *(thermos)* il thermos
flat l'appartamento *(m)*
flat piatto(a)
  flat battery la batteria scarica
  flat tyre la gomma a terra
flavour il gusto
  what flavour? che gusto?
flaw il difetto
fleas le pulci
flesh la carne
flex il filo flessibile
flight il volo
flip flops gli infradito
flippers le pinne
flood l'alluvione *(f)*
  flash flood l'inondazione *(f)*
floor *(of building)* il piano
  (of room) il pavimento
  which floor? a che piano?
  on the ground floor al pianterreno
  on the first floor al primo piano
  on the second floor al secondo piano
floorcloth lo straccio per pavimenti
Florence Firenze
florist's shop il fioraio
flour la farina
flowers i fiori
flu l'influenza *(f)*
fly la mosca
to fly volare
flysheet *(tent)* la tenda da campo
fog la nebbia
foggy nebbioso(a)
foil *(silver paper)* la carta stagnola
to fold ripiegare
to follow seguire
food il cibo
food poisoning l'intossicazione alimentare *(f)*

foot il piede
  on foot a piedi
football il calcio ; il pallone
football match la partita di calcio
football pitch il campo di calcio
football player il calciatore
footpath il sentiero
for per
  for me/us per me/noi
  for him/her per lui/lei
  for you per te/lei/voi
forbidden proibito(a)
forehead la fronte
foreign straniero(a)
foreigner lo/la straniero(a)
forest la foresta
forever per sempre
to forget dimenticare
fork *(for eating)* la forchetta
  (in road) il bivio
form *(document)* il modulo
fortnight quindici giorni
forward avanti
foul *(football)* il fallo
fountain la fontana
four-wheel drive con quattro ruote motrici
fox la volpe
fracture la frattura
fragile fragile
fragrance la fragranza
frame *(picture)* la cornice
France la Francia
free *(not occupied)* libero(a)
  (costing nothing) gratis
freezer il congelatore
French francese
  (language) il francese
French fries le patatine fritte
frequent frequente
fresh fresco(a)
fresh water l'acqua dolce *(f)*
Friday il venerdì
fridge il frigorifero
fried fritto(a)

friend l'amico(a)
friendly amichevole
frog la rana
from da
  from Scotland dalla Scozia
  from England dall'Inghilterra
front davanti
  in front of... di fronte a...
front door la porta d'ingresso
frost la brina
frozen *(food)* surgelato(a)
fruit la frutta
  dried fruit la frutta secca
fruit juice il succo di frutta
fruit salad la macedonia
to fry friggere
frying-pan la padella
fuel *(petrol)* la benzina
fuel gauge la spia della benzina
fuel pump la pompa
fuel tank il serbatoio della benzina
full pieno(a)
  (occupied) completo(a)
full board la pensione completa
fumes *(of car)* i gas di scarico
fun il divertimento
funeral il funerale
funfair il luna park
funny *(amusing)* divertente
fur il pelo
furnished ammobiliato(a)
furniture i mobili
fuse il fusibile
fuse box la scatola dei fusibili
future il futuro

G

gallery la galleria
game il gioco
  (meat) la selvaggina
garage *(private)* il garage
  (for repairs) l'autofficina *(f)*
  (for petrol) la stazione di servizio
garden il giardino

garlic l'aglio (m)
gas il gas
gas cooker la cucina a gas
gas cylinder la bombola del gas
gastritis la gastrite
gate il cancello
  (airport) l'uscita (f)
gay (person) gay
gear (car) la marcia
  first gear la prima
  second gear la seconda
  third gear la terza
  fourth gear la quarta
  neutral folle
  reverse la retromarcia
gearbox il cambio
generous generoso(a)
gents' (toilet) la toilette (per uomini)
genuine (leather, silver) vero(a)
  (antique, etc) autentico(a)
German tedesco(a)
  (language) il tedesco
German measles la rosolia
Germany la Germania
to get (obtain) ottenere
  (to receive) ricevere
  (to fetch) prendere
to get in/on (vehicle) salire in/su
to get off (bus, etc) scendere da
gift il regalo
gift shop il negozio di souvenir
girl (young child) la bambina
  (teenage) la ragazza
girlfriend la ragazza
to give dare
to give back restituire
glacier il ghiacciaio
glass (substance) il vetro
  (for drinking) il bicchiere
  a glass of water un bicchiere
  d'acqua
  a glass of wine un bicchiere di vino
glasses (specs) gli occhiali
glasses case la custodia degli
  occhiali
gloves i guanti

glue la colla
to go andare
  I'm going to... vado a...
  we're going to... andiamo a...
to go back ritornare
to go in entrare in
to go out (leave) uscire
goat la capra
God Dio
goggles gli occhialini
  (for skiing) gli occhiali da sci
gold l'oro (m)
golf il golf
golf ball la pallina da golf
golf clubs le mazze da golf
golf course il campo di golf
good buono(a)
  (pleasant) bello(a)
  very good ottimo(a)
good afternoon buon giorno
  (after 5pm) buona sera
goodbye arrivederci
good day buon giorno
good evening buona sera
good morning buon giorno
good night buona notte
goose l'oca (f)
gram il grammo
grandchild il/la nipote
granddaughter la nipotina
grandfather il nonno
grandmother la nonna
grandparents i nonni
grandson il nipotino
grapefruit il pampelmo
grapes l'uva (f)
grass l'erba (f)
grated grattugiato(a)
grater la grattugia
greasy grasso(a)
great (big) grande
  (wonderful) fantastico(a)
Great Britain la Gran Bretagna
green verde

green card (car insurance) la carta verde
greengrocer's il fruttivendolo
greetings card il biglietto d'auguri
grey grigio(a)
grill la griglia
to grill cuocere alla griglia
grilled alla griglia
grocer's il negozio di alimentari
ground la terra
ground floor il pianterreno
   on the ground floor a pianterreno
groundsheet il telone impermeabile
group il gruppo
guarantee la garanzia
guard (on train) il capotreno
guest (house guest) l'ospite (m/f)
   (in hotel) il/la cliente
guesthouse la pensione
guide (tourist) la guida
guidebook la guida
guided tour la visita guidata
guitar la chitarra
gun (pistol) la pistola
   (rifle) il fucile
gym (place) la palestra
gym shoes le scarpe da ginnastica

H

haemorrhoids le emorroidi
hail la grandine
hair i capelli
hairbrush la spazzola per capelli
haircut il taglio di capelli
hairdresser il parrucchiere/ la parrucchiera
hair dryer il fon
hair dye la tintura per capelli
hair gel il gel per capelli
hairgrip la molletta per capelli
hair mousse la spuma
hair spray la lacca per capelli
half la metà
   a half bottle of... una mezza bottiglia di...

half an hour mezz'ora
half board mezza pensione
half fare il ridotto
half-price metà prezzo
ham (cooked) il prosciutto cotto
   (cured) il prosciutto crudo
hamburger l'hamburger (m)
hammer il martello
hand la mano
handbag la borsa
handicapped disabile ; handicappato(a)
handkerchief il fazzoletto
handle il manico
handlebars il manubrio
hand luggage il bagaglio a mano
hand-made fatto a mano
hands-free phone il telefono viva voce
handsome bello(a)
hanger (coat hanger) la gruccia per abiti
hang gliding il volo con deltaplano
hangover i postumi della sbornia
to happen succedere
   what happened? cos'è successo?
happy felice
   happy birthday! buon compleanno!
harbour il porto
hard duro(a)
   (difficult) difficile
hardware shop il negozio di ferramenta
to harm nuocere
harvest il raccolto ; la vendemmia
hat il cappello
to have avere
   I have... ho...
   I don't have... non ho...
   we have... abbiamo...
   we don't have... non abbiamo...
   do you have...? ha/hai/avete...?
to have to dovere
hay fever il raffreddore da fieno
he egli ; lui

head la testa
headache il mal di testa
   I have a headache ho mal di testa
headlights i fari
headphones la cuffia
health la salute
health-food shop l'erboristeria *(f)*
healthy sano(a)
to hear sentire
hearing aid l'apparecchio acustico *(m)*
heart il cuore
heart attack l'infarto *(m)*
heartburn il bruciore di stomaco
to heat up *(food)* riscaldare
heater il termosifone
heating il riscaldamento
heavy pesante
heel il tallone
heel bar il banco del calzolaio
height l'altezza *(f)*
helicopter l'elicottero *(m)*
hello! salve! ; ciao!
   (on telephone) pronto
helmet il casco
help! aiuto!
to help aiutare
   can you help me? può aiutarmi?
hem l'orlo *(m)*
hepatitis l'epatite *(f)*
her il/la suo(a)
   her passport il suo passaporto
   her room la sua camera
herb l'erba aromatica *(f)*
herbal tea la tisana
here qui
   here is... ecco...
   here is my passport ecco il mio
   passaporto
hernia l'ernia *(f)*
hi! ciao!
to hide nascondere
high alto(a)
   (speed) forte
high blood pressure la pressione alta
high chair il seggiolone

hill la collina
hill-walking il trekking
him lui ; lo ; gli
hip l'anca *(f)*
hip replacement la protesi dell'anca
hire il noleggio
   car hire il noleggio auto
   bike hire il noleggio bici
   boat hire il noleggio barche
   ski hire il noleggio sci
to hire noleggiare
hired car la macchina a noleggio
his il/la suo(a)
   his passport il suo passaporto
   his room la sua camera
historic storico(a)
history la storia
to hit colpire
to hitchhike fare l'autostop
hobby il passatempo
to hold tenere
   (to contain) contenere
hold-up *(traffic)* l'ingorgo *(m)*
hole il buco
holiday la festa
   on holiday in vacanza
holiday rep il/la rappresentante
   dell'agenzia di viaggio
home la casa
   at home a casa
homesick: *to be homesick* avere
   nostalgia di casa
   I'm homesick ho nostalgia di casa
homosexual omosessuale
honest onesto(a)
honey il miele
honeymoon la luna di miele
hood *(on jacket)* il cappuccio
hook *(for fishing)* l'amo *(m)*
to hope sperare
   I hope so/not spero di sì/no
hors d'œuvre l'antipasto *(m)*
horse il cavallo
horse racing l'ippica *(f)*
to horse-ride andare a cavallo

hosepipe la canna dell'acqua
hospital l'ospedale (m)
hostel l'ostello (m)
hot caldo(a)
  I'm hot ho caldo
  it's hot (weather) fa caldo
hot-water bottle la borsa dell'acqua calda
hotel l'albergo (m) ; l'hotel (m)
hour l'ora (f)
  half an hour mezz'ora
  1 hour un'ora
  2 hours due ore
house la casa
housewife la casalinga
house wine il vino della casa
housework i lavori di casa
how? (in what way) come?
  how much? quanto(a)?
  how many? quanti(e)?
  how are you? come sta?
hungry: to be hungry avere fame
hunt la caccia
to hunt andare a caccia
hunting permit la licenza di caccia
hurry: I'm in a hurry ho fretta
to hurt fare male
  that hurts fa male
husband il marito
hut (bathing/beach) la cabina
  (mountain) la baita
hydrofoil l'aliscafo (m)
hypodermic needle l'ago ipodermico (m)

I

I io
ice il ghiaccio
  with ice con ghiaccio
  without ice senza ghiaccio
ice box il freezer
ice cream il gelato
iced coffee il caffè freddo
iced tea il tè freddo
ice lolly il ghiacciolo

ice rink la pista di pattinaggio su ghiaccio
to ice skate pattinare sul ghiaccio
ice skates i pattini da ghiaccio
idea l'idea (f)
identity card la carta d'identità
if se
ignition l'accensione (f)
ignition key la chiave dell'accensione
ill malato(a)
  I'm ill sto male
illness la malattia
immediately subito
immersion heater lo scaldabagno elettrico
immigration l'immigrazione (f)
immunisation l'immunizzazione (f)
to import importare
important importante
impossible impossibile
to improve migliorare .
in in
  in 2 hours in due ore
  in London a Londra
in front of davanti a
included compreso(a) ; incluso(a)
inconvenient scomodo(a)
to increase aumentare
  to increase volume alzare il volume
indicator (in car) la freccia
indigestion l'indigestione (f)
indigestion tablets le compresse per digerire
indoors dentro ; al chiuso
infection l'infezione (f)
infectious contagioso(a)
informal (clothes) sportivo(a)
information le informazioni
information office l'ufficio informazioni (m)
ingredients gli ingredienti
inhaler l'inalatore (m)
injection l'iniezione (f) ; la puntura
to injure ferire

injured ferito(a)
injury la lesione
ink l'inchiostro *(m)*
inn la locanda
inner tube la camera d'aria
inquiries le informazioni
insect l'insetto *(m)*
insect bite la puntura d'insetto
insect repellent l'insettifugo
inside dentro
instant coffee il caffè solubile
instead of invece di
instructor l'istruttore/l'istruttrice
insulin l'insulina *(f)*
insurance l'assicurazione *(f)*
insurance certificate il certificato
  di assicurazione
to insure assicurare
insured: *to be insured* essere
  assicurato(a)
to intend to avere intenzione di
interesting interessante
international internazionale
internet l'Internet *(m)*
internet café il cyber-café
interpreter l'interprete *(m/f)*
interval l'intervallo *(m)*
interview l'intervista *(f)*
into in
  into town in città
  into the centre in centro
to introduce someone to presentare
  qualcuno a
invitation l'invito *(m)*
to invite invitare
invoice la fattura
Ireland l'Irlanda *(f)*
Irish irlandese
iron *(for clothes)* il ferro da stiro
  (metal) il ferro
to iron stirare
ironing board l'asse da stiro
ironmonger's il negozio di
  ferramenta
is è

island l'isola *(f)*
it esse/essa ; lo/la
Italian italiano(a)
  (language) l'italiano *(m)*
Italy l'Italia *(f)*
to itch prudere
  my leg itches mi prude la gamba
  my eyes itch mi prudono gli occhi
item *(on bill)* la voce
itemised bill il conto dettagliato

J

jack *(for car)* il cric
jacket la giacca
  waterproof jacket il giaccone
  impermeabile
jam *(food)* la marmellata
jammed bloccato(a)
January gennaio
jar *(honey, jam, etc)* il vaso
jaundice l'itterizia *(f)*
jaw la mascella
jealous geloso(a) ; invidioso(a)
jeans i blue jeans
jelly *(dessert)* la gelatina
jellyfish la medusa
jet ski l'acqua-scooter *(m)*
jetty il molo
jeweller's la gioielleria
jewellery i gioielli
Jewish ebreo(a)
job il lavoro
to jog fare jogging
to join *(club)* iscriversi a
to join in *(game)* partecipare a
joint *(hip, etc)* l'articolazione *(f)*
joke la barzelletta
  (practical) lo scherzo *(m)*
to joke scherzare
journalist il/la giornalista
journey il viaggio
judge il/la giudice *(m/f)*
jug la brocca
juice il succo

a carton of juice un cartone di succo di frutta
orange juice il succo d'arancia
July luglio
to jump saltare
jumper il maglione
jump leads *(for car)* i cavi per far partire la macchina
junction *(road)* l'incrocio *(m)*
June giugno
just: *just two* solamente due
I've just arrived sono appena arrivato(a)

K

to keep *(retain)* tenere
keep the change! tenga il resto
kennel il canile
kettle il bollitore
key la chiave
card key il passe-partout
keyboard la tastiera
keyring il portachiavi
to kick dare calci a
kid *(child)* il bambino
kidneys *(in body)* i reni
to kill uccidere
kilo il chilo
a kilo of apples un chilo di mele
2 kilos due chili
kilogram il chilogrammo
kilometre il chilometro
kind *(sort)* il tipo
kind *(person)* gentile
king il re
kiosk l'edicola *(f)*
kiss il bacio
to kiss baciare
kitchen la cucina
kitchen paper la carta assorbente da cucina
kite l'aquilone *(m)*
knee il ginocchio
knee highs i gambaletti

knickers le mutandine
knife il coltello
to knit lavorare a maglia
to knock *(on door)* bussare
to knock down *(car)* investire
to knock over *(glass, vase)* rovesciare
knot il nodo
to know *(facts)* sapere
(to be acquainted with) conoscere
I don't know non lo so
to know how to sapere
to know how to swim saper nuotare
kosher kasher

L

label l'etichetta *(f)*
lace il pizzo
laces *(shoe)* i lacci
ladder la scala
ladies' *(toilet)* la toilette (per signore)
lady la signora
lager la birra (bionda)
lake il lago
lamb l'agnello *(m)*
lame zoppo(a)
lamp la lampada
lamppost il lampione
lampshade il paralume
land la terra
to land *(plane)* atterrare
landlady la padrona di casa
landlord il padrone di casa
landslide la frana
lane la stradina
(of motorway) la corsia
language la lingua
language school la scuola di lingue
laptop il laptop
large grande
last ultimo(a) ; scorso(a)
the last bus l'ultimo autobus
the last train l'ultimo treno
last night ieri notte
last week la settimana scorsa

last year l'anno scorso
last time l'ultima volta
late tardi
  the train's late il treno è in ritardo
  sorry we're late scusi il ritardo
later più tardi
to laugh ridere
launderette la lavanderia automatica
laundry il bucato
lavatory la toilette
lavender la lavanda
law la legge
lawn il prato inglese
lawyer *(m/f)* l'avvocato/l'avvocatessa
laxative il lassativo
layby la piazzola di sosta
lazy pigro(a)
lead *(electric)* il filo
lead *(metal)* il piombo
lead-free senza piombo
leaf la foglia
leak *(of gas, liquid)* la perdita
  (in roof) il buco
to leak: *it's leaking* perde
to learn imparare
lease *(rental)* l'affitto *(m)*
leather il cuoio ; la pelle
to leave *(leave behind)* lasciare
  (train, bus, etc) partire
  when does the bus leave? quando
  parte l'autobus?
  when does the train leave? quando
  parte il treno?
leeks i porri
left la sinistra
  on/to the left a sinistra
left-handed mancino(a)
left-luggage il deposito bagagli
left-luggage locker l'armadietto per
  despositare i bagagli *(m)*
leg la gamba
lemon il limone
lemonade la limonata
to lend prestare

length la lunghezza
lens *(camera)* l'obiettivo *(m)*
  (contact lens) la lente a contatto
lenses le lenti
lesbian lesbica
less meno
  less than meno di
lesson la lezione
to let *(allow)* permettere
  (to hire out) affittare
letter la lettera
letterbox la cassetta delle lettere
lettuce la lattuga
level crossing il passaggio a livello
library la biblioteca
licence il permesso
  (driving) la patente
lid il coperchio
to lie mentire
lie *(untruth)* la bugia
to lie down sdraiarsi
life belt il salvagente
lifeboat la scialuppa di salvataggio
lifeguard il bagnino
life insurance l'assicurazione sulla
  vita *(f)*
life jacket il giubbotto salvagente
life raft la zattera di salvataggio
lift *(elevator)* l'ascensore *(m)*
  (in car) il passaggio
light *(not heavy)* leggero(a)
  (colour) chiaro(a)
light la luce
  have you a light? ha da accendere?
light bulb la lampadina
lighter l'accendino *(m)*
lighthouse il faro
lightning il fulmine
like come
to like piacere
  I like coffee mi piace il caffè
  I don't like... non mi piace...
  I'd/we'd like... vorrei/ vorremmo...
lilo il materassino
lime *(fruit)* il cedro

line *(row, queue)* la fila
    (telephone) la linea
linen il lino
lingerie la biancheria intima
    da donna
lip reading la labiolettura
lips le labbra
lip salve il burro di cacao
lipstick il rossetto
liqueur il liquore
list l'elenco *(m)* ; la lista
to listen (to) ascoltare
litre il litro
    a litre of milk un litro di latte
litter *(rubbish)* i rifiuti
little *(small)* piccolino(a)
    a little... un po' di...
to live vivere ; abitare
    I live in London vivo a Londra
    he lives in a flat abita in un
    appartamento
liver il fegato
living room il salotto
loaf of bread la pagnotta
local locale
to lock chiudere a chiave
lock la serratura
    the lock is broken la serratura
    è rotta
locker l'armadietto *(m)*
locksmith il fabbro
log book *(car)* il libretto di
    circolazione
logs i ceppi
lollipop il lecca lecca
London Londra
    in/to London a Londra
long lungo(a)
    for a long time molto tempo
long-sighted presbite
to look after prendersi cura di
to look at guardare
to look for cercare
loose *(not fastened)* slegato(a)
    it's come loose *(knot)* si è allentato(a)

lorry il camion
to lose perdere
lost *(object)* perso(a)
    I've lost my... ho perso il/la...
    I'm lost mi sono smarrito(a)
    we're lost ci siamo smarriti(e)
lost property office l'ufficio oggetti
    smarriti *(m)*
lot: *a lot* molto
lottery la lotteria
loud forte
lounge *(in hotel)* il salone
    (in house) la sala
    (in airport) la sala d'attesa
love l'amore *(m)*
to love *(person)* amare
    I love you ti amo
    I love swimming mi piace nuotare
lovely bellissimo(a)
low basso(a)
    (standard, quality) scadente
low-alcohol a basso contenuto
    alcolico
to lower volume abbassare il volume
low-fat magro(a)
luck la fortuna
lucky fortunato(a)
luggage i bagagli
luggage rack il portabagagli
luggage tag l'etichetta *(f)*
luggage trolley il carrello
lump *(swelling)* il gonfiore
lunch il pranzo
lunch break l'intervallo del pranzo *(m)*
lung il polmone
luxury di lusso

M

machine la macchina
mad *(insane)* matto(a)
    (angry) arrabbiato(a)
magazine la rivista
maggot il verme
magnet la calamita

magnifying glass la lente d'ingrandimento

maid *(in hotel)* la cameriera

maiden name il nome da ragazza

mail la posta

main principale

main course *(meal)* il secondo

main road la strada principale

to make *(generally)* fare
  (meal) preparare

make-up il trucco

male maschio ; maschile

mallet la mazza

man l'uomo *(m)*

to manage *(be in charge of)* dirigere

manager il direttore ; il gerente

manual *(gear change)* cambio manuale

many molti(e)

map *(of country)* la carta geografica
  (city) la piantina

marble il marmo

March marzo

margarine la margarina

marina il porticciolo

mark *(stain)* la macchia ; il segno
  (brand) la marca

market il mercato
  where is the market? dov'è il mercato?
  when is the market? quando c'è il mercato?

marmalade la marmellata d'arance

married sposato(a)
  I'm married sono sposato(a)
  are you married? è sposato(a)?

marry: *to get married* sposarsi

marsh la palude

mascara il mascara

mass *(in church)* la messa

mast l'albero della barca a vela *(m)*

masterpiece il capolavoro

match *(game)* la partita

matches i fiammiferi

material il materiale
  (cloth) il tessuto

to matter importare
  it doesn't matter non importa
  what's the matter? cosa c'è?

mattress il materasso

May maggio

mayonnaise la maionese

mayor *(m/f)* il sindaco/la sindachessa

maximum il massimo

me me ; mi

meal il pasto

to mean *(signify)* voler dire
  what does it mean? cosa vuol dire?

measles il morbillo

to measure misurare

meat la carne

mechanic il meccanico

medical insurance l'assicurazione medica *(f)*

medical treatment le cure mediche

medicine la medicina

Mediterranean il Mediterraneo

medium rare *(steak)* poco cotto(a)

to meet incontrare
  pleased to meet you! piacere!

meeting la riunione
  (by chance) l'incontro *(m)*

meeting point il meeting point

melon il melone

to melt sciogliere

member *(of club, etc)* il/la socio(a)

membership card la tessera

memory la memoria
  (memories) i ricordi

memory card *(for camera)* la memory card

men gli uomini

to mend riparare

meningitis la meningite

menu il menù
  set menu il menù a prezzo fisso ;
  il menù turistico
  à la carte menu il menù alla carta

message il messaggio

metal il metallo

meter il contatore

metre il metro
metro (underground) la metropolitana
metro station la stazione del metrò
microwave oven il forno a microonde
midday il mezzogiorno
  at midday a mezzogiorno
middle il mezzo
middle-aged di mezz'età
midge il moscerino
midnight la mezzanotte
  at midnight a mezzanotte
migraine l'emicrania *(f)*
  I have a migraine ho l'emicrania
Milan Milano
mild dolce ; mite
milk il latte
  fresh milk il latte fresco
  hot milk il latte caldo
  long-life milk il latte a lunga
  conservazione
  powdered milk il latte in polvere
  whole milk il latte intero
  semi-skimmed milk il latte
  parzialmente scremato
  soya milk il latte di soia
  with/without milk con/senza latte
milkshake il frappé ; il frullato
millimetre il millimetro
mince *(meat)* la carne macinata
mind: *do you mind?* le dà fastidio?
  I don't mind non mi dà fastidio
mineral water l'acqua minerale *(f)*
minibar il minibar
minimum il minimo
minister *(church)* il sacerdote
  (political) il ministro
minor road la strada secondaria
mint *(herb)* la menta
mint tea il tè alla menta
minute il minuto
mirror lo specchio
to misbehave comportarsi male
miscarriage l'aborto spontaneo *(m)*
to miss *(train, etc)* perdere
Miss Signorina

missing *(thing)* smarrito(a)
  (person) scomparso(a)
mistake l'errore *(m)*
misty nebbioso(a)
misunderstanding il malinteso
to mix mescolare
mobile phone il cellulare
modem il modem
modern moderno(a)
moisturizer l'idratante *(m)*
mole *(on skin)* il neo
moment: *just a moment* un momento
monastery il monastero
Monday il lunedì
money i soldi
  I have no money non ho soldi
money belt il marsupio
money order il vaglia
month il mese
  this month questo mese
  last month il mese scorso
  next month il mese prossimo
monthly mensilmente
monument il monumento
moon la luna
mooring l'ormeggio *(m)*
mop lo straccio da terra
moped il motorino
more (than) più (di)
  more than 3 più di tre
  more wine ancora un po' di vino
morning la mattina
  in the morning di mattina
  this morning stamattina
  tomorrow morning domani mattina
morning-after pill la pillola del
  giorno dopo
mosquito la zanzara
mosquito net la zanzariera
mosquito repellent lo zanzarifugo
most il/la più ; il massimo
moth *(clothes)* la tarma
mother la madre
mother-in-law la suocera
motor il motore

motorbike la moto
motorboat il motoscafo
motorway l'autostrada *(f)*
mould la muffa
mountain la montagna
mountain bike la mountain bike
mountain rescue il soccorso alpino
mountaineering l'alpinismo *(m)*
mouse il topo
  (computer) il mouse
moustache i baffi
mouth la bocca
mouthwash il collutorio
move muoversi
  it isn't moving non si muove
movie il film
Mr Signor
Mrs Signora
Ms Signora
much molto
  too much troppo
muddy *(ground)* fangoso(a)
mugging lo scippo
mumps gli orecchioni
muscle il muscolo
museum il museo
mushrooms i funghi
music la musica
musical il musical
mussels le cozze
must *(to have to)* dovere
  I must devo
  we must dobbiamo
  I mustn't non devo
  we mustn't non dobbiamo
mustard la senape
my il/la mio(a)
  my passport il mio passaporto
  my room la mia camera

N

nail *(metal)* il chiodo
  (fingernail) l'unghia *(f)*
nailbrush lo spazzolino per le unghie

nail clipper il tagliaunghie
nail file la limetta per le unghie
nail polish/varnish lo smalto per
  le unghie
nail polish remover l'acetone *(m)*
nail scissors le forbicine
name il nome
  my name is... mi chiamo...
  what is your name? come si chiama?
nanny la bambinaia
napkin il tovagliolo
Naples Napoli
nappies i pannolini
narrow stretto(a)
national nazionale
national park il parco nazionale
nationality la nazionalità
natural naturale
nature la natura
nature reserve la riserva naturale
navy blue blu marino
near to vicino(a) a
  is it near? è vicino?
  near the bank vicino alla banca
necessary necessario(a)
neck il collo
necklace la collana
nectarine la nocepesca
to need avere bisogno di...
  I need... ho bisogno di...
  we need... abbiamo bisogno di...
needle l'ago *(m)*
  a needle and thread un ago e filo
negative *(photo)* il negativo
neighbour il/la vicino(a)
nephew il nipote
net la rete
  the Net l'Internet *(m)*
never mai
  I never drink wine non bevo mai
  il vino
new nuovo(a)
news le notizie
  (on television) il telegiornale
newsagent's il giornalaio

newspaper il giornale
newsstand l'edicola (f)
New Year il Capodanno
  happy New Year! buon Anno!
New Year's Eve la notte di San
  Silvestro ; l'ultimo dell'anno (m)
New Zealand la Nuova Zelanda
next prossimo(a)
  next to accanto(a) a
  next week la settimana prossima
  the next bus il prossimo autobus
  the next train il prossimo treno
  the next stop la prossima fermata
nice piacevole
  (person) simpatico(a)
niece la nipote
night la notte
  at night di notte
  last night ieri notte
  per night a notte
  tomorrow night domani sera
  tonight stasera
nightclub il nightclub
nightdress la camicia da notte
night porter il portiere notturno
no no
  no entry vietato l'ingresso
  no smoking vietato fumare
  no thanks no, grazie
  (without) senza
  no sugar senza zucchero
  no ice senza ghiaccio
  no problem non c'è problema
nobody nessuno
noise il rumore
noisy rumoroso(a)
  it's very noisy è molto rumoroso(a)
non-alcoholic analcolico(a)
none nessuno(a)
non-smoker non-fumatore
non-smoking per non-fumatori
north il nord
Northern Ireland l'Irlanda del Nord (f)
nose il naso
not non
  I do not know non lo so

note *(bank note)* la banconota
  (letter) il biglietto
note pad il bloc-notes
nothing niente
  nothing else nient'altro
notice l'avviso (m)
notice board la bacheca
novel il romanzo
November novembre
now adesso
nowhere da nessuna parte
nuclear nucleare
nudist beach la spiaggia nudista
number il numero
number plate *(car)* la targa
nurse l'infermiera/l'infermiere (f/m)
nursery *(children's)* l'asilo (m)
  (for plants) il vivaio
nursery slope la pista per
  principianti
nut *(to eat)* la noce
  (for bolt) il dado

O

oars i remi
oats l'avena (f)
to obtain ottenere
occupation *(work)* il lavoro
ocean l'oceano (m)
October ottobre
octopus il polpo
odd *(strange)* strano(a)
of di
  a bottle of wine una bottiglia di
    vino
  a glass of water un bicchiere
    d'acqua
  made of... fatto di...
off *(machine, etc)* spento(a)
  (milk, food) andato(a) a male
  this meat is off questa carne è
    andata a male
office l'ufficio (m)
often spesso
  how often? ogni quanto?

oil l'olio (m)
oil filter il filtro dell'olio
oil gauge l'indicatore del livello dell'olio (m)
ointment la pomata
OK! va bene!
old vecchio(a)
  how old are you? quanti anni ha?
  I'm ... years old ho ... anni
old age pensioner il/la pensionato(a)
olive oil l'olio d'oliva (m)
olives le olive
on (light, engine) acceso(a)
  (tap) aperto(a)
  on the table sulla tavola
  on time in orario
once una volta
  at once subito
one-way (street) a senso unico
onions le cipolle
only solo(a)
open aperto(a)
to open aprire
opera l'opera (f)
operation l'operazione (f)
operator (telephone) il/la centralinista
opposite di fronte a
  opposite the hotel di fronte all'albergo
  quite the opposite al contrario
optician's l'ottico (m)
or o
orange (colour) arancione
orange (fruit) l'arancia (f)
orange juice il succo d'arancia
orchestra l'orchestra (f)
order l'ordine (f)
  out of order fuori servizio
to order (food, etc) ordinare
oregano l'origano (m)
organic biologico(a)
to organize organizzare
ornament il soprammobile
other l'altro(a)
  the other one l'altro

have you any others? ce ne sono altri?
our il/la nostro(a)
  our car la nostra macchina
  our hotel il nostro albergo
out (light) spento(a)
  he/she's out è fuori
  he's gone out è uscito
outdoor (pool, etc) all'aperto
outside: it's outside è fuori
oven il forno
ovenproof dish la pirofila
over (on top of) sopra
to overbook accettare troppe prenotazioni
to overcharge far pagare troppo
overdone (food) troppo cotto(a)
overdose l'overdose (f)
to overheat surriscaldare
to overload sovraccaricare
to oversleep non svegliarsi in tempo
to overtake sorpassare
to owe dovere
  I owe you... le devo...
  you owe me... mi deve
owner il/la proprietario(a)
oxygen l'ossigeno (m)

P

pace il passo
pacemaker il pacemaker
to pack (suitcase) fare la valigia
package il pacco
package tour il viaggio organizzato
packet il pacchetto
padded envelope la busta imbottita
paddling pool la piscina per bambini
padlock il lucchetto
Padua Padova
page la pagina
paid pagato(a)
  I've paid ho pagato
pain il dolore

painful doloroso(a)
painkiller l'analgesico (m)
to paint (wall, etc) verniciare
   (picture) dipingere
painting (picture) il quadro
pair il paio
palace il palazzo
pale pallido(a)
pan (saucepan) la pentola
   (frying pan) la padella
pancake la crêpe
panties le mutandine
pants le mutande
panty liner il proteggislip
paper la carta
paper hankies i fazzolettini di carta
paper napkins i tovaglioli di carta
paragliding il parapendio
paralysed paralizzato(a)
parcel il pacco
pardon? scusi?
   I beg your pardon mi scusi
parents i genitori
park il parco
to park parcheggiare
parking disk il disco orario
parking meter il parchimetro
parking ticket (fine) la multa per
   sosta vietata
parmesan il parmigiano
   grated parmesan
   il parmigiano grattugiato
part la parte
partner (business) il/la socio(a)
   (boy/girlfriend) il/la compagno(a)
party (celebration) la festa
   (political) il partito
pass (mountain) il valico
   (bus, train) la tessera
passenger il/la passeggero(a)
passport il passaporto
passport control il controllo
   passaporti
password la password ; la parola
   d'ordine

pasta la pasta
pastry la pasta
   (fancy cake) il pasticcino
path il sentiero
patient (in hospital) il/la paziente
pavement il marciapiede
to pay pagare
   I want to pay vorrei pagare
   where do I pay? dove pago?
payment il pagamento
payphone il telefono pubblico
peace la pace
peaches le pesche
peak rate la tariffa nelle ore di punta
peanut allergy l'allergia alle arachidi (f)
pearls le perle
pears le pere
peas i piselli
pedal il pedale
pedalo il pedalò
pedestrian il pedone
pedestrian crossing il passaggio
   pedonale
to pee fare la pipì
to peel (fruit) sbucciare
peg (for clothes) la molletta
   (for tent) il picchetto
pen la penna
pencil la matita
penfriend l'amico(a) di penna
penicillin la penicillina
penis il pene
penknife il temperino
pension la pensione
pensioner il/la pensionato(a)
people la gente
pepper (spice) il pepe
   (vegetable) il peperone
per per
   per day al giorno
   per hour all'ora
   per week alla settimana
   per person a persona
   100 km per hour 100 km all'ora
perfect perfetto(a)

130

performance la rappresentazione
perfume il profumo
perhaps forse
period *(menstrual)* le mestruazioni
perm la permanente
permit il permesso
person la persona
personal organizer l'agenda elettronica *(f)*
personal stereo il walkman®
pet l'animale domestico *(m)*
pet food il cibo per gli animali domestici
pet shop il negozio di animali domestici
petrol la benzina
  4-star petrol la super
  unleaded petrol la benzina senza piombo
petrol cap il tappo del serbatoio
petrol tank il serbatoio della benzina
petrol pump la pompa della benzina
petrol station la stazione di servizio
pharmacy la farmacia
phone il telefono
  by phone per telefono
to phone telefonare
phonebook l'elenco telefonico *(m)*
phonebox la cabina telefonica
phonecard la scheda telefonica
photocopy la fotocopia
  I need a photocopy mi serve una fotocopia
to photocopy fotocopiare
photograph la foto
  to take a photo fare una foto
phrase book il manuale di conversazione
piano il pianoforte
to pick *(fruit, flowers)* cogliere
  (to choose) scegliere
pickpocket il borseggiatore
pickle i sottaceti
picnic il picnic

to have a picnic fare un picnic
picnic hamper il cestino per il picnic
picnic rug il plaid
picnic table il tavolo da picnic
picture *(painting)* il quadro
  (photo) la foto
pie *(sweet)* la torta
  (savoury) il pasticcio
piece il pezzo
pier il pontile
pig il maiale
pill la pillola
  to be on the pill prendere la pillola
pillow il guanciale ; il cuscino
pillowcase la federa
pilot il pilota
pin lo spillo
pink rosa
pipe *(water, etc)* il tubo
  (smoker's) la pipa
pity: *what a pity!* che peccato!
pizza la pizza
place il luogo
place of birth il luogo di nascita
plain *(obvious)* chiaro(a)
  (unflavoured) naturale
plait la treccia
plan il piano
to plan progettare
plane l'aereo *(m)*
plant la pianta
plaster *(sticking)* il cerotto
  (for broken limb) l'ingessatura
plastic *(made of)* di plastica
plastic bag il sacchetto di plastica
plate il piatto
platform *(railway)* il binario
  from which platform? da quale binario?
play *(theatre)* la commedia
to play *(games)* giocare
play area l'area giochi *(f)*
playground il parco giochi
play park il parco giochi
playroom la stanza dei giochi

pleasant piacevole
please per favore
pleased: *pleased to meet you* piacere
plenty l'abbondanza *(f)*
pliers le pinze
plug *(electrical)* la spina
  (for sink) il tappo
to plug in attaccare
plum la prugna ; la susina
plumber l'idraulico *(m)*
plumbing l'impianto idraulico *(m)*
plunger lo sturalavandini
p.m. del pomeriggio
poached *(egg)* in camicia
  (fish) bollito(a)
pocket la tasca
points *(in car)* le puntine
poison il veleno
poisonous velenoso(a)
police la polizia
policeman/woman il poliziotto/
  la donna poliziotto
police station il commissariato ;
  la questura
polish *(for shoes)* il lucido
  (for furniture) la cera
pollen il polline
polluted inquinato(a)
pony il pony
pony trekking le escursioni a cavallo
pool *(swimming)* la piscina
pool attendant il bagnino
poor povero(a)
pope il papa
pop socks i gambaletti
pork la carne di maiale
port *(seaport, wine)* il porto
porter il portiere
  (for luggage) il facchino
portion la porzione
Portugal il Portogallo
Portuguese portoghese
possible possibile
post: *by post* per posta

to post *(letters, etc)* imbucare
postbox la buca delle lettere
postcard la cartolina
postcode il codice postale
poster il poster
postman/woman il/la postino(a)
post office la posta ; l'ufficio postale
  (m)
to postpone rimandare
pot *(cooking)* la pentola
potato la patata
  baked potato la patata al forno
  boiled potatoes le patate lesse
  fried potatoes le patate fritte
  mashed potatoes il purè di patate
  roast potatoes le patate arrosto
potato masher lo schiacciapatate
potato peeler il pelapatate
potato salad l'insalata di patate *(f)*
pothole la buca
pottery la terracotta
pound *(money)* la sterlina
to pour versare
powder: *in powder form* in polvere
powdered milk il latte in polvere
power *(electricity)* l'elettricità
power cut l'interruzione di corrente *(f)*
pram la carrozzina
to pray pregare
to prefer preferire
pregnant incinta
  I'm pregnant sono incinta
to prepare preparare
to prescribe ordinare
prescription la ricetta
present *(gift)* il regalo
preservative il conservante
president il presidente
pressure: *tyre pressure* la pressione
  dei pneumatici
  blood pressure la pressione del
  sangue
pretty carino(a)
price il prezzo
price list il listino prezzi

132

priest il prete
print *(photo)* la foto
printer la stampante
prison il carcere ; la prigione
private privato(a)
prize il premio
probably probabilmente
problem il problema
professor il professore/
la professoressa
programme il programma
prohibited proibito(a)
promise la promessa
to promise promettere
to pronounce pronunciare
how's it pronounced? come si
pronuncia?
protein la proteina
Protestant protestante
to provide fornire
public pubblico(a)
public holiday la festa nazionale
pudding il dessert
to pull tirare
to pull over *(car)* accostare
pullover il pullover ; il maglione
pump la pompa
puncture la gomma a terra
puncture repair kit il kit per riparare
le gomme
puppet il burattino
puppet show lo spettacolo di
burattini
purple viola
purse il borsellino
to push spingere
pushchair il passeggino
to put *(to place)* mettere
to put back rimettere
pyjamas il pigiama

Q

quality la qualità
quantity la quantità

quarantine la quarantena
to quarrel litigare
quarter: *a quarter* un quarto
quay il molo
queen la regina
question la domanda
queue la coda
to queue fare la coda
quick veloce
quickly velocemente
quiet *(place)* tranquillo(a)
a quiet room una stanza tranquilla
quilt la trapunta
quite *(rather)* abbastanza
it's quite expensive è abbastanza
caro(a)
quite the opposite al contrario
quiz show il gioco a quiz

R

rabbit il coniglio
rabies la rabbia
race *(sport)* la gara
race course l'ippodromo *(m)*
racket *(tennis, etc)* la racchetta
radiator *(car)* il radiatore
(heater) il termosifone
radio la radio
railcard la tessera di riduzione
ferroviaria
railway station la stazione dei treni
rain la pioggia
to rain piovere
it's raining piove
raincoat l'impermeabile *(m)*
rake il rastrello
rape lo stupro
raped violentata
I've been raped sono stata violentata
rare *(unique)* raro(a)
(steak) al sangue
rash *(skin)* l'orticaria *(f)*
raspberries i lamponi
rate *(cost)* la tariffa

rate of exchange il cambio
raw crudo(a)
razor il rasoio
razor blades le lamette
to read leggere
ready pronto(a)
  to get ready prepararsi
real vero(a)
to realize rendersi conto di
rearview mirror lo specchietto retrovisore
receipt la ricevuta
receiver (phone) il ricevitore
reception (desk) la reception
receptionist l'addetto(a)
to recharge ricaricare
recharger (mobile) il caricatelefono
  (battery) il caricabatterie
recipe la ricetta
to recognize riconoscere
to recommend raccomandare
to record (programme) registrare
to recover (from illness) rimettersi
to recycle riciclare
red rosso(a)
to reduce ridurre
reduction la riduzione
to refer to (for information) rivolgersi a
refill (pen) il ricambio
  (lighter) la bomboletta di gas
refund il rimborso
to refuse rifiutare
regarding riguardo a
region la regione
register il registro
to register (letter) assicurare
  (car) immatricolare
  (for class) iscriversi
registered letter la lettera
registration form il modulo d'iscrizione
to reimburse rimborsare
relation (family) il/la parente
relationship il rapporto
to remain restare ; rimanere

to remember ricordare
  I don't remember non mi ricordo
remote control il telecomando
removal firm la ditta di traslochi
to remove togliere
rent l'affitto (m)
to rent (house) affittare
  (car) noleggiare
rental (house) l'affitto (m)
  (car) il nolo
repair la riparazione
to repair riparare
to repeat ripetere
to reply rispondere
report il resoconto
to report (crime) denunciare
request la richiesta
to request richiedere
to rescue salvare
reservation la prenotazione
to reserve prenotare
reserved prenotato(a)
resident residente
resort la località di vacanza
rest (repose) il riposo
  (remainder) il resto
to rest riposarsi
restaurant il ristorante
restaurant car il vagone ristorante
retired: I'm retired sono in pensione
to return (go back) ritornare
  (to give back) restituire
return ticket il biglietto di andata e ritorno
to reverse fare marcia indietro
to reverse the charges fare una telefonata al carico del destinatario
reverse charge call la chiamata a carico del destinatario
reverse gear la retromarcia
rheumatism il reumatismo
rib la costola
rice il riso
rich ricco(a)

134

ride *(in a car)* il giro in macchina
to ride a horse andare a cavallo
right *(correct)* giusto(a)
right la destra
  at/to the right a destra
  on the right sulla destra
right of way la precedenza
to ring *(bell)* suonare
  (phone) squillare
  it's ringing suona
ring l'anello *(m)*
ring road la circonvallazione
ripe maturo(a)
river il fiume
road la strada
road map la carta stradale
road sign il cartello stradale
roadworks i lavori stradali
roast arrosto
roll *(bread)* il panino
rollerblades i rollerblades
romantic romantico(a)
roof il tetto
roof-rack il portabagagli
room *(hotel)* la camera
  (space) lo spazio
  double room la camera doppia
  family room la camera per famiglia
  single room la camera singola
room number il numero di camera
room service il servizio in camera
root la radice
rope la corda
rose la rosa
rosé wine il vino rosato
rotten *(food)* marcio(a)
rough *(sea)* mosso(a)
round rotondo(a)
roundabout la rotatoria
row *(in theatre, etc)* la fila
to row *(boat)* remare
rowing boat la barca a remi
rubber *(eraser)* la gomma da cancellare
  (material) la gomma

rubber band l'elastico *(m)*
rubber gloves i guanti di gomma
rubbish la spazzatura
rubella la rosolia
rucksack lo zaino
rug *(carpet)* il tappeto
ruins le rovine
ruler *(to measure)* il righello
to run correre
runner beans i fagiolini
rush hour l'ora di punta *(f)*
rusty arrugginito(a)

S

sad triste
saddle la sella
safe *(for valuables)* la cassaforte
safe *(medicine, etc)* senza pericolo ; sicuro(a)
  is it safe? è senza pericolo?
safety la sicurezza
safetybelt la cintura di sicurezza
safety pin la spilla di sicurezza
to sail andare in barca
sailboard la tavola da windsurf
sailing la vela
sailing boat la barca a vela
saint il/la santo(a)
salad l'insalata *(f)*
  green salad l'insalata verde
  mixed salad l'insalata mista
  potato salad l'insalata di patate
  tomato salad l'insalata di pomodori
salad dressing il condimento per l'insalata
salami il salame
salary lo stipendio
sales *(reductions)* i saldi
salesman/woman il/la commesso(a)
sales rep il/la rappresentante
salt il sale
salt water l'acqua salata *(f)*
salty salato(a)
same stesso(a)

sample il campione
sand la sabbia
sandals i sandali
sandwich il panino ; il tramezzino
  toasted sandwich il toast
sanitary towels gli assorbenti
Sardinia la Sardegna
satellite dish l'antenna parabolica *(f)*
satellite TV la televisione via
  satellite
Saturday il sabato
sauce la salsa
  tomato sauce la salsa di pomodoro
saucepan la pentola
saucer il piattino
sauna la sauna
sausage la salsiccia
to save *(life)* salvare
  (money) risparmiare
savoury *(not sweet)* salato(a)
to say dire
scales *(weighing)* la bilancia
to scan scannerizzare
scan lo scan
scanner lo scanner
scarf la sciarpa
  (headscarf) il foulard
scenery il paesaggio
schedule il programma
  (timetable) l'orario *(m)*
school la scuola
  primary school la scuola elementare
  secondary school il liceo
scissors le forbici
score il punteggio
to score *(goal)* segnare
Scot lo/la scozzese
Scotland la Scozia
Scottish scozzese
scouring pad la paglietta
screen lo schermo
screen wash il liquido lavavetri
screw la vite
screwdriver il cacciavite
  phillips screwdriver il cacciavite
  a stella

scuba diving le immersioni
  subacquee
sculpture la scultura
sea il mare
seacat il catamarano
seafood i frutti di mare
seam *(of dress)* la cucitura
to search cercare
sea sickness il mal di mare
seaside: *at the seaside* al mare
season *(of year)* la stagione
  (holiday) il periodo delle vacanze
  in season di stagione
seasonal stagionale
seasoning il condimento
season ticket l'abbonamento
seat *(chair)* la sedia
  (theatre, plane, etc) il posto
seatbelt la cintura di sicurezza
seaweed le alghe
second *(time)* il secondo
second secondo(a)
second class la seconda classe
second-hand di seconda mano
secretary la segretaria
security guard la guardia giurata
sedative il sedativo
to see vedere
to seize afferrare
self-catering con uso di cucina
self-employed autonomo(a)
self-service il self-service
to sell vendere
  do you sell...? vende...?
sell-by date la data di scadenza
Sellotape® lo Scotch®
to send mandare ; spedire ; inviare
senior citizen l'anziano(a)
sensible pratico(a)
separated separato(a)
separately: *to pay separately* pagare
  separatamente
September settembre
septic tank la fossa settica

serious grave
  (not funny) serio(a)
to serve servire
service (in church) la funzione
  (in restaurant) il servizio
  is service included? il servizio
  è incluso?
service charge il servizio
service station la stazione di servizio
set menu il menù turistico
settee il divano
several alcuni(e)
to sew cucire
sewerage la fognatura
sex (gender) il sesso
  (intercourse) i rapporti sessuali
shade l'ombra (f)
  in the shade all'ombra
to shake (bottle) agitare
shallow basso(a)
shampoo lo shampoo
shampoo and set lo shampoo
  e messa in piega
to share dividere
sharp (razor, blade) affilato(a)
to shave farsi la barba
shaving cream la crema da barba
shawl lo scialle
she ella ; lei
sheep la pecora
sheet (bed) il lenzuolo
shelf la mensola
shell (seashell) la conchiglia
shellfish i frutti di mare
sheltered riparato(a)
to shine brillare
shingles (illness) il fuoco di
  sant'Antonio
ship la nave
shirt la camicia
shock (mental) lo shock
  (electric) la scossa
shock absorber l'ammortizzatore (m)
shoe la scarpa
shoelaces i lacci delle scarpe

shoe polish il lucido per scarpe
shoe repairer il calzolaio
shoe shop il negozio di calzature
shop il negozio
to shop fare la spesa
  to shop online fare la spesa su
  internet
shop assistant il/la commesso(a)
shop window la vetrina
shopping: to go shopping fare
  compere ; fare la spesa
shopping centre il centro
  commerciale
shore la riva
short corto(a)
  (person) basso(a)
short circuit il corto circuito
short cut la scorciatoia
shortage la carenza
shorts i calzoncini corti
short-sighted miope
shoulder la spalla
to shout gridare
show (theatre) lo spettacolo
to show mostrare
shower la doccia
  (rain) il rovescio
  to take a shower fare la doccia
shower cap la cuffia da doccia
shower gel il bagnoschiuma
to shrink restringersi
shrub l'arbusto (m)
shut (closed) chiuso(a)
shutter l'imposta (f)
shuttle service la navetta
Sicily la Sicilia
sick (ill) malato(a)
  (nauseous) nauseato(a)
  I feel sick mi sento male
side il lato
side dish il contorno
sidelight la luce di posizione
sidewalk il marciapiede
sieve il setaccio
sightseeing tour il giro turistico

sign il segno
   (on road) il segnale
to sign firmare
signature la firma
signpost il segnale
silk la seta
silver l'argento (m)
similar to simile a
since (time) da
to sing cantare
single (unmarried) non sposato(a)
   (not double) singolo(a)
   (ticket) di (sola) andata
single bed il letto a una piazza
single room la camera singola
sink il lavandino
sir Signore
sister la sorella
sister-in-law la cognata
to sit sedersi
   please, sit down prego, si accomodi
size (of clothes) la taglia
   (of shoes) il numero
to skate (on ice) pattinare sul
   ghiaccio
skateboard lo skateboard
skates (ice) i pattini da ghiaccio
   (roller) i pattini a rotelle
to ski sciare
skis gli sci
ski boots gli scarponi da sci
ski instructor il/la maestro(a) di sci
ski jump il trampolino
ski lift lo ski-lift
ski pass lo skipass
ski pole/stick la racchetta da sci
ski run la pista
ski suit la tuta da sci
skin la pelle
skirt la gonna
sky il cielo
sledge la slitta
to sleep dormire
to sleep in dormire fino a tardi
sleeper (on train) la cuccetta

sleeping bag il sacco a pelo
sleeping car il vagone letto
sleeping pill il sonnifero
slice (piece of) la fetta
sliced bread il pancarrè
slide (photo) la diapositiva
to slip scivolare
slippers le pantofole
slow lento(a)
to slow down rallentare
slowly lentamente
small piccolo(a)
   smaller (than) più piccolo (di)
smell l'odore (m)
   bad smell il puzzo
   nice smell il profumo
to smell (bad) puzzare
   to smell of avere odore di
smile il sorriso
to smile sorridere
smoke il fumo
to smoke fumare
   I don't smoke non fumo
   can I smoke? posso fumare?
smoke alarm l'allarme antincendio (m)
smoked (food) affumicato(a)
smokers (sign) fumatori
smooth liscio(a)
snack lo spuntino
   to have a snack fare lo spuntino
snake il serpente
   (grass) la biscia
snake bite il morso di vipera
to sneeze starnutire
snorkel il boccaglio
snow la neve
to snow: *it's snowing* nevica
snowboard lo snowboard
snowboarding: *to go snowboarding*
   andare a fare lo snowboard
snow chains le catene da neve
snow tyres i pneumatici da neve
snow plough lo spazzaneve
snowed up isolato(a) a causa della
   neve

soap il sapone
soap powder il detersivo in polvere
sober sobrio(a)
socket (electric) la presa
socks i calzini
soda water l'acqua di selz (f)
sofa il divano
sofa bed il divano letto
soft soffice ; morbido(a)
soft drink la bibita
software il software
soldier il soldato
sole (of foot, shoe) la suola
soluble solubile
some di (del/della)
   (a few) alcuni/alcune
someone qualcuno
something qualcosa
sometimes qualche volta
son il figlio
son-in-law il genero
song la canzone
soon presto
   as soon as possible il più presto
   possibile
sore throat il mal di gola
sorry: I'm sorry! mi scusi!
sort il tipo
   what sort? che tipo?
soup la minestra
sour aspro(a) ; agro(a)
soured cream la panna acida
south il sud
souvenir il souvenir
spa la stazione termale
space lo spazio
   (parking) il posteggio
spade il badile
Spain la Spagna
Spanish spagnolo(a)
spanner la chiave inglese
spare parts i pezzi di ricambio
spare room la stanza degli ospiti
spare tyre la gomma di scorta

spare wheel la ruota di scorta
sparkling frizzante
   sparkling water l'acqua gassata
   sparkling wine il vino frizzante
spark plugs le candele
to speak parlare
   do you speak English? parla inglese?
special speciale
specialist lo/la specialista
speciality la specialità
speech il discorso
speed la velocità
speedboat il motoscafo
speed limit il limite di velocità
   to exceed the speed limit superare
   il limite di velocità
speeding l'eccesso di velocità (m)
speeding ticket la multa per eccesso
   di velocità
speedometer il tachimetro
to spell scrivere
   how's it spelt? come si scrive?
to spend spendere
spice le spezie
spicy piccante
spider il ragno
to spill rovesciare
spinach gli spinaci
spin-dryer la centrifuga
spine la spina dorsale
spirits (alcohol) i liquori
splinter la scheggia
spoke (of wheel) il raggio
sponge la spugna
spoon il cucchiaio
sport lo sport
sports centre il centro sportivo
sports shop il negozio di articoli
   sportivi
spot (stain) la macchia
   (place) il posto
sprain la slogatura
spring (season) la primavera
   (metal) la molla
square (in town) la piazza

squash *(game)* lo squash
to squeeze premere ; stringere
squid il calamaro
stadium lo stadio
staff il personale
stage *(theatre)* il palcoscenico
stain la macchia
stained glass il vetro colorato
stain remover lo smacchiatore
stairs le scale
stale *(bread)* raffermo(a)
stalls *(in theatre)* la platea
stamp il francobollo
to stand stare in piedi
star la stella
starfish la stella marina
to start cominciare
starter *(food)* l'antipasto *(m)*
  (in car) il motorino d'avviamento
station la stazione
stationer's la cartoleria
statue la statua
stay il soggiorno
  enjoy your stay! buona permanenza!
to stay *(remain)* rimanere
  I'm staying at the Grand Hotel
  sono al Grand Hotel
steak la bistecca
to steal rubare
steamed al vapore
to steam cuocere a vapore
steel l'acciaio *(m)*
steep: *is it steep?* è in salita?
steeple il campanile
steering wheel il volante
step *(stair)* il gradino
stepdaughter la figliastra
stepfather il patrigno
stepmother la matrigna
stepson il figliastro
stereo lo stereo
sterling la sterlina
steward lo steward
stewardess la hostess

to stick *(with glue)* incollare
  (door) incepparsi
sticking plaster il cerotto
still *(motionless)* fermo(a)
  (water) naturale
  (yet) ancora
sting la puntura
to sting pungere
stitches i punti
stock cubes i dadi
stockings le calze
stolen rubato(a)
stomach lo stomaco ; la pancia
stomachache il mal di pancia
stone la pietra
to stop *(come to a halt)* fermarsi
  (stop doing something) smettere
stop sign lo stop
store *(shop)* il negozio
storey il piano
storm la tempesta ; il temporale
story il racconto
straightaway subito
straight on diritto
strange strano(a)
straw *(drinking)* la cannuccia
strawberries le fragole
stream il ruscello
street la strada
street map la piantina
strength *(of person)* la forza
  (of wine) la gradazione alcolica
stress lo stress
strike *(of workers)* lo sciopero
string lo spago
striped a strisce
stroke *(medical)* l'ictus *(m)*
  to have a stroke avere un ictus
strong forte
  strong coffee il caffè ristretto
  strong tea il tè forte
stuck bloccato(a)
student lo studente/la studentessa
student discount lo sconto per
  studenti

stuffed farcito(a)
stung punto(a)
stupid stupido(a)
subscription l'abbonamento (m)
subtitles i sottotitoli
subway (train) la metropolitana
  (passage) il sottopassaggio
suddenly all'improvviso
suede la pelle scamosciata
sugar lo zucchero
sugar-free senza zucchero
to suggest proporre
suit (man's) l'abito (m)
  (woman's) il tailleur
suitcase la valigia
sum (of money) la somma
summer l'estate (f)
summer holidays le vacanze estive
summit il vertice
sun il sole
to sunbathe prendere il sole
sunblock la protezione solare totale
sunburn la scottatura solare
Sunday la domenica
sunglasses gli occhiali da sole
sunny: it's sunny c'è il sole
sunrise l'alba (f)
sunroof (car) il tettuccio apribile
sunscreen la crema solare protettiva
sunset il tramonto
sunshade l'ombrellone (m)
sunstroke l'insolazione (f)
suntan l'abbronzatura (f)
suntan lotion la crema abbronzante
supermarket il supermercato
supper (dinner) la cena
supplement il supplemento
to supply fornire
sure sicuro(a) ; certo(a)
  I'm sure sono sicuro(a)
to surf fare il surf
  to surf the net navigare in internet
surfboard la tavola da surf
surgery (surgical treatment) la chirurgia

surname il cognome
  my surname is... di cognome
  mi chiamo...
surprise la sorpresa
suspension (in car) la sospensione
to survive sopravvivere
to swallow inghiottire
to swear (bad language) dire le
  parolacce
to sweat sudare
sweater il maglione
sweatshirt la felpa
sweet (not savoury) dolce
sweetener il dolcificante
sweets le caramelle
to swell gonfiare
to swim nuotare
swimming pool la piscina
swimsuit il costume da bagno
swing l'altalena (f)
Swiss svizzero(a)
switch l'interruttore (m)
to switch off spegnere
to switch on accendere
Switzerland la Svizzera
swollen gonfio(a)
synagogue la sinagoga
syringe la siringa

T

table la tavola
tablecloth la tovaglia
tablet (pill) la pastiglia
table tennis il ping pong
table wine il vino da tavola
tailor il sarto
to take (carry) portare
  (to grab, seize) prendere
  how long does it take? quanto
  tempo ci vuole?
takeaway (food) da asporto
to take off decollare
to take out (of bag) tirar fuori
talc il borotalco

to talk parlare
tall alto(a)
tampons gli assorbenti interni
tangerine il mandarino
tank la cisterna
  (car) il serbatoio
  (fish) l'acquario *(m)*
tap il rubinetto
tap water l'acqua del rubinetto *(f)*
tape il nastro
tape measure il metro a nastro
tape recorder il registratore
target lo scopo
tart la crostata
taste il sapore
to taste assaggiare ; provare
  can I taste some? ne posso
  assaggiare un pò?
tax la tassa ; l'imposta *(f)*
taxi il taxi
taxi driver il/la tassista
taxi rank il posteggio dei taxi
tea il tè
  herbal tea la tisana
  fruit tea il tè alla frutta
  lemon tea il tè al limone
  tea with milk il tè al latte
tea bag la bustina di tè
tea pot la teiera
to teach insegnare
teacher l'insegnante *(m/f)*
team la squadra
tear *(in material)* lo strappo
teaspoon il cucchiaino
teat *(on bottle)* la tettarella
tea towel lo strofinaccio per i piatti
teenager il/la teenager
teeth i denti
telegram il telegramma
telephone il telefono
to telephone telefonare
telephone box la cabina telefonica
telephone call la telefonata
telephone card la scheda telefonica
telephone directory l'elenco
  telefonico *(m)*

telephone number il numero
  di telefono
television la televisione
to tell dire
temperature la temperatura
  to have a temperature avere
  la febbre
temporary provvisorio(a)
tenant l'inquilino(a)
tendon il tendine
tennis il tennis
tennis ball la pallina da tennis
tennis court il campo da tennis
tennis racket la racchetta da tennis
tent la tenda
tent peg il picchetto
terminal *(airport)* il terminal
terrace la terrazza
terracotta la terracotta
to test *(try out)* provare
testicles i testicoli
tetanus jab l'antitetanica *(f)*
than di
to thank ringraziare
thank you grazie
  thanks very much molte grazie
that quel/quella/quello
  that one quello là
the *(sing)* il/lo/la
  (plural) i/gli/le
theatre il teatro
theft il furto
their il/la loro
them loro ; li ; le
there *(over there)* lì
there is/there are c'è/ci sono
thermometer il termometro
these questi/queste
  these ones questi qui
they loro ; essi/esse
thick spesso(a)
thief il/la ladro(a)
thigh la coscia
thin sottile
  (person) magro(a)

142

thing la cosa
  my things la mia roba
to think pensare
thirsty: *to be thirsty* avere sete
this questo/questa
  this one questo(a)
those quei/quelle/quegli
  those ones quelli(e)
thread il filo
throat la gola
throat lozenges le pastiglie per
  la gola
through attraverso
to throw away buttare via
thumb il pollice
thunder il tuono
thunderstorm il temporale
Thursday il giovedì
thyme il timo
ticket *(bus, train, etc)* il biglietto
  (entry fee) il biglietto d'ingresso
  a single ticket un biglietto di (sola)
  andata
  a return ticket un biglietto di
  andata e ritorno
  tourist ticket il biglietto turistico
  book of tickets il blocchetto di
  biglietti
ticket inspector il controllore
ticket office la biglietteria
tidy ordinato(a)
to tidy up fare ordine
tie la cravatta
tight stretto(a)
tights i collant ; la calzamaglia
tile *(floor)* la piastrella
till *(cash desk)* la cassa
till *(until)* fino a
  till 2 o'clock fino alle due
time il tempo
  (of day) l'ora *(f)*
  this time questa volta
  what time is it? che ore sono?
  do you have the time? ha l'ora?
timetable l'orario *(m)*
tin *(can)* la scatola ; la lattina

tinfoil la carta stagnola
tin-opener l'apriscatole *(m)*
tip *(to waiter, etc)* la mancia
to tip *(waiter)* dare la mancia
tired stanco(a)
tissues i fazzoletti di carta
to a
  to London a Londra
  to the airport all'aeroporto
toadstool il fungo velenoso
toast *(to eat)* il pane tostato
  (raising glass) il brindisi
tobacco il tabacco
tobacconist's il tabaccaio
today oggi
toe il dito del piede
together insieme
toilet la toilette
  toilet for disabled la toilette per
  i disabili
toilet brush lo spazzolino del
  gabinetto
toilet paper la carta igienica
toiletries gli articoli per l'igiene
token *(phone, etc)* il gettone
toll *(motorway)* il pedaggio
tomato il pomodoro
  peeled tomatoes i pelati
  a tin of tomatoes la scatola di pelati
tomato juice il succo di pomodoro
tomato purée il concentrato di
  pomodoro
tomato sauce la salsa di pomodoro
tomorrow domani
  tomorrow morning domani mattina
  tomorrow afternoon domani
  pomeriggio
  tomorrow evening domani sera
tongue la lingua
tonic water l'acqua tonica *(f)*
tonight stasera
tonsilitis la tonsillite
too *(also)* anche
  too big troppo grande
  too small troppo piccolo(a)

too hot troppo caldo(a)
too noisy troppo rumoroso(a)
tool l'attrezzo *(m)*
toolkit gli attrezzi
tooth il dente
toothache il mal di denti
toothbrush lo spazzolino da denti
toothpaste il dentifricio
toothpick lo stuzzicadenti
top: *the top floor* l'ultimo piano *(m)*
top la cima
  (clothing) il top
  on top of sopra di
topless topless
torch *(flashlight)* la pila
torn strappato(a)
total il totale
to touch toccare
tough *(meat)* duro(a)
tour il giro
  guided tour la visita guidata
tour guide la guida turistica
tour operator l'operatore turistico *(m)*
tourist il/la turista
tourist information le informazioni turistiche
tourist office l'ufficio turistico *(m)*
tourist route l'itinerario turistico *(m)*
tourist ticket il biglietto turistico
to tow rimorchiare
towbar la barra di rimorchio
tow rope il cavo da rimorchio
towel l'asciugamano *(m)*
tower la torre
town la città
town centre il centro città
town hall il municipio
town plan la piantina
toxic tossico(a)
toy il giocattolo
toy shop il negozio di giocattoli
tracksuit la tuta sportiva
traditional tradizionale
traffic il traffico

traffic jam l'ingorgo *(m)*
traffic lights il semaforo
traffic warden il vigile
trailer il rimorchio
train il treno
  the next train il prossimo treno
  the first train il primo treno
  the last train l'ultimo treno
trainers le scarpe da ginnastica
tram il tram
tranquillizer il tranquillante
to transfer trasferire
to translate tradurre
translation la traduzione
to travel viaggiare
travel agent's l'agenzia di viaggi *(f)*
travel documents i documenti di viaggio
travel guide la guida
travel insurance l'assicurazione di viaggio *(f)*
travel sickness *(sea)* il mal di mare
  (air) il mal d'aria
  (car) il mal d'auto
traveller's cheques i traveller's (cheque)
tray il vassoio
tree l'albero *(m)*
trip la gita ; il viaggio
trolley il carrello
trouble i problemi
trousers i pantaloni
truck il camion
true vero(a)
trunk *(luggage)* il baule
trunks *(swimming)* i calzoncini da bagno
to try provare
to try on *(clothes, etc)* provare
t-shirt la maglietta
Tuesday il martedì
tumble dryer l'asciugatrice *(f)*
tunnel la galleria
Turin Torino
to turn *(handle, wheel)* girare

to turn around girarsi

to turn off *(light, etc)* spegnere *(tap)* chiudere

to turn on *(light, etc)* accendere *(tap)* aprire

turquoise *(colour)* turchese

tweezers le pinzette

twice due volte ; il doppio

twin beds i letti gemelli

twins i gemelli

to type battere a macchina

typical tipico(a)

tyre la gomma ; il pneumatico

tyre pressure la pressione delle gomme

U

ugly brutto(a)

ulcer *(stomach)* l'ulcera *(f)* *(mouth)* l'afta *(f)*

umbrella l'ombrello *(m)* *(sunshade)* l'ombrellone *(m)*

uncle lo zio

uncomfortable scomodo(a)

unconscious svenuto(a)

under sotto

undercooked poco cotto(a)

underground *(metro)* la metropolitana

underpants le mutande

underpass il sottopassaggio

to understand capire
I don't understand non capisco
do you understand? capisce?

underwear la biancheria intima

to undress spogliarsi

unemployed disoccupato(a)

to unfasten slacciare

United Kingdom il Regno Unito

United States gli Stati Uniti

university l'università *(f)*

unleaded petrol la benzina senza piombo ; la benzina verde

unlikely improbabile

to unlock aprire

to unpack disfare la valigia

unpleasant sgradevole

to unplug staccare

to unscrew svitare

until fino a

unusual raro(a)

up: *to get up* alzarsi

upside down sottosopra

upstairs di sopra

urgent urgente

urine l'urina *(f)*

us ci ; noi

to use usare

useful utile

usual solito(a)

usually di solito

U-turn l'inversione a U *(f)*

V

vacancy *(in hotel)* la camera libera

vacant libero(a)

vacation la vacanza

vaccination la vaccinazione

vacuum cleaner l'aspirapolvere *(m)*

vagina la vagina

valid valido(a)

valley la valle

valuable di valore

valuables gli oggetti di valori

value il valore

valve la valvola

van il furgone

vase il vaso

VAT l'IVA *(f)*

vegan vegetaliano(a)
I'm vegan sono vegetaliano(a)

vegetables le verdure

vegetarian vegetariano(a)
I'm vegetarian sono vegetariano(a)

vehicle il veicolo

vein la vena

Velcro® il velcro®

vending machine il distributore automatico
venereal disease la malattia venerea
Venice Venezia
ventilator il ventilatore
very molto
vest la canottiera
vet il/la veterinario(a)
via passando per
to video *(from TV)* registrare su videocassetta
video il video
video camera la videocamera
video cassette/tape la videocassetta
video game il videogioco
video recorder il videoregistratore
view la vista
villa la villa
village il paese
vinegar l'aceto *(m)*
vineyard la vigna
viper la vipera
virus il virus
visa il visto
visit la visita
to visit visitare
visiting hours l'orario delle visite *(m)*
visitor il visitatore/la visitatrice
vitamin la vitamina
voice la voce
volcano il vulcano
volleyball la pallavolo
voltage il voltaggio
to vomit vomitare
voucher il buono

W

wage il salario ; la paga
waist la vita
waistcoat il gilè
to wait (for) aspettare
waiter/waitress il cameriere/ la cameriera

waiting room la sala d'aspetto
to wake up
   (someone) svegliare
   (oneself) svegliarsi
Wales il Galles
walk la passeggiata
to walk andare a piedi
walking boots gli scarponcini
walking stick il bastone
Walkman® il walkman®
wall il muro ; la parete
wallet il portafoglio
to want volere
   I want... voglio...
   we want... vogliamo...
war la guerra
ward *(hospital)* il reparto
wardrobe l'armadio *(m)*
warm caldo(a)
   it's warm fa caldo
to warm up *(milk, etc)* riscaldare
warning triangle il triangolo d'emergenza
to wash lavare
   (to wash oneself) lavarsi
wash and blow dry lo shampoo e messa in piega
washbasin il lavandino
washing machine la lavatrice
washing powder il detersivo in polvere
washing-up bowl la bacinella
washing-up liquid il detersivo per i piatti
wasp la vespa
wasp sting la puntura di vespa
waste bin il bidone della spazzatura
watch l'orologio *(m)*
to watch guardare
watchstrap il cinturino dell'orologio
water l'acqua *(f)*
   bottled water l'acqua in bottiglia *(f)*
   drinking water l'acqua potabile
   mineral water l'acqua minerale
   sparkling water l'acqua gassata

still water l'acqua naturale
water heater lo scaldabagno
watermelon l'anguria *(f)*
waterproof impermeabile
to water-ski fare lo sci nautico
watersports gli sport acquatici
waterwings i braccioli salvagente
waves *(on sea)* le onde
waxing *(hair removal)* la ceretta
way in l'entrata *(f)* ; l'ingresso *(m)*
way out l'uscita *(f)*
we noi
weak *(person)* debole
  (tea, coffee, etc) leggero(a)
to wear portare
weather il tempo
weather forecast le previsioni
  del tempo
website il sito web
wedding il matrimonio
wedding anniversary l'anniversario
  di matrimonio *(m)*
wedding present il regalo di
  matrimonio
wedding ring la fede
Wednesday mercoledì
week la settimana
  last week la settimana scorsa
  next week la prossima settimana
  per week alla settimana
  this week questa settimana
  during the week durante la
  settimana
weekday il giorno feriale
weekend il fine settimana
  next weekend il prossimo fine
  settimana
  this weekend questo fine settimana
weekly settimanale
  weekly pass l'abbonamento
  settimanale *(m)*
to weigh pesare
weight il peso
welcome benvenuto
well bene

well *(for water)* il pozzo
well-done *(steak)* ben cotto(a)
wellington boots gli stivali di
  gomma
Welsh gallese
west ovest
wet bagnato(a)
wetsuit la muta
what cosa
  what is it? cos'è?
wheat il grano
wheel la ruota
wheelchair la sedia a rotelle
wheel clamp il ceppo bloccaruote
when quando
where dove
which qual/quale
while mentre
  in a while fra poco
whipped cream la panna montata
whisky l'whisky *(m)*
white bianco(a)
who chi
whole tutto
wholemeal bread il pane integrale
whose: *whose is it?* di chi è?
why perché
wide largo(a) ; ampio(a)
widow la vedova
widower il vedovo
width la larghezza
wife la moglie
wig la parrucca
to win vincere
wind il vento
windbreak *(camping)* il frangivento
windmill il mulino a vento
window la finestra
  (shop) la vetrina
  (car) il finestrino
windscreen il parabrezza
windscreen wiper il tergicristallo
to windsurf fare il windsurf
windy: *it's windy* c'è vento

wine il vino
  red wine il vino rosso
  white wine il vino bianco
  dry wine il vino secco
  sweet wine il vino dolce
  rosé wine il vino rosato
  sparkling wine il vino frizzante
  house wine il vino della casa
wine list la lista dei vini
wing *(of bird)* l'ala *(f)*
  (of car) la fiancata
wing mirror lo specchietto laterale
winter l'inverno *(m)*
wire il filo
with con
  with ice con ghiaccio
  with milk con latte
  with sugar con zucchero
without senza
  without ice senza ghiaccio
  without milk senza latte
  without sugar senza zucchero
witness il/la testimone
woman la donna
wonderful meraviglioso(a)
wood *(material)* il legno
  (forest) il bosco
wooden di legno
wool la lana
word la parola
work il lavoro
to work *(person)* lavorare
  (machine, car, etc) funzionare
  it doesn't work non funziona
work permit il premesso di lavoro
world il mondo
worried preoccupato(a)
worse peggio
worth *(value)* il valore
  it's worth £5 vale cinque sterline
to wrap up *(parcel)* incartare
wrapping paper la carta da regalo
wrinkles le rughe
wrist il polso
to write scrivere
  please write it down lo scriva per
  favore

writing paper la carta da lettere
wrong sbagliato(a)
  what's wrong? cosa c'è?
wrought iron il ferro battuto

X

x-ray la radiografia
to x-ray radiografare

Y

yacht lo yacht
year l'anno *(m)*
  this year quest'anno
  next year l'anno prossimo
  last year l'anno scorso
yearly *(every year)* annualmente
yellow giallo(a)
Yellow Pages le pagine gialle®
yes sì
yesterday ieri
yet: *not yet* non ancora
yoghurt lo yogurt
  plain yoghurt lo yogurt naturale
yolk il tuorlo
you tu ; voi ; lei
young giovane
your il/la suo(a) ; il/la tuo(a) ; il/la
  vostro(a)

Z

zebra crossing le strisce pedonali
zero lo zero
zip la cerniera
zone la zona
zoo lo zoo
zoom lens lo zoom

A

a at ; in
abbaglianti *mpl* full-beam headlights
abbiamo... we have...
  non abbiamo... we don't have...
abbigliamento *m* clothes
abbonamento *m* subscription ; season ticket
abbronzatura *f* suntan
abito *m* dress ; man's suit
aborto *m* abortion
  aborto spontaneo miscarriage
abuso *m* misuse
a.C. B.C.
accamparsi to camp
accanto (a) beside ; next (to)
acceleratore *m* accelerator
accendere to turn on ; to light
  accendere i fari switch on your headlights
accendino *m* cigarette lighter
accensione *f* ignition
accento *m* accent *(pronunciation)*
acceso(a) on *(light, engine)*
accesso *m* access
  divieto di accesso no access
accettazione *f* reception
  accettazione bagagli check-in
accomodarsi to make oneself comfortable
  si accomodi do take a seat
accompagnare to accompany
accordo *m* agreement
aceto *m* vinegar
acetone *m* nail polish remover
ACI *m* Automobile Association
acqua *f* water
  acqua calda hot water
  acqua corrente running water
  acqua distillata distilled water
  acqua gassata sparkling water
  acqua minerale mineral water
  acqua naturale still water
  acqua potabile drinking water
acquisto *m* purchase

addetto(a) person in charge
adesso now
adulto(a) adult
aereo *m* plane ; aircraft
aeroplano *m* airplane
aeroporto *m* airport
affari *mpl* business
  per affari on business
affittare to rent ; to let
  affittasi for rent
affitto *m* lease ; rent
affogare to drown
agenda *f* diary
agenzia *f* agency
  agenzia di viaggi travel agent
  agenzia immobiliare estate agent
aggredire to attack
aglio *m* garlic
ago *m* needle
  ago ipodermico hypodermic needle
agosto *m* August
AIDS *m* AIDS
aiutare to help
aiuto! help!
alba *f* dawn
albergo *m* hotel
albero *m* tree ; mast
albicocca *f* apricot
alcolici *mpl* alcoholic drinks
alcolico(a) alcoholic
alcool *m* alcohol
alcuni(e) some ; a few
alcuno(a) any ; some
alimentari *mpl* groceries
allacciare to fasten *(seatbelt, etc)*
allarme *m* alarm
  allarme antincendio fire alarm
allergia *f* allergy
allergico(a) a allergic to
alloggio *m* accommodation
alluvione *f* flood
Alpi *fpl* Alps
alpinismo *m* climbing
alt stop

altezza f height
alto(a) high ; tall
  alta stagione high season
  alta marea high tide
altro(a) other
  altri passaporti other passports
alzarsi to get up ; to stand up
amabile sweet *(wine)*
amare to love *(person)*
amarena f sour black cherry
amaro(a) bitter *(taste)*
ambasciata f embassy
ambiente m environment
ambulanza f ambulance
ambulatorio m surgery ; out-patients
America f America
americano(a) American
amico(a) m/f friend
ammalato(a) ill
amministratore delegato m
  managing director
ammontare m total amount
ammortizzatore m shock absorber
amo m bait
amore m love
analisi del sangue f blood test
analcolico m soft drink
analcolico(a) non-alcoholic
analgesico m painkiller
ananas m pineapple
anatra f duck
anca f hip
anche too ; also ; even
ancora still ; yet ; again
  ancora un po'? a little more?
  non ancora not yet
ancora f anchor
andare to go
  andare a cavallo to ride a horse
  andare a piedi to go on foot
  andare bene to fit *(clothes)*
  andare in macchina to go by car
andata: *andata e ritorno* return *(ticket)*
  di (sola) andata single *(ticket)*
andiamo! let's go!

  andiamo a... we're going to...
anestetico m anaesthetic
angina pectoris f angina
anguria f watermelon
anice m aniseed
animale m animal
  animale domestico pet
annata f vintage ; year
  vino d'annata vintage wine
anniversario m anniversary
anno m year
  buon anno! happy New Year!
annuale annual
annullamento m cancellation
annullare to cancel
annuncio m announcement ; advert
antibiotico m antibiotic
anticipo m advance *(loan)*
  in anticipo in advance ; early
anticoncezionale m contraceptive
antifurto m burglar alarm
antigelo m antifreeze ; de-icer
antipasto m starter ; hors d'œuvre
antisettico m antiseptic
antistaminico m antihistamine
anziano(a) m/f senior citizen
ape f bee
aperitivo m apéritif
aperto(a) open
  all'aperto open-air
appartamento m flat ; apartment
appendicite f appendicitis
appuntamento m appointment ; date
apribottiglie m bottle opener
aprile m April
aprire to open ; to turn on *(tap)*
apriscatole m tin-opener
arachide f peanut
arancia f orange
aranciata f orangeade
arancione orange *(colour)*
area f area
  area di servizio service area
argento m silver

aria condizionata *f* air-conditioning
armadio *m* cupboard ; wardrobe
arrabbiato(a) angry
arredato(a) furnished
arrestare to arrest
arrivare to arrive
arrivederci goodbye
arrivo *m* arrival
  arrivi nazionali domestic arrivals
  arrivi internazionali international
  arrivals
arrosto *m* roast
arte *f* art ; craft
articolo *m* article
  articoli da dichiarare goods to
  declare
  articoli da regalo gifts
artigiano(a) *m/f* craftsperson
artista *m/f* artist
artrite *f* arthritis
ascensore *m* lift ; elevator
ascesso *m* abscess
asciugamano *m* towel
asciugare to dry
asciugatrice *f* tumble dryer
ascoltare to listen (to)
asma *f* asthma
asparagi *m* asparagus
aspettare to wait (for) ; to expect
aspirapolvere *m* vacuum cleaner
aspirina *f* aspirin
assaggiare to taste
asse *m* axle *(car)*
  asse da stiro ironing board
assegno *m* cheque
assicurato(a) insured
assicurazione *f* insurance
assistente *m/f* assistant
assistenza *f* assistance ; aid
associazione *f* association
assorbenti *mpl* sanitary towels
  assorbenti interni tampons
ATM public transport service of
  Milan

attaccare to attach ; to attack ;
  to fasten
attacco *m* fit *(seizure)*
  attacco cardiaco heart attack
attendere to wait for
attento(a) careful
attenzione *f* caution
  fare attenzione to be careful
atterraggio *m* landing *(of plane)*
atterrare to land *(plane)*
attestare to declare
attore *m* actor
attracco *m* mooring ; berth
attraente attractive
attraversare to cross
attraverso through
attrazione *f* attraction
attrezzatura *f* equipment
attrezzo *m* tool
attrice *f* actress
auguri! best wishes!
aumentare to increase
Australia *f* Australia
australiano(a) Australian
austriaco(a) Austrian
autentico(a) genuine
autista *m/f* driver
auto *f* car
autobus *m* bus
autofficina *f* garage *(for repairs)*
autoforniture *fpl* car parts and
  accessories
autonoleggio *m* car hire
autore *m* author
autorimessa *f* garage
autorizzazione *f* authorization
autostop *m* hitchhiking
autostrada *f* motorway
autunno *m* autumn
avanti in front ; forward(s)
  avanti! come in!
avere to have
  avere bisogno di to need
  avere fame to be hungry
  avere sete to be thirsty

avvertire to warn
avvisare to inform ; to warn
avviso *m* notice ; advertisement
azienda *f* business ; firm
  azienda di soggiorno local tourist
  board
azzardo *m* risk ; hazard
azzurro(a) light blue

B

babbo *m* daddy
  Babbo Natale Father Christmas
baciare to kiss
bacinella *f* washing-up bowl
bacio *m* kiss
  baci! love and kisses *(in letter)*
baffi *mpl* moustache
bagagli *mpl* luggage
bagagliaio *m* boot *(of car)*
bagaglio *m* luggage
  bagaglio a mano hand luggage
bagnarsi to bathe ; to get wet
bagnino *m* lifeguard
bagno *m* bath ; bathroom
balcone *m* balcony
ballare to dance
balletto *m* ballet
ballo *m* dance
balneazione *f* bathing
  divieto di balneazione no swimming
balsamo *m* hair conditioner
bambino(a) *m/f* child ; baby
bambini *mpl* children
  per bambini for children
bambola *f* doll
banana *f* banana
banca *f* bank
bancarella *f* stall ; stand
banchina *f* platform ; quay
banco *m* counter ; desk
  banco informazioni enquiry desk
Bancomat® *m* cash dispenser
banconota *f* banknote
bandiera *f* flag

bar *m* bar ; café
barattolo *m* tin ; jar
barba *f* beard
barbiere *m* barber
barca *f* boat
barista *m/f* barman/barmaid
basso(a) low ; short
  bassa marea low tide
basta that's enough
battello *m* boat
batteria *f* battery *(car)*
  batteria scarica flat battery
  batteria ricaricabile rechargeable
baule *m* trunk *(luggage)*
bavaglino *m* bib
bello(a) beautiful ; fine ; lovely
benda *f* bandage
bene well ; all right ; OK
benvenuto welcome
benzina *f* petrol
  fare benzina to get petrol
bere to drink
bevanda *f* drink
biancheria *f* linen *(for beds, table)*
  biancheria intima underwear
bianco(a) white ; blank
  lasciate in bianco leave blank
biberon *m* baby's bottle
bibita *f* soft drink
  bibite soft drinks
bicchiere *m* glass *(for drinking)*
bici *f* bike *(pushbike)*
bicicletta *f* bicycle
bidet *m* bidet
bidone *m* bin ; dustbin ; can
biglietteria *f* ticket office
biglietto *m* ticket ; note ; card
  biglietto d'auguri greetings card
  biglietto da visita business card
bin. abbreviation of binario
binario *m* platform
biologico(a) organic
biondo(a) blond *(person)*
biro *f* biro
birra *f* beer

birra alla spina draught beer
birra bionda lager
birra chiara lager
birreria f bar ; pub
biscotto m biscuit
bisogno m need
avere bisogno di to need
bistecca f steak
bloccare to block
bloccare un assegno to stop
a cheque
blocchetto di biglietti m book
of tickets
blocco m block ; notepad
blu blue
blue jeans mpl jeans
boa f buoy
bocca f mouth
boccaglio m snorkel
bocce fpl bowls (game)
bolletta f bill
bollire to boil
bollitore m kettle
bomba f bomb
bombola del gas f gas cylinder
bombolone m doughnut
borotalco m talc
borsa f bag ; handbag ; briefcase
borsa termica cool-box (for picnic)
borseggiatore m pickpocket
borsellino m purse ; wallet
borsetta di plastica f plastic bag
bosco m wood ; forest
bottega f shop
botteghino m box office
bottiglia f bottle
bottone m button
boxer mpl boxer shorts
braccialetto m bracelet
braccio m arm
braccioli mpl armbands (swimming)
braciola f steak ; chop
brindisi m toast (raising glass)
brioche f croissant
britannico(a) f British

bronchite f bronchitis
bruciare to burn
masterizzare to burn (CD)
bruciore di stomaco m heartburn
brutto(a) bad (weather, news) ; ugly
buca delle lettere f postbox
bucato m washing ; laundry
bucato in lavatrice machine wash
bucato a mano hand washing
buco m hole ; leak
buono(a) good
buon appetito! enjoy your meal!
buon compleanno! happy birthday!
buon giorno good morning/
afternoon
buona notte good night
buona sera good afternoon/evening
a buon mercato cheap
buono m voucher ; coupon ; token
burattino m puppet
burrasca f storm
burro m butter
burro di cacao m lip salve
bussare to knock (on door)
busta f envelope
bustina di tè f tea bag
buttare via to throw away

C

cabina f beach hut ; cabin
cabina telefonica phonebox
cacciavite m screwdriver
cadere to fall
caffè m coffee (espresso)
caffè corretto espresso with spirit
such as grappa
caffè macchiato espresso with a
little warm milk
caffè solubile instant coffee
caffellatte milky coffee
caffettiera f espresso-maker
calamita f magnet
calciatore m football player
calcio m football ; kick
calcolatrice f calculator

caldo(a) hot
calendario m calendar
calle f street *(in Venice dialect)*
callo m corn *(on foot)*
calmante m sedative
calmo(a) calm
calpestare to tread on
calvo(a) bald
calza f stocking ; sock
calzamaglia f tights
calzature fpl shoeshop
calze fpl stockings
calzini mpl socks
calzolaio m shoe mender
calzoleria f shoe mender's
calzoncini corti mpl shorts
  calzoncini da bagno swimming
  trunks
cambiamento m change
cambiare to change
  cambiare autobus/treno to change
  bus/train
  cambiare soldi to change money
  cambiarsi to change one's clothes
cambio m exchange ; gear
camera f room *(in house, hotel)*
  camera da letto bedroom
  camera doppia double room
  camera libera vacancy *(in hotel)*
  camera per famiglia family room
  camera singola single room
  camere vacancies
cameriera f chambermaid
cameriere m waiter
camiceria f shirt shop
camicetta f blouse
camicia f shirt
  camicia da notte nightdress
camion m lorry
camminare to walk
camoscio m chamois
campagna f countryside ; campaign
campanello m bell
campeggiare to camp
campeggio m camping ; campsite

campeggio libero free campsite
camping gas m gas da campeggio
campione m sample ; champion
campo m field ; court
  campo da tennis tennis court
  campo di calcio football pitch
  campo di golf golf course
  campo sportivo sports ground
camposanto m cemetery
Canada m Canada
canadese Canadian
canale m canal ; channel
cancellare to erase ; to cancel
cancellazione f cancellation
cancro m cancer
candeggina f bleach
candela f candle ; spark plug
candida f thrush *(candida)*
cane m dog
canile m kennel
canna da pesca f fishing rod
cannuccia f straw *(for drinking)*
canoa f canoe
canottaggio m rowing
canottiera f vest
canotto m dinghy *(rubber)*
cantante m/f singer
cantare to sing
cantiere m building site
cantina f cellar ; wine cellar
canzone f song
capelli mpl hair
capire to understand
  capisce? do you understand?
  non capisco I don't understand
capitale f capital *(city)*
capitolo m chapter
capo m head ; leader ; boss
Capodanno m New Year's day
capogruppo m group leader
capolavoro m masterpiece
capolinea m terminus
capoluogo m county town
capotreno m guard *(on train)*

cappella f chapel
cappello m hat
cappotto m overcoat
cappuccino m cappuccino
capra f goat
carabiniere m policeman
caraffa f carafe
caramelle fpl sweets
carbone m coal ; charcoal
carburante m fuel
carburatore m carburettor
carcere m prison
caricare to charge (battery)
carico m load ; shipment ; cargo
carino(a) pretty ; lovely ; nice
carne f meat
carnevale m carnival
caro(a) dear ; expensive
carote fpl carrots
carrello m trolley
carriera f career
carro m cart
  carro attrezzi breakdown van
carrozza f carriage
  carrozze cuccette couchettes
  carrozza letto sleeper
carrozzeria f bodywork
carrozzina f pram
carta f paper ; card ; map
  carta assegni cheque card
  alla carta à la carte
  carta d'argento senior citizen's
  rail card
  carta di credito credit card
  carta famiglia family rail card
  carta d'identità identity card
  carta igienica toilet paper
  carta d'imbarco boarding card
  carta stradale road map
  carta verde green card
carte da gioco fpl playing cards
cartella f briefcase ; folder
cartello m sign ; signpost
cartine fpl cigarette papers
cartoccio m paper bag

cartoleria f stationer's
cartolina f postcard
casa f house ; home
  a casa at home
casalinga f housewife
casalinghi mpl household articles
cascata f waterfall
casco m helmet
casella postale f post-office box
casinò m casino
caso: in caso di in case of
cassa f till ; cash desk
  cassa chiusa position closed
cassaforte f safe (for valuables)
cassetta f cassette
  cassetta delle lettere letterbox
cassetto m drawer
cassiere(a) m/f cashier ; teller
castello m castle
catena f chain ; mountain range
  catene (da neve) snow chains
cattedrale f cathedral
cattivo(a) bad ; nasty ; naughty
cattolico(a) Catholic
causa f cause ; case (lawsuit)
  a causa di because of
cavalcare to ride (horse)
cavallo m horse
cavatappi m corkscrew
cavo m cable
  cavo da rimorchio tow rope
cavolfiore m cauliflower
CD m CD
  (blank) CD vuoto
c'è there is
cedro m cedar ; lime (fruit)
CE f EC
celibe m single man (not married)
cellulare m mobile phone
cena f dinner (evening meal)
cenare to have dinner
cenone m New Year's Eve dinner
centesimo m cent (euro)
centimetro m centimetre
cento hundred

centrale **central**

centralino m **switchboard**

centro m **centre**
  centro città **city centre**
  centro commerciale **shopping centre**
  centro storico **old town**

ceppo bloccaruote m **wheel clamp**

cera f **wax** (for furniture)

ceramica f **ceramics** ; **pottery**

cercare **to look for**

ceretta f **waxing** (hair removal)

cerini mpl **matches**

cerniera f **zip**

cerotto m **sticking plaster**

certificato m **certificate**
  certificato di nascita **birth certificate**

cervello m **brain**

cestino m **basket** ; **waste paper bin**

cetriolo m **cucumber**

che **what** ; **who** ; **which**
  che gusto? **what flavour?**
  che ore sono? **what time is it?**

cherosene m **paraffin**

chi? **who?**
  di chi è? **whose is it?**

chiamare **to call**
  chiamare per telefono **to phone**

chiamarsi **to be called** (name)
  come si chiama? **what's your name?**

chiamata f **call** (telephone)

chiave f **key**
  chiave inglese **spanner**

chiedere **to ask** ; **to ask for**

chiesa f **church**

chilo m **kilo**

chilogrammo m **kilogram**

chilometraggio m **mileage** (in km)

chilometro m **kilometre**

chiodo m **nail** (metal)

chirurgia f **surgery** (operations)

chitarra f **guitar**

chiudere **to close** ; **to turn off** (tap)
  chiudere a chiave **to lock**

chiuso(a) **closed**

  chiuso per turno **closed for weekly day off**
  chiuso per ferie **closed for holidays**

chiusura centralizzata f **central locking** (car)

ciabatta f **flat bread** ; **slipper**

ciao! **hi!** ; **bye!**

cibo m **food**

cielo m **sky**

ciliegia f **cherry**

cinghia della ventola f **fan belt**

cintura f **belt**
  cintura di sicurezza **seatbelt**

cinturino dell'orologio m **watchstrap**

cioccolato m **chocolate**

cipolla f **onion**

circo m **circus**

circolare **to move** (traffic)

circolazione f **traffic**

circonvallazione f **ring road**

cisterna f **cistern** ; **tank**

cisti f **cyst**

cistite f **cystitis**

citofono m **intercom**

città f **city** ; **town**

cittadinanza f **citizenship**

cittadino(a) **citizen**

classe f **class**

clavicola f **collar bone**

cliente m/f **customer**

climatizzato(a) **air-conditioned**

clinica f **clinic**

cocco m **coconut**

cocomero m **watermelon**

coda f **tail** ; **queue**

codice m **code**
  codice a barra **barcode**
  codice postale **postcode**
  codice stradale **highway code**

cofano m **bonnet** (car)

cognata f **sister-in-law**

cognato m **brother-in-law**

cognome m **surname**
  di cognome mi chiamo... **my surname is...**

coincidenza f **connection** (train, etc)

colazione f **breakfast** ; **lunch**

collana f **necklace**

collant mpl **tights**

collega m/f **colleague**

colletto m **collar**

collina f **hill**

collo m **neck** ; **package**

colluttorio m **mouthwash**

colomba f **dove** ; **Easter cake**

colore m **colour**

Colosseo m **Coliseum**

colpa f **fault**
  non è colpa mia **it's not my fault**

coltello m **knife**

combustibile m **fuel**

come **like** ; **as** ; **how**
  come? **how?** (in what way)
  come si chiama? **what's your name?**
  come si pronuncia? **how is it
  pronounced?**
  come si scrive? **how is it spelt?**
  come sta? **how are you?**
  come va? **how's it going?**

cominciare **to begin**

commesso(a) m/f **assistant** ; **clerk**

commissariato m **police station**

commozione cerebrale f **concussion**

comodo(a) **comfortable**

compagnia f **company**
  compagnia aerea **airline**

compilare **to fill in** (form)

compleanno m **birthday**

completo(a) **no vacancies** ; **full**

comporre **to dial** (number)

comprare **to buy**

compreso(a) **included**

compressa f **tablet**

computer m **computer**

comune m **town hall** ; **commune**

con **with**
  con bagno **with bathroom**
  con filtro **filter-tipped**
  con ghiaccio **with ice**

concerto m **concert**

conchiglia f **seashell**

condimento m **seasoning** ;
  dressing (for food)

conducente m/f **driver** (taxi, bus)

confermare **to confirm**

confine m **boundary** ; **border**

congelatore m **freezer**

congratulazioni! **congratulations!**

congresso m **conference**

cono m **cone**
  cono gelato **ice-cream cone**

conoscere **to know** (to be acquainted
  with)

consegna f **consignment** ; **delivery**

conservante m **preservative**

consigliare **to advise**

consiglio m **advice**

consumare **to use up**
  da consumarsi entro **best before**

consumazione f **drink**

contanti mpl **cash**
  pagare in contanti **to pay cash**

contatore m **electricity meter**

contento(a) **happy**

continuare **to continue**

conto m **account** ; **bill**
  conto corrente **current account**
  conto dettagliato **itemised bill**
  conto in banca **bank account**

contorno m **vegetable side dish**

contrabbando m **smuggling**

contratto m **contract**

contravvenzione f **fine**

contro **against** ; **versus**

controllare **to check**

controllo m **check** ; **control**
  controllo passaporti **passport
  control**

controllore m **ticket collector**

convalida f **date stamp**

convalidare **to validate** (ticket)

convincere **to persuade**

coperta f **blanket**

coperto m **place setting** ; **cover
  charge**

copertura f cover (insurance)

coppa gelato f ice cream served in goblet/tub

coppia f couple (two people)

copriletto m bedspread

coraggioso(a) brave

corda f rope

cornetto m ice cream cone

corpo m body

corrente f current (electric, water)
  corrente d'aria draught

correre to run

corridoio m corridor

corriere m courier

corsa f race ; journey
  corsa semplice single fare

corsia f lane ; hospital ward ; route
  corsia di emergenza hard shoulder
  corsia di sorpasso outside lane

corso m course ; avenue
  corso dei cambi exchange rates
  corso intensivo crash course

cortile m courtyard

corto(a) short

cos'è? what is it?
  cos'è successo? what happened?

cosa f thing
  cosa? what?

coscia f thigh

così so ; thus (in this way)

cosmetici mpl cosmetics

costa f coast
  Costa Azzurra French Riviera

costare to cost

costoletta f chop

costoso(a) expensive

costruire to build

costume m custom ; costume
  costume da bagno swimsuit

cotone m cotton
  cotone idrofilo cotton wool

cotto(a) cooked
  poco cotto(a) medium rare (steak)

cotton fioc® m cotton bud

crampi mpl cramps

cravatta f tie

credere to believe

credito m credit
  non si fa credito no credit given

crema f cream ; custard
  crema da barba shaving cream

crescere to grow

crespella f fried pastry twist

cric m jack (for car)

crisi epilettica f epileptic fit

cristallo m crystal
  di cristallo made of crystal

croccante f crisp

croce f cross

crocevia m crossroads

crociera f cruise

crollo m collapse

cronaca f news

cruciverba m crossword puzzle

crudo(a) raw

cuccetta f couchette ; sleeper

cucchiaino m teaspoon

cucchiaio m spoon ; tablespoon

cucina f cooker ; kitchen ; cooking
  cucina a gas gas cooker

cucinare to cook

cucire to sew

cuffia f bathing cap

cuffie fpl earphones

cugino(a) m/f cousin

culla f cradle

cuocere to cook
  cuocere a vapore to steam
  cuocere alla griglia to grill

cuoco m chef

cuoio m leather

cuore m heart

cupola f dome

curva f bend ; corner

cuscino m cushion

custode m caretaker

custodia f case ; holder

cyber-café m internet cafe

D

da from ; by ; with ; worth
  da asporto take-away
  dall'Inghilterra from England
  dalla Scozia from Scotland
  da vedere worth seeing
  da 100 euro worth 100 euros
dadi *m* stock cubes
danneggiare to spoil ; to damage
danno *m* damage
dappertutto everywhere
dare to give
  dare su to overlook ; to give onto
  dare la precedenza give way
  dare da mangiare to feed
  dare la mancia to tip *(waiter, etc)*
data *f* date
  data di nascita date of birth
  data di scadenza sell-by date
dati *mpl* data
dattero *m* date *(fruit)*
davanti a in front of ; opposite
dazio *m* customs duty
d.C. A.D.
debito *m* debt
decaffeinato(a) decaffeinated
decollare to take-off
decollo *m* takeoff
delizioso(a) delicious
dente *m* tooth
dentiera *f* dentures
dentifricio *m* toothpaste
dentro in ; indoors ; inside
deodorante *m* deodorant
  deodorante per ambienti air
  freshener
deposito bagagli *m* left-luggage
descrivere to describe
descrizione *f* description
desiderare to want ; to desire
destinazione *f* destination
destra *f* right
detergente *m* cleanser
detersivo *m* detergent

detersivo in polvere soap powder
detersivo per i piatti washing-up
liquid
detrazione *f* deduction
dettagli *mpl* details
deviazione *f* detour ; diversion
di of ; some
  di cristallo/plastica made of
  crystal/plastic
  di Giovanni Giovanni's
  di lusso luxury *(hotel, etc)*
  di mattina in the morning
  di pomeriggio in the afternoon
  di moda fashionable
  di notte at night
  di stagione in season
  di valore of value ; valuable
diabete *m* diabetes
diabetico(a) diabetic
diaframma *m* cap *(diaphragm)*
dialetto *m* dialect
diamante *m* diamond
diapositiva *f* slide *(photo)*
diarrea *f* diarrhoea
dicembre *m* December
dichiarare to declare
dichiarazione *f* declaration
dieta *f* diet
  essere a dieta to be on a diet
dietro behind ; after
  dietro di behind
difetto *m* fault
difficile difficult
diga *f* dam ; dyke
digerire to digest
digestivo *m* after-dinner liqueur
dimenticare to forget
Dio *m* God
dipinto(a) painted
diramazione *f* fork *(in road)*
dire to say ; to tell
diretto(a) direct
  treno diretto through train
direttore *m* manager ; director
direzione *f* management ; direction

dirigere to manage (be in charge of)
diritto(a) straight
  sempre diritto straight on
disabile disabled (person)
disastro m disaster
dischetto m floppy disk ; diskette
disco m disk ; record
  disco orario parking disk
discoteca f disco
disdire to cancel
disegno m drawing
disfare la valigia to unpack
disinfettante m disinfectant
disoccupato(a) unemployed
dispiacere: mi dispiace I'm sorry
disponibile available
distaccare to detach ; to unplug
distante far ; distant
distanza f distance
distorsione f sprain
distributore m dispenser
  distributore di benzina petrol station
disturbare to disturb
disturbo m trouble
dito m finger
  dito del piede toe
ditta f firm ; company
diurno(a) day(time)
divano m sofa ; divan
  divano letto sofa bed
diversi(e) several ; various
diverso(a) different
divertente funny (amusing)
divertimento m entertainment ; fun
divertirsi to enjoy oneself
dividere to share
divieto forbidden ; not allowed
  divieto di sorpasso no overtaking
  divieto di sosta no parking
divisa f uniform
divorziato(a) divorced
dizionario m dictionary
DOC abbreviation of
  denominazione di origine
  controllata (guarantee of wine quality)

doccia f shower
docente m/f lecturer
DOCG abbreviation of
  denominazione di origine
  controllata e garantita (guarantee
  of wine quality)
documenti mpl papers (passport)
dogana f customs
dolce sweet (not savoury) ; mild
dolce m sweet ; dessert ; cake
dolcelatte m creamy blue cheese
dolcificante m sweetener
dolciumi mpl sweets
dollari mpl dollars
dolore m pain ; grief
doloroso(a) painful
domanda f question
domandare to ask (a question)
domani tomorrow
  domani mattina tomorrow morning
  domani pomeriggio tomorrow
  afternoon
  domani sera tomorrow
  evening/night
domattina tomorrow morning
domenica Sunday
donna f woman
  donne ladies ; women
dopo after ; afterward(s)
dopobarba m aftershave
dopodomani the day after
  tomorrow
doppio(a) double
dormire to sleep
dove? where?
dovere to have to
droga f drugs (narcotics)
drogheria f grocery shop
duepezzi m two-piece suit ; bikini
duomo m cathedral
durante during
durare to last
duro(a) hard ; tough ; harsh

E

e and
E **east** *(abbreviation)*
è **is** (to be)
ebreo(a) **Jewish**
ecc. **etc.**
eccedenza f **excess ; surplus**
eccesso m **excess**
  eccesso di velocità **speeding**
eccezionale **exceptional**
eccezione f **exception**
ecco **here is/are**
economico(a) **cheap**
edicola f **newsstand ; kiosk**
edificio m **building**
effetto m **effect**
  effetti personali **belongings**
egregio(a) **dear** *(in formal letter)*
elastico m **rubber band**
elenco m **list**
  elenco telefonico **phone directory**
elettricista m/f **electrician**
elettricità f **electricity**
elettrico(a) **electric(al)**
elettrodomestici mpl **electrical goods**
emergenza f **emergency**
emicrania f **migraine**
emorroidi fpl **haemorrhoids**
enoteca f **wine shop ; wine bar**
ente m **corporation ; body**
entrambi(e) **both**
entrare **to come/go in ; to enter**
entrata f **entrance**
  entrata abbonati **season ticket holders' entrance**
  entrata libera **free admission**
epatite f **hepatitis**
epilessia f **epilepsy**
epilettico(a) **epileptic**
equitazione f **horse-riding**
erba f **grass**
ernia f **hernia**
errore m **mistake**
esame m **examination**

esatto(a) **exact ; accurate**
esaurimento nervoso m **nervous breakdown**
esaurito(a) **exhausted ; out of print**
  tutto esaurito **sold out**
esca m **fishing bait**
escluso(a) **excluding**
escursione f **excursion**
esente **exempt**
  esente da dogana **duty-free**
esempio **example**
  per esempio **for example**
esercizio m **exercise ; business**
esigenza f **requirement**
esperto(a) **expert ; experienced**
esplosione f **explosion**
esportare **to export**
esposto(a) **exposed**
  esposto(a) a nord **north-facing**
espresso m **express train ; coffee**
espresso(a) **express** *(parcel, etc)*
essere **to be**
  essere assicurato(a) **to be insured**
  essere capace (di) **to be able (to)**
  essere d'accordo **to agree**
  essere nato(a) **to be born**
est m **east**
estate f **summer**
esterno(a) **outside ; external**
estero(a) **foreign**
  all'estero **abroad**
estintore m **fire extinguisher**
estivo(a) **summer**
età f **age**
etichetta f **luggage tag ; label**
euro **euro**
euro cent m **centesimo**
eurocheque m **Eurocheque**
Europa f **Europe**
eventuale **possible**
evitare **to avoid**

F

fa **ago**
  un anno fa **a year ago**

fabbrica f factory
fabbricare to manufacture
faccia f face
facile easy
fagiano m pheasant
fagiolini m runner beans
fallire to fail
fallito(a) bankrupt
fallo m foul (football)
falso(a) fake
fame f hunger
  avere fame to be hungry
famiglia f family
familiare family ; familiar
famoso(a) famous
fanale m light
fanalino dello stop m brake light
fango m mud
farcito(a) stuffed ; filled
fare to do ; to make
  fare attenzione to be careful
  fare la spesa to go shopping
  fare la spesa su internet to shop
  online
farfalla f butterfly
fari mpl headlights
farina f flour
farmacia f chemist's ; pharmacy
  farmacie di turno duty chemists
farmaco m drug (medicine)
faro m headlight ; lighthouse
fascia f band ; bandage
fastidio: non mi dà fastidio I don't
  mind
fatelo da voi m DIY
fatto a mano hand-made
fatto di ... made of ...
fattoria f farm ; farmhouse
fattura f invoice
favore m favour
  per favore please
fax m fax
fazzoletto m handkerchief
  fazzoletto di carta tissue

febbraio February
febbre f fever
  avere la febbre to have
  a temperature
  febbre da fieno hay fever
fede f wedding ring
federa f pillowcase
fegato m liver
felice happy
felpa f sweatshirt
femmina f female
feriale workday (Monday-Saturday)
ferie fpl holiday(s)
  essere in ferie to be on holiday
ferire to injure
ferita f wound ; injury ; cut
ferito(a) injured
fermare to stop
fermata f stop
  fermata dell'autobus bus stop
fermo(a) still ; off (machine)
  stare fermo to stay still
ferro da stiro m iron (for clothes)
ferrovia f railway
festa f festival ; holiday ; party
  festa nazionale public holiday
festivo(a) sundays/public holiday
fetta f slice
fiamma f flame
fiammifero m match
fico m fig
fidanzato(a) engaged (to marry)
fieno m hay
fiera f fair (trade)
figlia f daughter
figlio m son
fila f line (row, queue)
  fare la fila to queue
filiale f branch ; subsidiary
film m film (at cinema)
filo m thread ; wire
  filo interdentale dental floss
filtro m filter
  filtro dell'olio oil filter
finanza f finance

Guardia di finanza Customs and Excise
fine f end
  fine settimana weekend
  fine stagione end of season
fine elegant ; fine
finestra f window
finestrino m window *(car, train)*
finire to finish
finito(a) finished
fino a until ; as far as
  fino alle due till 2 o'clock
fior di latte m cream *(ice cream flavour)*
fiori mpl flowers
fiorista m/f florist
Firenze Florence
firma f signature
firmare to sign
  firmare il registro to sign the register
fiume m river
focaccia f flat salted bread
foglia f leaf *(of tree, etc)*
fogna f sewer ; drain
folla f crowd
folle mad
  in folle in neutral *(car)*
fon m hairdryer
fondo m back *(of room)* ; bottom
fontana f fountain
fonte f source
foratura f puncture
forbici fpl scissors
  forbicine nail scissors
forchetta f fork *(for eating)*
foresta f forest
forfora f dandruff
formaggio m cheese
fornaio m baker
fornello m stove ; hotplate
fornitore m supplier
forno m oven
  forno a microonde microwave
forse perhaps

forte strong ; loud ; high *(speed)*
fortunato(a) lucky
forza f strength ; force
foto f photo
fotocamera digitale f digital camera
fotocopia f photocopy
fotocopiare to photocopy
fototessera f passport-type photo
foulard m headscarf
fra between ; among(st)
  fra 2 giorni in 2 days
  fra poco in a while
fragile breakable
fragola f strawberry
frana f landslide
francese French
francese m French *(language)*
Francia f France
francobollo m stamp
frappé m milk shake
fratello m brother
frattura f fracture
frazione f village
freccia f indicator *(car)* ; arrow
freddo(a) cold
frenare to brake
freno m brake
  freno a mano handbrake
frequente frequent
fretta f hurry
  avere fretta to be in a hurry
friggere to fry
frigorifero m refrigerator
frittata f omelette
fritto(a) fried
frizione f clutch *(car)*
frizzante fizzy ; sparkling
fronte f forehead ; front
  di fronte a facing ; opposite
frontiera f frontier ; border
frullato m milkshake
frutta f fruit
  frutta secca dried fruit
frutti di mare mpl seafood

fruttivendolo *m* greengrocer

FS Italian State Railways

fuga *f* escape ; leak *(gas)*

fuggire to escape

fulmine *m* lightning

fumare to smoke
　non fumo I don't smoke

fumatori smokers

fumo *m* smoke

funerale *m* funeral

funghi *mpl* mushrooms
　funghi porcini boletus mushrooms
　funghi secchi dried mushrooms

funicolare *f* funicular railway

funzionare to work *(mechanism)*
　non funziona it doesn't work

fuoco *m* fire ; focus
　fuochi d'artificio fireworks

fuori outside ; out
　fuori servizio out of order

furgone *m* van

furto *m* theft

fuseaux *mpl* leggings

fusibile *m* fuse

futuro *m* future

G

gabinetto *m* lavatory
　gabinetto biologico chemical toilet
　gabinetto medico doctor's surgery

galleria *f* tunnel ; gallery ; arcade ;
circle *(theatre)*
　galleria d'arte art gallery

Galles *m* Wales

gallese Welsh

gamba *f* leg

gara *f* race *(sport)*

garanzia *f* guarantee ; warranty

gas *m* gas

gasolio *m* diesel

gassato(a) fizzy

gassosa *f* lemonade

gastrite *f* gastritis

gatto *m* cat

gay gay *(person)*

gel per capelli *m* hair gel

gelateria *f* ice-cream shop

gelatina *f* jelly

gelato *m* ice cream

gelo *m* frost

geloso(a) jealous

gemelli *mpl* twins ; cufflinks

genere *m* kind *(type)* ; gender

genero *m* son-in-law

genitori *mpl* parents

Genova *f* Genoa

gentile kind *(person)*

Germania *f* Germany

gesso *m* chalk ; plaster *(for limb)*

gettare to throw
　non gettare rifiuti no dumping

gettone *m* token
　gettone di presenza attendance fee

ghiaccio *m* ice

ghiacciolo *m* ice lolly

giacca *f* jacket

giallo *m* thriller *(book or film)*

giallo(a) yellow ; amber *(light)*

giardiniere *m* gardener

giardino *m* garden

gilè *m* waistcoat

gin *m* gin
　gin tonic gin and tonic

ginocchio *m* knee

giocare to play ; to gamble

giocattolo *m* toy

gioco *m* game
　gioco a quiz quiz show

gioielleria *f* jeweller's

gioielli *mpl* jewellery

gioielliere *m* jeweller

giornalaio *m* newsagent

giornale *m* newspaper

giornalista *m/f* journalist

giornata *f* day

giorno *m* day
　giorni feriali Monday-Saturday
　giorni festivi Sundays/holidays

giovane young
giovedì m Thursday
girare to turn ; to spin
  girarsi to turn around
girasole m sunflower
girella f scrunchie
giro m tour ; turn
  fare un giro a piedi to go for a stroll
  giro turistico sightseeing tour
gita f trip ; excursion
  gita in barca boat trip
  gita in pullman coach trip
giù down ; downstairs
giubbotto salvagente m life jacket
giudice m judge
giugno m June
giusto(a) fair ; right *(correct)*
gli the ; to him/it
globale inclusive *(costs)*
goccia f drop *(of liquid)* ; drip
gola f throat ; gorge
golfo m gulf
gomito m elbow
gomma f rubber ; tyre
  gomma a terra flat tyre
  gomma da cancellare eraser
gommone m dinghy *(inflatable)*
gonfiare to inflate
gonfio(a) swollen
gonfiore m lump *(swelling)*
gonna f skirt
gradazione f content *(of alcohol)*
gradevole pleasant
gradino m step ; stair
Gran Bretagna f Great Britain
grana f parmesan cheese
granaio m barn
granchio m crab
grande large ; great ; big
grande magazzino m department store
grandine f hail
granita f water ice *(flavoured)*
grappa f strong spirit *(often drunk with coffee)*

grasso(a) fat ; greasy
gratis free of charge
grattacielo m skyscraper
grattugia f grater
grattugiato(a) grated
gratuito(a) free of charge
  il servizio è gratuito service included
grave serious
grazie thank you
gridare to shout
grigio(a) grey
griglia f grill
  alla griglia grilled
grissini mpl breadsticks
grosso(a) big ; thick
grucce fpl crutches
gruccia f coat hanger
gruppo m group
  gruppo sanguigno blood group
guadagnare to earn
guanciale m pillow
guanto m glove
  guanto da forno oven glove
  guanto di spugna facecloth
  guanti di gomma rubber gloves
guardacoste m coastguard
guardare to look (at) ; to watch
guardaroba m cloakroom
guardia f guard
  Guardia di finanza Customs and Excise
guasto out of order
guerra f war
guida f guide *(person or book)* ; directory
  guida a sinistra left-hand drive
  guida telefonica telephone directory
  guida turistica tour guide
guidare to drive ; to steer
guidatore m driver
guinzaglio m lead *(for dog)*
gustare to taste ; to enjoy
gusto m flavour

H

ha...? do you have...?
  ha l'ora? do you have the time?
hamburger m burger
herpes m cold sore ; herpes
ho... I have...
  ho ... anni I'm ... years old
  ho bisogno di... I need...
  ho fame I'm hungry
  ho fretta I'm in a hurry
  ho sete I'm thirsty
hostess f stewardess

I

i the
identificare to identify
idratante m moisturizer
idraulico m plumber
ieri yesterday
il the
imbarcarsi to embark
imbarcazione f boat
imbarco m boarding
  carta d'imbarco boarding card
imbottigliato(a) bottled
imbucare to post *(letter, etc)*
immediatamente at once
immergere to dip *(into liquid)*
immersioni subacquee fpl scuba
  diving
immondizie fpl rubbish
immunizzazione f immunisation
impanato coated in breadcrumbs
imparare to learn
impasto m mixture
imperatore m emperor
impermeabile m raincoat
impero m empire
impiego m use ; employment
impiegato(a) m/f employee ; white-
  collar worker
importante important
importare to import ; to matter
  non importa it doesn't matter

importo m (total) amount
impossibile impossible
imposta f tax *(on income)* ; shutter
  imposta sul valore aggiunto (IVA)
  value-added tax (VAT)
improbabile unlikely
in in ; to
  in Spagna to Spain
  in vacanza on holiday
inalatore m inhaler
inadempienza f negligence
incantevole charming
incaricarsi di to take charge of
incartare to wrap up *(parcel)*
incassare to cash *(a cheque)*
incendio m fire
inchiostro m ink
incidente m accident
incinta pregnant
incluso(a) included ; enclosed
incontrare to meet
incontro m meeting *(by chance)*
incrocio m crossroads ; junction
indicatore m indicator ; gauge
  indicatore del livello dell'olio
  oil gauge
indicazioni fpl directions
indice m index ; contents
indietro backwards ; behind
indirizzo m address
infarto m heart attack
infatti in fact ; actually
infermeria f infirmary
infermiera f nurse
infezione infection
infiammabile inflammable
infiammazione f inflammation
influenza f flu
informare to inform
  informarsi (di) to inquire (about)
informazioni fpl information
infuso di erbe f herbal tea
ingessatura f plaster cast
Inghilterra f England
inghiottire to swallow

inglese **English**

ingorgato(a) **blocked** *(pipe, sink)*

ingorgo *m* **blockage ; hold-up**
  ingorgo stradale **traffic jam**

ingresso *m* **entry/entrance**
  ingresso gratuito **free entry**

iniezione *f* **injection**

inizio *m* **start**

innocuo(a) **harmless**

inondazione *m* **flood**

inoltre **besides**

inquinato(a) **polluted**

insalata *f* **salad**
  insalata di patate **potato salad**
  insalata di pomodori **tomato salad**
  insalata mista **mixed salad**
  insalata verde **green salad**

insegnante *m/f* **teacher**

insegnare **to teach**

inserire **to insert**
  inserire le banconote una per volta
  insert banknotes one at a time

insettifugo *m* **insect repellent**

insetto *m* **insect**

insieme **together**

insieme *m* **whole outfit**

insolazione *f* **sunstroke**

insulina *f* **insulin**

interessante **interesting**

internazionale **international**

Internet *m* **Internet**

interno *m* **inside ; extension** *(phone)*

intero(a) **whole**

interpretazione *f* **interpretation**

interprete *m/f* **interpreter**

interruttore *m* **switch**

intervallo *m* **half-time ; interval**

intervento *m* **operation**

inversione *f* **U-turn**

intervista *f* **interview**

intestato(a) **a registered in the name of**

intimi donna *mpl* **ladies' underwear**

intorno **around**

intossicazione alimentare *f* **food-poisoning**

introdurre **to introduce**

inutile **unnecessary ; useless**

invalido(a) **disabled ; invalid**

invece di **instead of**

invernale **winter**

inverno *m* **winter**

investire **to knock down** *(car)*

inviare **to send**

invitare **to invite**

invito *m* **invitation**

io **I**

ipermercato *m* **hypermarket**

ipermetrope **long-sighted**

Irlanda *f* **Ireland**
  Irlanda del Nord **Northern Ireland**

irlandese **Irish**

iscritto *m* **member**
  per iscritto **in writing**

iscriversi a **to join** *(club)*

iscrizione *f* **inscription ; enrolment**

isola *f* **island**

istituto *m* **institute**

istruttore(trice) *m/f* **instructor**

istruzioni *fpl* **instructions**

Italia *f* **Italy**

italiano(a) **Italian**

itinerario *m* **route**
  itinerario turistico **scenic route**

itterizia *f* **jaundice**

IVA *f* **VAT**

J

jolly *m* **joker** *(cards)*

L

la **the ; her ; it ; you**

là **there**
  per di là **that way**

labbra *fpl* **lips**

lacca *f* **lacquer ; hair spray**

ladro *m* **thief**

lago m lake
lamette fpl razor blades
lampada f lamp
lampadina f lightbulb
lampone m raspberry
lana f wool
largo(a) wide ; broad
lasciare to leave ; to let (allow)
lassativo m laxative
lassù up there
latte m milk
  latte a lunga conservazione
  long-life milk
  latte di soia soya milk
  latte fresco fresh milk
  latte in polvere powdered milk
  latte intero whole milk
  latte scremato skimmed milk
  latte parzialmente scremato semi-
  skimmed milk
lattuga f lettuce
lavabile washable
lavaggio m washing
  lavaggio auto car wash
  per lavaggi frequenti for frequent
  use
lavanderia f laundry (place)
  lavanderia automatica launderette
lavandino m sink
lavare to wash
  lavare a secco to dry-clean
lavarsi to wash (oneself)
lavasecco m dry-cleaner's
lavastoviglie f dishwasher
lavatrice f washing machine
lavorare to work (person)
lavoro m job ; occupation ; work
  lavori stradali road works
  lavori in corso road works
le the ; them ; to her ; to you
legge f law
leggere to read
leggero(a) light (not heavy) ; weak
legno m wood (material)
lei she ; her ; you

lentamente slowly
lente f lens (of glasses)
  lente d'ingrandimento magnifying
  glass
  lenti a contatto contact lenses
lento slow
lenzuolo m sheet (bed)
lesbica lesbian
lesione f injury
lettera f letter
  lettera raccomandata registered
  letter
lettino m cot
letto m bed
  letto a una piazza single bed
  letto matrimoniale double bed
  letti gemelli twin beds
  letti a castello bunk beds
lettore CD m CD player
lì there (over there)
libero(a) free/vacant
libreria f bookshop
libretto m booklet
  libretto degli assegni cheque book
libro m book
licenza f licence ; permit
  licenza di caccia hunting permit
  licenza di pesca fishing permit
limetta per le unghie f nail file
limite m limit ; boundary
  limite di velocità speed limit
limone m lemon
linea f line ; route
  linea aerea airline
lingua f language ; tongue
lino m linen
liquido m liquid
  liquido dei freni brake fluid
  liquido lavavetri screen wash
  liquido per lenti a contatto contact
  lens solution
liquore m liqueur
liquori mpl spirits (alcohol)
liscio(a) straight ; smooth
lista f list
  lista dei vini wine list

listino prezzi m price list
litro m litre
livello m level
lo him ; it
locale local
locale m room ; place ; local train
  locale notturno nightclub
località di vacanza f resort
locanda f inn
Londra f London
lontano(a) far
lozione f lotion
  lozione solare suntan lotion
lucchetto m padlock
  lucchetto della bici bike lock
luce f light
lucertola f lizard
luglio m July
lui him
lumaca f snail
luna f moon
  luna di miele honeymoon
luna park m funfair
lunedì m Monday
lunghezza f length
lungo(a) long
  lungo la strada along the street
  a lungo for a long time
lungomare m promenade ; seafront
luogo m place
  luogo di nascita place of birth
lupo m wolf
lusso m luxury
  di lusso luxury (hotel, etc)

M
ma but
macchia f stain ; mark
macchina f car ; machine
  macchina a noleggio hire car
  macchina fotografica camera
  fotocamera digitale digital camera
  macchina sportiva sports car
macedonia f fruit salad
macellaio m butcher's

macinato(a) ground (coffee, meat)
madre f mother
magazzino m warehouse
maggio m May
maggiore larger ; greater ; older ;
  largest ; greatest ; oldest
maglietta f t-shirt
maglione m jumper ; sweater
magro(a) thin (person) ; low-fat ;
  lean (meat)
mai never ; ever
maiale m pig ; pork
maionese f mayonnaise
mal see male
malato(a) ill ; sick
malattia f disease
  malattia venerea venereal disease
male badly (not well)
male m pain ; ache
  mal d'aria air sickness
  mal d'auto car sickness
  mal d'orecchi earache
  mal di denti toothache
  mal di gola sore throat
  mal di mare sea sickness
  mal di pancia stomachache
  mal di testa headache
maltempo m bad weather
mamma f mum(my)
mancia f tip (to waiter, etc)
mandare to send
  mandare per fax to fax
mangiare to eat
  mangiare fuori to eat out
manica f sleeve
  la Manica the English Channel
mano f hand
  fatto(a) a mano handmade
Mantova f Mantua
manuale di conversazione m phrase
  book
manzo m beef
marca f brand (make)
marcia f gear (car) ; march
marciapiede m pavement
mare m sea ; seaside

Mare del Nord **North Sea**
margarina f margarine
margherita f daisy
marina f navy
marito m husband
marmellata f jam
  marmellata d'arance marmalade
marrone m brown ; chestnut
marsupio m bumbag ; money belt
martedì m Tuesday
  martedì grasso Shrove Tuesday
martello m hammer
marzo m March
maschera f mask ; fancy dress
maschile masculine ; male
massimo(a) maximum
masticare to chew
materassino m airbed ; lilo
materasso m mattress
materiale m material
matrigna f stepmother
matrimonio m wedding
mattina f morning
  di mattina in the morning
matto(a) mad
mazza f mallet
  mazze da golf golf clubs
meccanico m mechanic ; repair shop
medicina f medicine
medico m doctor
Mediterraneo m Mediterranean
medusa f jellyfish
meglio better ; best
  meglio di better than
mela f apple
melanzana f aubergine ; eggplant
melone m melon
membro m member
meningite f meningitis
meno less ; minus
mensa f canteen
mensile monthly
mensilmente monthly
mensola f shelf

menta f mint
mento m chin
mentre while ; whereas
menù m menu
  menù alla carta à la carte menu
  menù a prezzo fisso set-price menu
  menù turistico set menu
meraviglioso(a) wonderful
mercatino dell'usato m flea market
mercato m market
merce f goods
merci fpl freight ; goods
mercoledì m Wednesday
merenda f snack
meridionale southern
mese m month
messa f mass *(in church)*
messaggio m message
mestruazioni fpl period *(menstrual)*
metà f half
  metà prezzo half-price
metro m metre
  metro a nastro tape
  measure
metropolitana f underground ;
  metro
mettere to put ; to put on *(clothes)*
  mettersi in contatto con to contact
mezzanotte f midnight
mezzi mpl means ; transport
mezzo m middle
mezzo(a) half
  mezza pensione half board
mezzogiorno m midday ; noon
  il Mezzogiorno the south of Italy
mezz'ora f half an hour
mi me ; to me ; myself
mia my
miele m honey
migliorare to improve
migliore better ; best
Milano Milan
miliardo m billion
milione m million
mille thousand

millimetro *m* millimetre
minestra *f* soup
minimo *m* minimum
ministro *m* minister *(political)*
minorenne underage
minori *mpl* minors
minuto *m* minute
mio my
miscela *f* blend
misto(a) mixed
mittente *m/f* sender
MM metro ; underground (in Milan)
mobili *mpl* furniture
moda *f* fashion
moderno(a) modern
modo *m* way ; manner
modulo *m* form *(document)*
    modulo d'iscrizione registration
    form
moglie *f* wife
molletta *f* clothes peg
    molletta per capelli hairgrip
molo *m* jetty ; quay ; pier
molti(e) many
    molte grazie thanks very much
molto much ; a lot ; very
    molto tempo for a long time
    molta gente lots of people
monastero *m* monastery
moneta *f* coin ; currency
montagna *f* mountain
monumento *m* monument
mordere to bite
morire to die
morsicare to bite
morsicato(a) bitten
morso *m* bite
morso(a) bitten
morto(a) dead
mosca *f* fly
moscerino *m* midge ; gnat
moschea *f* mosque
mosso(a) rough *(sea)* ; ruffled
mostra *f* exhibition

mostrare to show
moto *f* motorbike
motore *m* engine ; motor
motorino *m* moped
motorino d'avviamento *m*
    starter motor
multa *f* fine *(to be paid)*
municipio *m* town hall
muro *m* wall
museo *m* museum
musica *f* music
muta *f* wetsuit
mutande *fpl* underpants
mutandine *fpl* knickers ; panties

N

N north *(abbreviation)*
nafta *f* diesel
Napoli Naples
nascita *f* birth
naso *m* nose
nastro *m* tape ; ribbon
nato(a) born
nauseato(a) nauseous
nave *f* ship
nave-traghetto *f* ferry
nazionale national ; domestic *(flight)*
nazionalità *f* nationality
nazione *f* nation
né ... né neither ... nor
nebbia *f* fog
necessario(a) necessary
negativo *m* negative *(photo)*
negozio *m* shop
nero(a) black
nessuno(a) no ; nobody ; none
netto *m* net
    al netto di IVA net of VAT
neve *f* snow
nevicare to snow
niente nothing
    niente da dichiarare nothing
    to declare
nipote *m/f* nephew/niece

nipotina f granddaughter
nipotino m grandson
noce f walnut
nocivo(a) harmful
nodo m knot ; bow
  nodo ferroviario junction (railway)
noi we
noleggiare to hire
noleggio m hire
  noleggio auto car hire
  noleggio barche boat hire
  noleggio bici bike hire
  noleggio sci ski hire
nolo m hire
nome m name ; first name
  nome da ragazza maiden name
non not
  non ancora not yet
  non c'é there isn't
  non funziona it doesn't work
  non capisco I don't understand
  non pericoloso(a) safe
non-fumatore m/f non-smoker
nonna f grandmother
nonno m grandfather
nord m north
nostro(a) our
notare to notice
notizie fpl news
notte f night
  notte di San Silvestro New Year's Eve
  di notte at night
novembre m November
nubile single (woman)
nulla nothing ; anything
nullo(a) void (contract)
numero m number ; size (of shoe)
  numero di camera room number
  numero del conto account number
  numero di telefono phone number
nuora f daughter-in-law
nuotare to swim
Nuova Zelanda f New Zealand
nuovo(a) new
  di nuovo again
nuvoloso(a) cloudy

O

o or
O west (abbreviation)
obbligatorio(a) compulsory
oceano m ocean
occasione f opportunity ; bargain
occhiali mpl glasses
  occhiali da sci skiing goggles
  occhiali da sole sunglasses
occhio m eye
occupato(a) busy/engaged
odore m smell
offerta f offer
officina f workshop ; repair shop
oggetto m object
oggi today
ogni each ; every
  ogni giorno every day ; daily
  ogni quanto? how often?
  ogni tanto occasionally
olio m oil
  olio solare suntan oil
  olio di girasole sunflower oil
  olio d'oliva olive oil
olive fpl olives
oltre beyond ; besides
ombra f shade
  all'ombra in the shade
ombrello m umbrella
ombrellone m sun umbrella
ombretto m eye shadow
omogeneizzati mpl baby food
omosessuale homosexual
onde fpl waves
onestà f honesty
onesto(a) honest
opera f opera
operatore turistico m tour operator
operazione f operation (surgical)
opuscolo m brochure
ora now
ora f hour
  ora di punta rush hour
  che ore sono? what's the time?

orario *m* timetable
  in orario on time
  orario di apertura opening hours
  orario di cassa banking hours
  orario visite visiting hours
ordinare to order ; to prescribe
ordine *f* order *(in restaurant)*
ordinato(a) tidy
orecchini *mpl* earrings
orecchio *m* ear
orecchioni *mpl* mumps
oreficeria *f* jeweller's
orina *f* urine
ormeggiare to moor
ormeggio *m* mooring
oro *m* gold
  placcato oro gold-plated
orologeria *m* watchmaker's
orologio *m* clock ; watch
orticaria *f* rash *(skin)*
ortografia *f* spelling
ospedale *m* hospital
ospite *m/f* guest ; host/hostess
osso *m* bone
ostello *m* hostel
  ostello della gioventù youth hostel
osteria *f* inn
ottenere to get ; obtain
  ottenere la linea to get through
  (on phone)
ottimo(a) excellent
ottobre *m* October
otturazione *f* filling *(in tooth)*
ovest *m* west

P

pacchetto *m* packet
pacco *m* package ; parcel
padella *f* frying-pan
Padova Padua
padre *m* father
padrone(a) *m/f* owner
paesaggio *m* scenery ; countryside
paese *m* country *(nation)* ; village

pagare to pay ; to pay for
pagato(a) paid
pagina *f* page
paio *m* pair
palazzo *m* building ; block of flats ;
  palace
palestra *f* gym
palla *f* ball
pallina *f* ball *(small)*
  pallina da golf golf ball
  pallina da tennis tennis ball
pallone *m* football
pandoro *m* Italian Christmas cake
pane *m* bread ; loaf
  pane integrale wholemeal bread
  pane carré sandwich bread
  pane e coperto cover charge
  pane di segale rye bread
panettone *m* Italian Christmas cake
panetteria *f* baker's
pangrattato *m* breadcrumbs
panificio *m* bakery
panino *m* bread roll
  panino imbottito sandwich
paninoteca *f* sandwich bar
panna *f* cream
panno *m* cloth ; fabric
pannolini *mpl* nappies
pantaloni *mpl* trousers
  pantaloni corti shorts
pantofole *fpl* slippers
papa *m* pope
papà *m* daddy
parabrezza *m* windscreen
paraurti *m* bumper *(on car)*
parcheggiare to park
parcheggio *m* car park
  parcheggio custodito supervised
  car-park
  parcheggio libero free parking
  parcheggio sotterraneo
  underground car park
parchimetro *m* parking meter
parco *m* park
  parco nazionale national park

parente *m/f* relation ; relative

Parigi *f* Paris

parlare to speak ; to talk

parmigiano *m* parmesan
  parmigiano grattugiato grated
  parmesan

parola *f* word
  parola d'ordine password

parolaccia *f* swear word

parrucchiere(a) *m/f* hairdresser

parte *f* share ; part ; side

partenza *f* departures
  partenze internazionali
  international departures
  partenze nazionali domestic
  departures

partire to depart ; to leave

partita *f* match ; game
  partita di calcio football match

passaggio *m* passage ; lift *(in car)*
  dare un passaggio to give a lift

passaporto *m* passport

passeggiata *f* walk ; stroll

passeggino *m* pushchair

passo *m* pace ; pass *(mountain)*
  passo carrabile keep clear
  passo chiuso pass closed
  fare quattro passi to go for a stroll

pasticcino *m* cake *(small, fancy)*

pastiglia *f* tablet *(pill)*

pasto *m* meal

pastorizzato pasteurised

patata *f* potato

patatine *fpl* crisps
  patatine fritte chips

patente *f* permit ; driving licence

patrigno *m* stepfather

pavimento *m* floor

paziente *m/f* patient

pecora *f* sheep

pedaggio *m* toll *(motorway)*

pedale *m* pedal

pedalò *m* pedalboat

pedicure *m* chiropodist

pedoni *mpl* pedestrians

peggio worse

pelati *mpl* tinned tomatoes

pelle *f* skin ; hide ; leather

pellegrino *m* pilgrim

pelletterie *fpl* leather goods

pellicola *f* film *(for camera)*
  pellicola a colori colour film
  pellicola in bianco e nero black and
  white film

pelo *m* fur

pene *m* penis

penicillina *f* penicillin

penisola *f* peninsula

penna *f* pen

pensare to think

pensione *f* guesthouse
  pensione completa full board
  mezza pensione half board
  pensione familiare bed and
  breakfast

pentola *f* saucepan

pepe *m* pepper *(spice)*

peperone *m* pepper (vegetable)

per for ; per ; in order to
  per esempio for example
  per favore please
  per via aerea air mail

pera *f* pear

perché why ; because ; so that

percorso *m* walk ; journey ; route
  percorso panoramico scenic route

perdere to lose ; to miss *(train, etc)*

perdita *f* leak *(of gas, liquid)*

pericolante unsafe

pericolo *m* danger

pericoloso(a) dangerous
  non pericoloso(a) safe

periferia *f* outskirts ; suburbs

permanente continua parking
  restrictions still apply

permanenza *f* stay ; residency

permesso *m* licence ; permit
  permesso! excuse me! *(to get by)*

permesso di soggiorno residence permit

permettere to allow

perso(a) lost *(object)* ; missed *(train, plane, etc)*

persona f person

personale m staff

pesante heavy

pesare to weigh

pesca f angling ; fishing ; peach
  divieto di pesca no fishing

pescare to fish

pesce m fish

pesche f peaches

pescivendolo m fishmonger's

peso m weight

pettine m comb

petto m chest ; breast
  petto di pollo chicken breast

pezzo m piece ; bit ; cut *(of meat)*

piacere to please
  le piace? do you like it?
  piacere! pleased to meet you!

piangere to cry *(weep)*

piano slowly ; quietly

piano m floor *(of building)* ; plan

pianta f map ; plan ; plant

pianterreno m ground floor

piantina f street map

piatto m dish ; course ; plate
  primo piatto first course

piazza f square *(in town)*

piazzale m large square

piazzola (di sosta) f lay-by

piccante spicy ; hot

picchetto m tent peg

piccolo(a) little ; small

piede m foot
  a piedi on foot

pieno(a) full

pietra f stone

pigiama m pyjamas

pigro(a) lazy

pila f battery ; torch

pillola f pill

pinne fpl flippers

pino m pine

pinze fpl pliers

pinzette fpl tweezers

pioggia f rain

piombo m lead *(metal)*

piovere to rain

piscina f swimming pool
  piscina per bambini paddling pool

piselli m peas

pista f track ; race track
  pista da ballo dance floor
  pista da sci ski run

più more ; most ; plus
  più di more than
  più economico(a) cheaper
  più tardi later

piumino m duvet

pizzeria m pizza restaurant

pizzico m pinch ; sting

pizzo m lace

plastica f plastic
  di plastica made of plastic

pneumatico m tyre

po' a little *(shortened form of poco)*

pochi(e) few

poco(a) little ; not much
  un po' a little

poi then

polizia f police
  polizia stradale traffic police

poliziotto m policeman

polizza f policy

pollo m chicken

polmone m lung

poltrona f armchair ; seat in stalls

pomata f ointment

pomeriggio m afternoon
  di pomeriggio in the afternoon

pomodoro m tomato

pompa f pump

pompelmo m grapefruit

ponte m bridge ; deck
  ponte macchine car deck

pontile m jetty ; pier

porcellana f china
porri m leeks
porta f door ; gate ; goal
  porta di sicurezza emergency exit
portabagagli m luggage rack ;
  porter *(at airport, station, etc)*
portacenere m ashtray
portafoglio m wallet
portare to carry/bring ; to wear
portiere m porter *(doorkeeper)* ;
  goalkeeper
portineria f caretaker's lodge
porto m port ; harbour
  porto di scalo port of call
Portogallo m Portugal
porzione f portion ; helping
posate fpl cutlery
posologia f dosage
possiamo we can
  non possiamo we cannot
posso I can
  non posso I cannot
posta f post office ; mail
  posta elettronica e-mail
  posta raccomandata registered mail
posteggio m car park
  posteggio taxi taxi rank
posto m place ; job ; seat
  posti in piedi standing room
  posti a sedere seating capacity
  posti prenotati reserved seats
potabile ok to drink
potere to be able
pranzo m lunch
pré-maman m maternity dress
preavviso m advance notice
precotto(a) ready-cooked
predeterminare l'importo
  desiderato select required amount
preferire to prefer
preferito(a) favourite
prefisso m prefix ; area code
  prefisso telefonico dialling code
pregare to pray
  si prega... please...

prego don't mention it!
prelievo m collection ; sample
premere to push ; to press
premio m prize
prendere to take ; to catch *(bus, etc)*
  prendere il sole to sunbathe
  prendere in prestito to borrow
prenome m first name
prenotare to book ; to reserve
prenotato(a) reserved
prenotazione f reservation
preoccupato(a) worried
preparare to prepare ; to get ready
presa f socket *(electric)*
preservativo m condom
pressione del sangue f blood
  pressure
prestare to lend
presto early ; soon
prete m priest
previsione f forecast
  previsioni del tempo weather
  forecast
previsto(a) scheduled ; expected
  come previsto as expected
prezzo m price
  prezzo al dettaglio retail price
  prezzo fisso set price
  prezzo di catalogo list price
  prezzo al minuto retail price
  prezzo d'ingresso entrance fee
prima di before
primavera f spring *(season)*
primo(a) first ; top ; early
  primo piano first floor
  primo piatto first course
principale main
principiante m/f beginner
privato(a) private
problema m problem
professione f profession
professore m/f teacher ; professor
profondità f depth
profondo(a) deep
profumeria f perfume shop

progettare to plan

programma m programme ; syllabus ; schedule

proibire to ban ; to prohibit

proibito(a) forbidden ; prohibited

prolunga f extension (electrical)

promettere to promise

pronto(a) ready
  pronto! hello! (on telephone)
  pronto soccorso casualty

proprietario(a) m/f owner

proprio(a) own

prosciutto cotto m ham (cooked)

prosciutto crudo m ham (cured)

prossimamente coming soon

prossimo(a) next

proteggislip m panty liner

protesi dell'anca f hip replacement

protestante Protestant

provare to try ; to test (try out) ; to try on (clothes)

provvisorio(a) temporary

prugna f plum

PTP abbreviation of Posto Telefonico Pubblico

pubblicità f advertisement

pubblico m audience ; public

pulce f flea

pulito(a) clean

pulizia f cleaning
  pulizia del viso facial

pullman m coach

pulmino m minibus

punteggio m score

puntine fpl points

punto m point ; stitch ; full stop
  punto d'incontro meeting place

puntura f bite ; sting ; injection

puzzle m jigsaw

puzzo m bad smell

Q

qua here

quaderno m exercise book

quadro m picture ; painting

qual(e) what ; which ; which one

qualche some
  qualche volta sometimes

qualcosa something ; anything

qualcuno someone ; somebody

qualificato(a) qualified

qualità f quality

qualsiasi any

qualunque any

quando? when?

quanto(a)? how much?
  quanti(e)? how many?

quartiere m district

quarto m quarter
  quarto d'ora quarter of an hour

quattro four

quei those ; those ones

quel(la) that ; that one

quelli(e) those ; those ones

quello(a) that ; that one

questi(e) these ; these ones

questo(a) this ; this one

questura f police station

qui here

quindi then ; therefore

quindici giorni fortnight

quotidiano m daily (paper)

quotidiano(a) daily

R

rabarbaro m rhubarb

rabbia f anger ; rabies

racchetta f racket ; bat
  racchetta da neve snowshoe
  racchetta da sci ski pole

raccomandare to recommend

racconto m story

radiatore m radiator

radio f radio

radiografia f x-ray

raffreddore m cold (illness)
  raffreddore da fieno hay fever

ragazza f young woman ; girlfriend

ragazza alla pari au pair
ragazzo *m* young man ; boyfriend
RAI *f* Italian State Broadcasting
rallentare to slow down
rapido *m* express train
rapido(a) high-speed ; quick
rasoio *m* razor
  rasoio elettrico electric razor
reato *m* crime
recarsi alla cassa pay at cash desk
recentemente recently
reclamo *m* complaint
recupero monete returned coins
regalo *m* present ; gift
reggiseno *m* bra
regione *f* region ; district ; area
registrare to record
registratore *m* cassette player
registro *m* register
Regno Unito *m* United Kingdom
regolamento *m* regulation
regolare regular ; steady
remare to row *(boat)*
rendersi conto di to realize
rene *m* kidney
reparto *m* department ; ward
restare to stay ; to remain
restituire to return ; to give back
restituzione *f* return ; repayment
resto *m* remainder ; change *(money)*
restringersi to shrink
rete *f* net ; goal
  rete portabagagli rack *(luggage)*
retro *m* back
  vedi retro please turn over
retromarcia *f* reverse gear
reumatismo *m* rheumatism
ricambio *m* spare part ; refill
ricaricare to recharge *(battery)*
  caricatelefono m recharger *(mobile)* ;
  caricabatterie (battery)
ricetta *f* prescription ; recipe
ricevere to receive ; to welcome
ricevitore *m* receiver *(phone)*

ricevuta *f* receipt
richiedere to require
richiesta *f* request
riciclare to recycle
riconoscere to recognize
riconoscimento *m* identification
ricordare to remember
  non mi ricordo I don't remember
ricordo *m* souvenir ; memory
ricorrere a to resort to
ricoverare to admit *(to hospital)*
ridere to laugh
ridurre to reduce
riduttore *m* adaptor
riduzione *f* reduction
riempire to fill
rientro *m* return ; return home
rifare to do again ; to repair
rifiutare to refuse
rifiuti *mpl* rubbish ; waste
rifugio *m* mountain inn ; shelter
righello *m* ruler *(for measuring)*
rigore *m* penalty *(football)*
riguardo *m* care ; respect
  riguardo a... regarding...
rilasciato(a) a issued at
rimandare to postpone
rimanere to stay ; to remain
rimborsare to reimburse
rimborso *m* refund
rimessa *f* remittance ; garage
rimettere to put back
rimettersi to recover *(from illness)*
rimorchiare to tow
rimorchio *m* trailer
  a rimorchio on tow
rimozione *f* removal ; towing away
Rinascimento *m* Renaissance
rinfreschi *mpl* refreshments
ringraziare to thank
rinnovare to renew
rinunciare to give up
riparare to repair
riparato(a) sheltered ; repaired

riparazione f repair
ripetere to repeat
ripido(a) abrupt ; steep
ripiegare to fold
ripieno m stuffing
riposarsi to rest
riposo m rest (repose)
risalita f reascent
risarcimento m compensation
riscaldamento m heating
riscaldare to heat up (food)
rischio m risk
risciacquare to rinse
riscuotere to collect ; to cash
riserva f reserve ; reservation
  riserva di caccia private hunting
  riserva naturale nature reserve
riservare to reserve
riservato(a) reserved
riso m rice ; laugh
risotto m rice cooked in stock
risparmiare to save (money)
rispondere to answer ; to reply
risposta f answer
ristorante m restaurant
ritardo m delay
ritirare to withdraw
ritiro m retirement ; withdrawal
  ritiro bagagli baggage reclaim
ritornare to return (go back)
ritorno m return
riunione f meeting
riuscita f result ; outcome
riva f bank ; shore
riviera f riviera
rivista f magazine ; revue
rivolgersi a to refer to (for info)
roba f stuff ; belongings
roccia f rock
rognoni mpl kidneys
romanico(a) Romanesque
romanzo m novel
  romanzo rosa romantic novel
rompere to break

rondine f swallow (bird)
rosa pink
rosa f rose
rosmarino m rosemary
rosolia f German measles ; rubella
rossetto m lipstick
rosso(a) red
rosticceria f shop selling cooked
  food
rotonda f roundabout
rotondo(a) round
rotto(a) broken
roulotte f caravan
rovesciare to spill ; to knock over
rovine fpl ruins
rtd delay
rubare to steal
rubinetto m tap
rubrica f address book
ruggine f rust
rughe fpl wrinkles
rullino m roll of film
rum m rum
rumore m noise
rumoroso(a) noisy
ruota f wheel
  ruota di scorta spare wheel
rupe f mountain cliff
ruscello m stream
russare to snore

S

S south (abbreviation)
sabato Saturday
sabbia f sand
saccarina f saccharin
sacchetto m small bag
  sacchetto di carta paper bag
  sacchetto di plastica plastic bag
sacco m large bag
  sacco a pelo sleeping bag
  sacco della spazzatura bin bag
sacerdote m priest
sagra f local food festival

sala f hall ; auditorium
  sala da pranzo dining room
  sala d'aspetto waiting room
  sala partenze departure lounge
salame m salami
salario m wage
salato(a) salted ; savoury
saldare to settle (bill) ; to weld
saldi sale
saldo m payment ; balance
sale m salt
salire to rise ; to go up
  salire in to get in (vehicle)
salita f climb ; slope
  in salita uphill
salmone m salmon
  salmone affumicato smoked salmon
salone m lounge ; salon
salotto m living room ; lounge
salsa f sauce
salsiccia f sausage
saltare to jump
saltato(a) sautéed
salumeria f delicatessen
salumi mpl cured pork meats
salute f health
  salute! cheers!
saluto m greeting
salvagente m life belt
salvare to rescue ; to save (life)
salvavita m circuit breaker
salve! hello!
salvia f sage (herb)
salvietta f serviette
salviettine per bambini fpl baby
  wipes
salvo except ; unless
sandali mpl sandals
sangue m blood
  al sangue rare (steak)
sanguinare to bleed
sapere to know
sapone m soap
sapore m flavour ; taste
saporito(a) tasty

Sardegna f Sardinia
sarto m tailor
sartoria f tailor's ; dressmaker's
sasso m stone
sauna f sauna
sbagliato(a) wrong
sbaglio m mistake
sbarco m landing (boat)
sbrigare to hurry
scadente low (standard, quality)
scadenza f expiry
scadere to expire (ticket, etc)
scaduto(a) out-of-date ; expired
scala f scale ; ladder ; staircase
  scala antincendio fire escape
  scala mobile escalator
scalare to climb
scaldabagno m water heater
scaldare to heat up
scale fpl stairs
scalino m step
scalo m stopover
scaloppina f veal escalope
scannerizzare to scan
  lo scan scan
  lo scanner scanner
scarico(a) flat (battery)
scarpa f shoe
  scarpe da ginnastica trainers
scarponcini mpl walking boots
scarponi da sci mpl ski boots
scatola f box ; tin
  scatola di pelati tinned tomatoes
scegliere to choose
scelta f range ; selection ; choice
scendere to go down
  scendere da to get off (bus, etc)
scheda f slip (of paper) ; card
  scheda telefonica phonecard
schiena f back (of body)
sci m ski ; skiing
  sci di fondo cross-country skiing
  sci nautico water-skiing
scialuppa di salvataggio f lifeboat
sciare to ski

sciarpa f scarf
sciogliere to melt
sciopero m strike
sciovia f ski-lift
scivolare to slip
scomodo(a) inconvenient ;
  uncomfortable
scomparire to disappear
scompartimento m compartment
scongelare to defrost
sconto m discount
  sconti reductions
scontrino m ticket ; receipt ; chit
scopa f broom (brush)
scorso(a) last
scossa f shock (electric)
scottatura f burn
  scottatura solare sunburn
Scozia f Scotland
scozzese Scottish
scrivania f desk
scrivere to write ; to spell
scultura f sculpture
scuola f school
  scuola di sci ski school
  scuola materna nursery school
scuro(a) dark (colour)
scusare to excuse ; to forgive
scusarsi to apologise
scusi? pardon?
se if ; whether
sé oneself
seconda f second gear
secondo m second (time) ; main
  course (meal)
secondo(a) second ; according to
  seconda classe second class
  di seconda mano secondhand
sedano m celery
sede f head office
sedersi to sit down
sedia f chair
  sedia a rotelle wheelchair
  sedia a sdraio deckchair
sedile per bambini m babyseat (car)

seggiolone m highchair
seggiovia f chair-lift
segnale m signal ; road sign
segnare to score (goal)
segreteria telefonica f answering
  machine
seguente following
seguire to follow ; to continue
sella f saddle
selvatico(a) wild
semaforo m traffic lights
semifreddo m dessert made with
  ice cream
seminterrato basement
semplice plain ; simple
sempre always ; ever
  per sempre for ever
senape f mustard
senso unico one-way street
  senso vietato no entry
sentiero m path ; footpath
sentire to hear
sentirsi to feel
senza without
separato(a) separated
sera f evening
serbatoio m tank (car)
  serbatoio dell'acqua cistern
serio serious (not funny)
serpente m snake
serratura f lock
servire to serve
servizio m service ; report (in press)
  servizio al tavolo waiter service
  servizio compreso service included
servizi mpl facilities ; bathroom
sesso m sex
seta f silk
sete f thirst
  avere sete to be thirsty
settembre m September
settentrionale northern
settimana f week
  settimana bianca week's skiing
  holiday

181

settimanale **weekly**

sfida f **challenge**

sfuso(a) **loose ; on tap** *(wine)*

sganciare **to lift receiver**

si **yes**

Sicilia f **Sicily**

sicurezza f **safety ; security**

sicuro(a) **sure**

sidro m **cider**

Sig. **Mr** *abbreviation of Signor*

Sig.ra **Mrs/Ms** *abbreviation of Signora*

sigaretta f **cigarette**

sigaro m **cigar**

Sig.na **Miss** *abbreviation of Signorina*

Signor: *il Signor Grandi* **Mr Grandi**

signora f **lady ; madam ; Mrs ; Ms**
 signore **ladies**

signore m **gentleman ; sir**
 signori **gents**

signorina f **young woman ; Miss**

silenzio m **silence**

simile a **similar to**

simpatico(a) **pleasant ; nice**

sindacato m **trade union**

sindaco m **mayor**

singolo(a) **single**

sinistra f **left**

sistemare **to arrange**

sito m **site**
 sito web **website**

skipass m **skipass**

slacciare **to unfasten ; to undo**

slavina f **snowslide ; landslide**

slegato(a) **loose** *(not fastened)*

slogatura f **sprain**

smarrito(a) **missing** *(thing)*

smettere **to stop doing something**

soccorso m **assistance ; help**
 soccorso alpino **mountain rescue**

socio m **associate ; member**

soggiorno m **stay ; sitting room**

soldi mpl **money**

sole m **sun ; sunshine**

solito: *di solito* **usually**

sollevare **to raise ; to relieve**

sollievo m **relief**

solo(a) **alone ; only**

solubile **soluble**
 caffè solubile **instant coffee**

sonnifero m **sleeping pill**

sono **I am (to be)**

sopra **on ; above ; over**
 di sopra **upstairs**

sopracciglia fpl **eyebrows**

sopravvivere **to survive**

sorella f **sister**

sorpassare **to overtake** *(in car)*

sorpresa f **surprise**

sorridere **to smile**

sorriso m **smile**

sospeso(a) **suspended ; postponed**

sosta f **stop**
 divieto di sosta **no parking**

sott'acqua **underwater**

sotterraneo(a) **underground**

sotto **underneath ; under ; below**

Spagna f **Spain**

spagnolo(a) **Spanish**

spalla f **shoulder**

sparire **to disappear**

spazzatura f **rubbish**

spazzola f **brush**
 spazzola per capelli **hairbrush**
 spazzolino da denti **toothbrush**

speciale **special**

specialità f **speciality**

specialmente **especially**

spedire **to send ; to dispatch**

spegnere **to turn off ; to put out**

spendere **to spend** *(money)*

spento(a) **turned off ; out** *(light, etc)*

sperare **to hope**

spese fpl **shopping ; expenses**

spesso **often**

spettacolo m **show ; performance**

spezzatino m **stew**

spiaggia f **beach ; shore**
 spiaggia privata **private beach**

spiccioli *mpl* **small coins ; change**
  non ho spiccioli **I've no change**
spiegare **to explain**
spina *f* **bone** *(of fish)* **; plug** *(electric)*
spinaci *m* **spinach**
spingere **to push**
spirale *f* **coil** *(IUD)*
spogliatoio *m* **dressing room**
sporco(a) **dirty**
sportello *m* **counter ; window**
sportivo(a) **informal** *(clothes)*
sposarsi **to get married**
sposato(a) **married**
  non sposato(a) **single**
spremuta *f* **freshly squeezed juice**
spugna *f* **sponge**
spuma *f* **hair mousse**
spumante *m* **sparkling wine**
spuntino *m* **snack**
squadra *f* **team**
squillare **to ring** *(phone)*
Srl **Ltd**
stabilimento *m* **factory**
stadio *m* **stadium**
stagione *f* **season**
  di stagione **in season**
stalla *f* **stable**
stampatello *m* **block letters**
stanco(a) **tired**
stanza *f* **room**
  stanza da bagno **bathroom**
  stanza dei giochi **playroom**
stare **to be**
  stare attento(a) a... **beware of..**
  stare bene **to be well**
  stare in piedi **to stand**
  come sta? **how are you?**
stasera **tonight ; this evening**
Stati Uniti *mpl* **United States**
stazione *f* **station ; resort**
  stazione balneare **seaside resort**
  stazione dell'autobus **bus station**
  stazione di servizio **petrol station**
  stazione ferroviaria **train station**
stella *f* **star**

sterlina *f* **sterling ; pound**
stesso(a) **same**
stirare **to iron**
stitichezza *f* **constipation**
stitico(a) **constipated**
stivali *mpl* **boots**
storia *f* **history**
storico(a) **historic(al)**
  centro storico **old town**
strada *f* **road ; street**
  strada chiusa **road closed**
  strada panoramica **scenic route**
  strada sbarrata **road closed**
  strada statale **main road**
  strada senza uscita **no through road**
stradina *f* **lane**
straniero(a) **foreign ; foreigner**
strano(a) **strange**
stupido(a) **stupid**
su **on ; onto ; over ; about ; up**
sua **his ; her(s) ; its ; your(s)**
  (with f sing)
subito **at once ; immediately**
succedere **to happen**
succo *m* **juice**
  succo d'arancia **orange juice**
  succo di frutta **fruit juice**
  succo di mela **apple juice**
  succo di pomodoro **tomato juice**
succursale *m* **branch** *(of bank, etc)*
sud *m* **south**
sue **his ; her(s) ; its ; your(s)** *(with f pl)*
suo(i) **his ; her(s) ; its ; your(s)** *(with m pl)*
suocera *f* **mother-in-law**
suocero *m* **father-in-law**
suola *f* **sole** *(of foot, shoe)*
suonare **to ring ; to play**
suono *m* **sound**
superare **to exceed ; to overtake**
supermercato *m* **supermarket**
supplemento *m* **supplement**
supposta *f* **suppository**
surf *m* **surf**
surgelato(a) **frozen**
sveglia *f* **alarm clock/call**

183

svegliare to wake up
svenire to faint
sviluppare to develop *(photos)*
Svizzera f Switzerland
svizzero(a) Swiss
svolta f turn

T

tabaccaio m tobacconist's
tacco m heel
tachimetro m speedometer
taglia f size *(of clothes)*
tagliare to cut
tailleur m women's suit
tallone m heel
tangenziale f by-pass
tanti(e) so many
tanto(a) so much ; so
tappo m cork ; plug ; cap
  tappo del serbatoio petrol cap
tardi late
targa f numberplate *(car)*
tariffa f tariff ; rate
  tariffa economica cheap rate
  tariffa festiva rate on holidays
  tariffa ore di punta peak rate
tartufo m truffle
tasca f pocket
tassa f tax
tasso m rate
  tasso di cambio exchange rate
tavola f table ; plank ; board
  tavola calda hot snacks
  tavola da surf surfboard
  tavola a vela windsurfing board
taxi m taxi
tazza f cup
tè m tea
  tè al latte tea with milk
  tè al limone lemon tea
  tè freddo iced tea
teatro m theatre ; drama
tedesco(a) German
telecomando m remote control

telefonare to (tele)phone
telefonata f phone call
telefonino m mobile phone
telefono m telephone
  telefono pubblico payphone
televisione f television
telone impermeabile m groundsheet
temperatura f temperature
temperino m penknife
tempesta f storm
tempio m temple
tempo m weather ; time
temporale m thunderstorm
tenda f curtain ; tent
tendine m tendon
tenere to keep ; to hold
tenore m tenor *(singer)*
tenore alcolico m alcohol content
tergicristallo m windscreen wiper
terminal m terminal *(airport)*
termometro m thermometer
termosifone m heater
terra f earth ; ground
terrazza f terrace
terremoto m earthquake
terza f third gear
terzi mpl third party
terzo(a) third
tessera f pass ; season ticket
tesserino m pass *(bus, train)*
tessuto m fabric
testa f head
testicoli mpl testicles
tettarella f dummy *(for baby)*
tetto m roof
tettuccio apribile m sunroof *(car)*
Tevere m Tiber
thermos m thermos flask
thriller m thriller
timone m rudder
tirare to pull
toccare to touch ; to feel
  non toccare do not touch
togliere to remove ; to take away

toilette f toilet
tonno m tuna
topo m mouse
Torino f Turin
tornare to return ; to come/go back
torneo m tournament
toro m bull
torre f tower
torrone m nougat
torta f cake ; tart ; pie
Toscana f Tuscany
tosse f cough
tossico(a) toxic
tossire to cough
totale m total (amount)
tovaglia f tablecloth
tovagliolo m napkin
tra between ; among(st) ; in
tradizionale traditional
tradurre to translate
traduzione f translation
traffico m traffic
traghetto m ferry
tramezzino m sandwich
trampolino m diving board ; ski jump
tranquillante m tranquillizer
tranquillo(a) quiet (place)
trasferire to transfer
trasporto m transport
trattoria f restaurant
traveller's cheque mpl traveller's
  cheque
traversata f crossing ; flight
treno m train
  treno merci goods train
triangolo d'emergenza m warning
  triangle
tribuna f stand (stadium)
tribunale m law court
trimestre m term (school)
triste sad
tritare to mince ; to chop
troppi(e) too many
troppo too much ; too

trovare to find
trucco m make-up
tu you (familiar)
tubo m pipe ; tube
  tubo di scappamento exhaust
tuffarsi to dive
turno m turn ; shift
  di turno on duty
tuta sportiva f tracksuit
tutti (e) all ; everybody
  tutte le direzioni all routes
tutto everything ; all

U

ubriaco(a) drunk
uccello m bird
uccidere to kill
UE European Union
ufficio m office ; church service
  ufficio informazioni information
  bureau
  ufficio oggetti smarriti lost property
  office
  ufficio postale post office
ufficio turistico tourist office
uguale equal ; even
ulcera f ulcer
ultimo(a) last
un a ; an ; one
unghia f nail (finger, toe)
unione f union
  Unione Europea European Union
Unità Sanitaria Locale local health
  centre
università f university
uno(a) a ; an ; one
uomo m man
  uomini gents
uova mpl eggs
uovo m egg
  uovo di Pasqua Easter egg
  uovo sodo hard-boiled egg
uragano m hurricane
urgente urgent

usare to use
uscire to go/come out
uscita f exit/gate
  uscita di sicurezza emergency exit
USL abbreviation of Unità Sanitaria
  Locale
uso m use
utile useful
uva f grapes

V

va bene all right (agreed)
vacanza f holiday(s)
  vacanze estive summer holidays
vaccinazione f vaccination
vagina f vagina
vaglia m money order
vagone m carriage ; wagon
  vagone letto sleeper
  vagone ristorante restaurant car
valanga f avalanche
valico m pass (mountain)
valido(a) valid
  valido fino a... valid until...
valigia f suitcase
valore m value; worth
  di valore valuable
valuta f currency
valvola f valve
varicella f chickenpox
vasetto m jar
vaso m vase
vassoio m tray
vecchio(a) old
vedere to see
vedova f widow
vedovo m widower
vegetaliano(a) vegan
vegetariano(a) vegetarian
veicolo m vehicle
vela f sail ; sailing
veleno m poison
velenoso(a) poisonous
veloce quick

velocemente quickly
velocità f speed
vena f vein
vendere to sell
  vendesi for sale
vendita f sale
  vendita al minuto retail
  vendita a rate hire purchase
venerdì m Friday
venerdì santo m Good Friday
Venezia f Venice
venire to come
ventaglio m fan (hand-held)
ventilatore m electric fan
vento m wind
verde green
verdura f vegetables
verità f truth
vermut m vermouth
vernice f paint
verniciare to paint
vero(a) true ; real ; genuine
versamento m payment ; deposit
versare to pour
vertice m summit
vescica f blister
vespa f wasp
vestaglia f dressing gown
vestirsi to get dressed
vestiti mpl clothes
vestito m dress
vetrina f shop window
vetro m glass (substance)
via f street ; by (via)
  per via aerea by air mail
viaggiare to travel
viaggiatore m traveller
viaggio m journey ; trip ; drive
  viaggio d'affari business trip
  viaggio organizzato package tour
viale m avenue
vicino (a) near ; close by
vicolo m alley ; lane
  vicolo cieco cul-de-sac
videocamera f videocamera

videocassetta *f* videocassette
videogioco *m* computer game
videoregistratore *m* video recorder
vietato forbidden
  vietato accendere fuochi do not light fires
  vietato fumare no smoking
  vietato l'ingresso no entry
  vietato ingresso veicoli no entry for vehicles
  vietato scendere no exit
vigili del fuoco fire brigade
vigilia *f* eve
  Vigilia di Natale Christmas Eve
vigna *f* vineyard
vincere to win
vino *m* wine
  vino bianco white wine
  vini da pasto table wines
  vino da tavola table wine
  vini pregiati quality wines
  vino rosso red wine
violentare to rape
virus *m* virus
visita *f* visit
  visite guidate guided tours
visitare to visit
vista *f* view
visto *m* visa
vita *f* life ; waist
  vita notturna night life
vitamina *f* vitamin
vite *f* vine ; screw
vivere to live
vivo(a) live ; alive
voce *f* voice
volante *m* steering wheel
volare to fly
voler dire to mean *(signify)*
volere to want
volo *m* flight
  volo di linea scheduled flight
  volo charter charter flight
volta *f* time
  una volta once
  due volte twice

voltaggio *m* voltage
vomitare to vomit
vongola *f* clam
vostro(a) your ; yours
vulcano *m* volcano
vuoto(a) empty

Z
zanzara *f* mosquito
zanzariera *f* mosquito net
zia *f* aunt
zio *m* uncle
zona *f* zone
  zona blu restricted parking zone
  zona pedonale pedestrian
zucchero *m* sugar
zucchini *mpl* courgettes
zuppa *f* soup
  zuppa inglese type of trifle

Grammar

NOUNS

In Italian all nouns are either *masculine* or *feminine*. Where in English we say **the apple** and **the book**, in Italian it is **la mela** and **il libro** because **mela** is *feminine* and **libro** is *masculine*. The gender of nouns is shown in the *article* (**il, la, un, una**, etc.):

THE: *masc. sing.*   **il**   *fem. sing.*   **la**

                                 l' (+vowel)   **l'** (+vowel)

                                 lo (+z, gn, pn, ps, x, s +consonant)

          masc. plur.   **i**

                                 gli (+vowel, +z, gn, pn, s +consonant)   *fem. plur.*   **le**

A, AN: *masc.*   **un**   *fem.*   **una**

                                 uno (+z, gn, pn, s +consonant)   **un'** (+vowel)

NOTE: definite articles (**il, la, i, le**, etc.) used after the prepositions **a** (**to, at**), **da** (**by, from**), **su** (**on**), **di** (**of, some**) and **in** (**in, into**) contract as follows:

a + il = al	da + il = dal	su + il = sul
a + lo = allo	da + lo = dallo	su + lo = sullo
a + l' = all'	da + l' = dall'	su + l' = sull'
a + la = alla	da + la = dalla	su + la = sulla
a + i = ai	da + i = dai	su + i = sui
a + gli = agli	da + gli = dagli	su + gli = sugli
a + le = alle	da + le = dalle	su + le = sulle

di + il = del	in + il = nel
di + lo = dello	in + lo = nello
di + l' = dell'	in + l'' = nell'
di + la = della	in + la = nella
di + i = dei	in + i = nei
di + gli = degli	in + gli = negli
di + le = delle	in + le = nelle

e.g. **alla** casa (**to the** house)   **sul** tavolo (**on the** table)

NOUNS: FORMATION OF PLURALS

For most nouns, the singular ending changes as follows:

masc. sing.	masc. plur.	example	
o	i	libro	libri
e	i	padre	padri
a	i	artista	artisti

NOTE:nouns ending in e can be either masculine or feminine. In the plural they all end in **i**, e.g.

la televisione	le televisioni
il mare	i mari

NOTE:most nouns ending in **co** and **go** become **chi** and **ghi** in the plural to keep the **c** and **g** hard sounding. Some exceptions occur in the masculine, e.g. **amico – amici**

fem. sing.	fem. plur.	example	
a	e	mela	mele
e	i	madre	madri

NOTE:nouns ending in **ca** and **ga** become **che** and **ghe** in the plural to keep the **c** and **g** hard sounding. Nouns ending in **cia** and **gia** often becomes **ce** and **ge** to keep the **c** and **g** soft sounding.

ADJECTIVES

Adjectives normally follow the noun they describe in Italian,e.g. **la mela rossa** (**the red apple**)

Some common exceptions which precede the noun are:**bello** beautiful, **breve** short, **brutto** ugly, **buono** good, **cattivo** bad, **giovane** young, **grande** big, **lungo** long, **nuovo** new, **piccolo** small, **vecchio** old e.g. **una bella giornata** (**a beautiful day**)

Italian adjectives have to reflect the gender of the noun they describe. To make an adjective *feminine*, an **a** replaces the **o** of the *masculine*, e.g. ross<u>o</u> - ross<u>a</u>. Adjectives ending in **e**, e.g. **giovane**, can be either *masculine* or *feminine*. The plural forms of the adjective change in the way described for nouns (above).

MY, YOUR, HIS, HER

These words also depend on the gender and number of the noun they accompany, and not on the sex of the 'owner'.

	with masc. sing. noun	with fem. sing. noun	with masc. plur. noun	with fem. plur. noun
my	il mio	la mia	i miei	le mie
your (polite)	il suo	la sua	i suoi	le sue
your (plural)	il vostro	la vostra	i vostri	le vostre
his/her	il suo	la sua	i suoi	le sue

PRONOUNS

SUBJECT		OBJECT	
I	io	**me**	me/mi
you	tu	**you**	te/ti
you	lei	**you**	la
he	lui/egli	**him**	lo/l' (+vowel)

she	**lei/ella**	**her**	**la/l'** (+vowel)
it (masc.)	**esso**	**it** (masc.)	**lo/l'** (+vowel)
it (fem.)	**essa**	**it** (fem.)	**la/l'** (+vowel)
we	**noi**	**us**	**ci**
you	**voi**	**you**	**vi**
they	**loro**	**them** (masc.)	**li**
(things:masc.)	**essi**	**them** (fem.)	**le**
(things:fem.)	**esse**		

The object pronouns shown above are also used to mean to me, to us, etc., except:

to him/to it	= **gli**
to her/to it/to you	= **le**
to them	= **loro**

Pronoun objects (other than **loro**) usually precede the verb:

lo vedo	*but*	**scriverò loro**
I see him		I will write to them

When used with an infinitive (the verb form given in the dictionary), the pronoun follows and is attached to the infinitive less its final **e**:

voglio comprarlo (comprare)   **I want to buy it**

Subject pronouns (**io**, **tu**, **egli**, etc.) are often omitted before verbs, since the verb ending generally distinguishes the person:

parlo	<u>I</u> speak
parliamo	<u>we</u> speak
parlono	<u>they</u> speak

Lei is the polite form for **you**; **voi** is the plural form. **Tu**, the familiar form for **you**, should only be used with people you know well, or children.

VERBS

There are three main patterns of endings for verbs in Italian – those ending **are**, **ere** and **ire** in the dictionary. Two examples of the **ire** verbs are shown, since two distinct groups of endings exist. Subject pronouns are shown in brackets because these are often not used:

	PARL<u>ARE</u>	TO SPEAK	VEND<u>ERE</u>	TO SELL
(io)	**parlo**	I speak	**vendo**	I sell
(tu)	**parli**	you speak	**vendi**	you sell
(lui/lei)	**parla**	(s)he speaks	**vende**	(s)he sells
(noi)	**parliamo**	we speak	**vendiamo**	we sell
(voi)	**parlate**	you speak	**vendete**	you sell
(loro)	**parlano**	they speak	**vendono**	they sell

	DORMIRE	TO SLEEP	FINIRE	TO FINISH
(io)	dormo	I sleep	finisco	I finish
(tu)	dormi	you sleep	finisci	you finish
(lui/lei)	dorme	(s)he sleeps	finisce	(s)he finishes
(noi)	dormiamo	we sleep	finiamo	we finish
(voi)	dormite	you sleep	finite	you finish
(loro)	dormono	theysleep	finiscono	they finish

IRREGULAR VERBS

Among the most important irregular verbs are the following:

	ESSERE	TO BE	AVERE	TO HAVE
(io)	sono	I am	ho	I have
(tu)	sei	you are	hai	you have
(lui/lei)	è	(s)he is	ha	(s)he has
(noi)	siamo	we are	abbiamo	we have
(voi)	siete	you are	avete	you have
(loro)	sono	they are	hanno	they have

	ANDARE	TO GO	FARE	TO DO
(io)	vado	I go	faccio	I do
(tu)	vai	you go	fai	you do
(lui/lei)	va	(s)he goes	fa	(s)he does
(noi)	andiamo	we go	facciamo	we do
(voi)	andate	you go	fate	you do
(loro)	vanno	they go	fanno	they do

	POTERE	TO BE ABLE	VOLERE	TO WANT
(io)	posso	I can	voglio	I want
(tu)	puoi	you can	vuoi	you want
(lui/lei)	può	(s)he can	vuole	(s)he wants
(noi)	possiamo	we can	vogliamo	we want
(voi)	potete	you can	volete	you want
(loro)	possono	they can	vogliono	they want

PAST TENSE

To form the simple past tense, **I spoke/I have spoken, I sold/I have sold,** etc. combine the present tense of the verb **avere – to have** with the past participle of the verb, e.g.

ho parlato	I spoke/I have spoken
ho venduto	I sold/I have sold

PARL**ARE** *(past)*

ho parlato	I spoke
hai parlato	you spoke
ha parlato	(s)he spoke
abbiamo parlato	we spoke
avete parlato	you spoke
hanno parlato	they spoke

VEND**ERE** *(past)*

ho venduto	I sold
hai venduto	you sold
ha venduto	(s)he sold
abbiamo venduto	we sold
avete venduto	you sold
hanno venduto	they sold

DORM**IRE** *(past)*

ho dormito	I slept
hai dormito	you slept
ha dormito	(s)he slept
abbiamo dormito	we slept
avete dormito	you slept
hanno dormito	they slept

FIN**IRE** *(past)*

ho finito	I finished
hai finito	you finished
ha finito	(s)he finished
abbiamo finito	we finished
avete finito	you finished
hanno finito	they finished

NOTE: not all verbs take **avere** (**ho**, **hai**, etc.) as their auxiliary verb, some verbs take **essere** (**sono**, **sei**, etc.). These are mainly verbs of motion or staying: **andare – to go**, **stare – to be** (located at), e.g.

sono andato	I went
sono stato a Roma	I was in Rome

When the auxiliary verb **essere** is used, the past participle (**andato**, **stato**) becomes an adjective and should agree with the subject of the verb, e.g.

sono andata	I went *(female)*
siamo stati	we went *(plural)*